COASTAL ZONE MANAGEMENT

COASTAL ZONE MANAGEMENT

A Study of the Political Economy of Sustainable Development

(Volume 1)

Dr. Ramakrishana Korakandy

Publications

KALPAZ PUBLICATIONS

DELHI - 110052

Coastal Zone Management

A Study of the Political Economy of Sustainable Development

Rs. 1800 (Set)

ISBN : 81-7835-302-4 (Set)
ISBN : 81-7835-303-2 (Vol. 1)

Published in 2005 in India by
Kalpaz Publication,
C-30, Satyawati Nagar,
Delhi-110 052
Email : kalpaz@hotmail.com

Lasertype Setting by: Tact Computer Graphics, Delhi
Printed at: Mehra Offset Press, Delhi

Dedication

This work is dedicated to the pioneers from whom I learnt the basic concepts and approach

Contents

Preface

Coastal Zone Management has evolved ever since the US Coastal Zone Management Act was passed in 1972. With the adoption of chapter 17 agenda 21 of the United Nations Conference on Environment and, Development at Rio de Jeneiro in 1992, integrated management of coastal zones acquired a new dimension. The multiple use conflicts prevailing in the coast affecting the ecological, economic and social sustainability of coastal societies began to be considered as manageable and needing only an integrated approach to coastal zone management. The United Nations also took the lead in propagating the message of Integrated Coastal Zone Management, world wide. It, alongwith the developed nations, strived to promote programmes for coastal zone management, with technical programmes for global 'partnerships' and 'capacity building' for integrated coastal zone management.

Much before the UNCED in 1992, coastal states were encouraged to initiate programmes for ICM, by the United States, European Economic Community and the United Nations. Programmes were afoot in the ASEAN, Mediterranean and other coasts which were supported by these agencies. By 1992, the FAO as the chief agency of the UN had put forward the idea of integrating fisheries management with coastal zone management. The idea has been since extended to agriculture and forestry. Presently the World Bank is also assisting in implementing integrated coastal zone management programmes, especially in the African coasts.

A major component of the United Nation's programme for coastal zone management is the building of capacity for ICM world wide, by providing technical support to planning, education and implementation of ICM plans in developing coastal states. Legal and institutional changes are also being promoted by the UN for ICM.

It is noteworthy that the Government of India initiated a programme for the conservation of the Indian coast in 1991, when it introduced the Coastal Regulation Zone Notification under the provisions of the Environment (Protection) Act of 1986. Curiously, it took another five years for the Government of Kerala to publicise the same for implementation in 1996. This notification, since 1996, has been bogged in controversy in Kerala and it is seldom sought to be understood by the public, the stakeholders or the 'state' and rarely implemented in letter and spirit. The genesis of the present study is to be found here.

The present study was initiated in 2000 as a major research project funded by the UGC. The project initially sought to examine the controversy over the implementation of the CRZ notification in Kerala as a pure political economy crisis. With the inception of the study, it, however, had to widen its ambit and truely look into the political economy of sustainable development of the coast where in the ICM is considered as the main tool or a necessary condition. A sufficient condition for sustainable development has to be sought elsewhere.

This study is presented in ten chapters. The first chapter introduces the theme and background of the study, its need, objectives, hypothesis, methodology, data base, limitations and prospects. The second chapter is devoted to a review of literature, which is presented in two sections, one dealing with the domestic literature and the other, with the international. Chapter three gives the conceptual framework of ICM with definitions, goals, strategy, programmes and a review of development world wide. Chapter four makes the rationale for ICM clear, which is presented in four sections as corresponding to the ecological, economic, socio-cultural and other factors. Chapter five outlines the coastal resource base of Kerala as the starting point for any ICM approach to sustainable development of the coast. Chapter six is earmarked for a detailed account of coastal zone activities of Kerala, ranging from agriculture to aquaculture, fisheries, forestry, mining, manufacturing, tourism, transport, shipping, port, municipal development, etc. Chapter seven discusses the major coastal issues of Kerala as pointing to the need for an ICZM solution. Chapter eight makes a review of coastal zone management efforts in Kerala in the past and at present. Chapter nine which carries the title of this study drives home the need for ICM, the master plan framework, the components of the master plan for ICM in Kerala and the need for a precautionary approach. Chapter ten, being the last chapter, gives the summary of findings and conclusion of this study. A post-script has pointed out the deficiency of the ICZM approach to sustainable development.

The present study is unique in certain respects. It is perhaps the first attempt to analyse the coastal issues and prescribe ICM solutions for that in any part of the country.

This study is also unique in that it has tried to present the semantics of ICM and the political economy of sustainable development of the coast in some detail. In this regard, it is expected to be a valuable addition to the limited national literature on the subject. Another facet of this study is that it has found some chinks in the ICM approach to sustainable development and also a possible linkage between ICM and globalisation.

Dr. Ramakrishan Korakandy
School of Industrial Fisheries
Cochin University of Science and Technology,
Fine Arts Avenue
Cochin-682016

Acknowledgements

As in all my previous efforts, the present work has also been made possible with the unstinted support which I received from several sources. It is time to reckon them. First of all, I wish to record my deep gratitude to Professor (Dr.) N. Unnikrishnan Nair, the present Vice-Chancellor of the Cochin University of Science and Technology, who as Registrar of the University in 1998 had been very positive in recommending my application for project funding by the UGC, under its major research projects. The present Registrar of the University Dr. K. V. Kunhikrishnan has also been equally swift in sending my requests to the UGC to get the grants released from New Delhi in time. It goes without saying that the financial wherewithal for this study was provided by the UGC and I am greatly indebted to it for that as before.

Among the other individuals whose kind regards helped me much in the proposal stage of this work are my former colleagues Professor (Dr.) M. Shahul Hameed, the then Director of the School, Dr. C. Hridayanathan, then Professor in the School, and Professor (Dr.) K.C. Sankaranarayanan, then, Head of the Department of Applied Economics, all of whom unanimously approved the project proposal for presentation to the UGC. I acknowledge their services with gratitude. My present colleagues in the school, Dr. Saleena Mathew, Dr. B. Madhusoodana Kurup, Dr. K.T. Thomson and Sri John Mohan were also concerned with the progress of this work. I owe them all for this. Dr. A. Ramachandran, presently, Controller of Examinations, at the University was equally interested in the coastal issues of Kerala which is the theme of this study. Dr. Kuruvila Mathew, my retired colleague also had the same passion.

The completion of this study has been made possible with the active help received from Mr. Rajesh, K. Project Fellow in collecting the literature and data for this study. Mr. Zubair, A.A., Mr. Sreekanth, P.R., Miss Swarna Janardhanan and Miss Nija, M.A. had assisted me as project investigators for short periods. Their services are acknowledged on this occasion.

Another major source of support for this study was the staff of the library of the School of Marine Sciences, Central Institute of Fisheries Technology and Central Marine Fisheries Research Institute, who all helped me in garnering information for this study. Here I must admit that I have drawn extensively from the global literature on ICZM, all of which have been acknowledged at the very instance.

Incidentally, it is my friend Sriman K.V.Chandran who gave this work its present shape by fine typing. It was his finger tips and intelligence that brought the many scattered lines of writing and tattered pieces of papers into binding sheets and bonding thoughts. I owe it entirely to his commitment to quality and perfection of his work.

The anchorage at home, as usual, was provided by my wife Dr. Chandraprabha and son Amarkrishna both of whom bore the brunt of my depravity of curtailing their freedom for facilitating this work. I owe it to their forbearance. Finally my great indelated to Sri Amit Garg for Volunteering to publish this work. With this I also acknowledge that the shortcomings of this work are solely due to my own constraints.

Dr. Ramakrishnan Korakandy

School of Industrial Fisheries

Cochin University of Science and Technology,

Fine Arts Avenue

Cochin 682 016.

List of Tables

List of Acronyms

ASEAN	—	Association of South East Asian Nations
BAU	—	Business As Usual
CAM	—	Coastal Area Management
CAMP	—	Coastal Area Management Plan
CAMPNET	—	Coastal Area Management and Planning Network
CBCRM	—	Community Based Coastal Resource Management
CESS	—	Centre for Earth Science Studies
COFI	—	Committee on Fisheries (of FAO)
CRM	—	Coastal Resource Management
CRMP	—	Coastal Resource Management Plan
CRZ	—	Coastal Regulation Zone
EU	—	European Union
CZM	—	Coastal Zone Management
FAO	—	Food and Agriculture Organisation
FCCC	—	Framework Convention on Climate Change
GESAMP	—	Joint Group of Experts on Scientific Aspects of Marine Environmental Protection
ICAM	—	Integrated Coastal Area Management
ICLARM	—	International Centre for Living Aquatic Resource Management
ICOM	—	Integrated Coastal and Ocean Management
ICM	—	Integrated Coastal Management
ICZM	—	Integrated Coastal Zone Management
IMCAM	—	Integrated Marine and Coastal Area Management
IUCN	—	World Conservation Union (formerly

		International Union for Conservation of Nature and Natural Resources)
KWBSP	—	Kuttanad Water Balance Study Project
MAP	—	Mediterranean Action Programme
NDZ	—	No Development Zone
OECD	—	Organisation for Economic Cooperation and Development
UNCED	—	United Nations Conference on Environment and Development
UNCLOS	—	United Nations Conference on the Law of the Sea
UNEP	—	United Nations Environmental Programme
UNESCO	—	United Nations Educational, Scientific and Cultural Organisation
USAID	—	United States Agency for International Development
WCC	—	World Coast Conference
WCED	—	World Commission on Environment and Development

1
Introduction

1.1 The theme and background of the study

The theme of this study is 'Coastal Zone Management in Kerala—A Study of the Political Economy of Sustainable Development'. This theme was submitted to the University Grants Commission in 1998 seeking financial support for undertaking a major research project in this area. The Commission was quite gracious to sanction a project on this topic in June 2000. The present book is the culmination of this study.

Two factors had led to the choice of this topic, which was not quite directly related to my professional field (fisheries economics). One factor was the growing global concern for fisheries management and the emerging trend in the FAO circle to prescribe the need for integration of fisheries management with coastal area management. The second was the fact that in the meantime in 1996, the Government of Kerala had announced the implementation of the Coastal Regulation Zone (CRZ) notification of Government of India issued in 1991. This period also witnessed growing conflicts of interests and protests against the implementation of CRZ notification in Kerala. The traditional fishermen, the major stakeholders of the Kerala coast were generally in favour of implementing the regulations which they considered will be helpful in protecting their traditional fishing and other rights over the coasts. The regulations were, however, objected by many other sectors like aquaculture, mining, tourism, transport, housing, hotel and construction (real estate).

The fact that the major investments planned by the new industrial sectors in the coast were suddenly thwarted by the CRZ rules had in fact emboldened the new entrants to business to declare that the CRZ regulations were anti-developmental and against the interests of Kerala. This lobby, in fact, interestingly, asked the Government of Kerala, which was not quite committed to the implementation of CRZ rules, to plead to the Central Government to exempt Kerala from implementing many of the provisions of the CRZ rules. It may be noted in retrospective that this lobby has more or less succeeded in delaying and diluting the environmental protection measures by legal amendments and expert manoeuvring strategy (Das, 1999).

It is also noted in perspective here that the theory and practice of Coastal Zone Management, never more the concept of Integrated Coastal Zone Management, was ever familiar to the planners, scholars, and the business community in Kerala or the country, till recently, and the spirit of the CRZ notification was thoroughly misunderstood by most, and the state government kept a lackadaisical attitude towards CRZ implementation. It was precisely during this period that the idea of integrating fisheries management with coastal area management as put forward by the FAO (FAO, 1996a Nadia, 1998) and the political economy of the objections to the implementation of CRZ notification in Kerala began to agitate my mind. It actually forced me to write a single page article in the Southern Economist in January 1997 (Korakandy, 1997) which was not a matter of interest to the local English Press at that time. The prevailing mood and the raging controversy over the need for coastal zone management in Kerala prompted me to submit the research proposal to the UGC with the earlier noted title in 1998. As already noted, the project was sanctioned by the UGC in June 2000.

1.2. Need for the study

The need for the present study arose primarily from the prevailing crisis in the coastal zones of Kerala and the academic curiosity in studying the coastal issues and the prospect of prescribing some management solutions to the coastal problems. The coastal zones, as Scura, *et al.* put it, 'form the interface between land and sea, the complex physical and biological process played out there testifying to the close terrestrial-aquatic links. Ecologically, coastal areas contain a number of critical terrestrial and aquatic habitats, which comprise unique coastal ecosystems, containing a valuable assortment of natural resources. These interrelated ecosystems are also closely linked with the socio-economic systems to form resource systems' (Scura, *et al.*, 1992, p.16). These critical coastal systems are, however, threatened by overuse and abuse by man and are in need for careful management actions.

The significance of the coastal and ocean environment and the evolving scenario on the coast, world wide, have been summarised by Barcena at the UNCED, 1992. Barcena noted that 'the marine environment forms an integrated whole that is an essential component of the global life support system. The oceans cover 70 per cent of the surface of the globe and play a dominant and decisive role in the biogeochemical processes of the planet on local, regional and global scales. The global energy, climate and weather, the hydrological and carbon cycles, atmospheric and physical processes are critically influenced by the properties of the oceanic processes. Yet our understanding of these processes is less well developed than those occurring in the terrestrial environment and atmosphere. Long-term management and sustainable development of the world's resources must be based on a sound understanding of the role of the ocean in shaping conditions on the globe and on a proper evaluation of the benefits of the marine resource base for sustainable development. Degradation of the marine environment can result from a wide range of activities on land, either from a lack of, or an excess of, economic and industrial growth. Human populations, land use, agriculture, forestry, fisheries, urban development, tourism and industry, all impact on the marine environment.

Oceans have crucial importance as a lead sector in international law and in providing a model for management for sustainable development. Ocean management policy must be integrated horizontally, across disciplines, departments and specialised agencies and between the public and private sector, as well as vertically, across levels of governance, national, regional and global in a coherent system. Its full implementation requires new approaches that are integrated in content, and precautionary and anticipatory in ambit to ocean and coastal area management and development, at the national, regional and international levels' (Barcena, 1992, p.15).

The coastal situation is further vividly portrayed by Clark. Clark writes that 'the transitional strip of land and sea that straddles the coastline contains some of the most productive and valuable habitats of the biosphere, including estuaries, lagoons, coastal wetlands, and fringing coral reefs. It is also a place of natural dynamism where huge amounts of natural energy are released and a great abundance of life is nurtured. It is a place of high priority interest to people, to commerce, to the military, and to a variety of industries. Because it contains, dense populations, the coast undergoes great environmental modifications and deterioration through landfill, dredging, and pollution caused by urban, industrial, and agricultural development' (Clark, 1998, p.1).

It is also observed by Clark that 'the history of coastal occupancy and coastal development around the globe shows a pattern of depletion of coastal resources and loss of biodiversity. Critical habitats have been destroyed, ecosystem process disrupted, and waters heavily polluted. But with the ecological knowledge that we have now accumulated and the techniques that are available for coastal zone management, this trend, can be reversed. Appropriate actions are available by which coastal communities can both conserve their natural resources and invigorate their economies' (ibid, p.8).

The coastal system and its dynamics have been convincingly described by Cicin-Sain and Knecht as well. They observed that 'the place where the waters of the seas meet the land—the coasts–are indeed unique places in our global geography. They are unique in a very real economic sense as sites for port and harbour facilities that capture the large monetary benefits associated with water-borne commerce and as locations for industrial processes requiring water cooling, such as power generation plants. The coasts are highly valued and greatly attractive as sites for resorts and as vacation destinations and they are valuable in many other ways as well. The combination of freshwater and saltwater in coastal estuaries creates some of the most productive and richest habitats on earth; the resulting bounty in fishes and other marine life can be of great value to coastal nations. In many locations, the coastal topography formed over the millennia provides significant protection from hurricanes, typhoons, and other ocean-related disturbances. Hence, for most coastal nations, the coasts are an asset of incalculable value, an important part of the national patrimony.

But these values can be diminished or even lost. Pollution of coastal waters can greatly reduce the production of fish, as can degradation of coastal nursery grounds and other valuable wetland habitat. The storm protection offered by fringing coral reefs and mangrove forests can be lost if the corals die or the mangroves are removed. Inappropriate development and accompanying despoilment can reduce the attractiveness of the coastal environment, greatly affecting tourism potential. Even ports and harbours require active and informed management if they are to remain productive and successful enterprises over the long term.

Beyond these values, and perhaps more important the coasts are home to more than half of the world's population. Two thirds of the world's largest cities are located on coasts and populations of coastal areas are growing faster than inland populations.

The presence of large and growing populations in the world's coastal areas creates major problems. In developed countries, needs are generated for ever larger sewage treatment plants, expanded land fills for the disposal of solid wastes, and increased recreational facilities, to mention only a few. In developing countries, with less infrastructure in place, more people in the coastal zones means more pollution of coastal waters, more pressure on nearby natural resources (for example, mangrove forests for firewood and beach sand for construction), and pressure on fishery resources. Clearly, the tendency for even greater numbers of people to migrate to the world's coasts is exerting serious pressure on these areas that could put the value and productivity of many of them at risk. Unless effective steps to manage these areas are taken soon, losses of considerable consequence will occur (Cicin-Sain and Knecht, 1998, pp.15-16).

It is also noted here that the coastal zones are the thresholds for bearing the 'ecological footprints' or 'sustainability gaps' in development arising from global expansion in trade (Ekins, 2000, p.149).

What is apparent from the above descriptions and observations is the widespread global concern for coastal resources and their management. The prevailing situation in the Kerala coast being no way different from the global scenario noted above, and the academic and administrative initiative in tackling the coastal issues of Kerala being very tardy and invisible, there is an absolute need for a study of this sort.

1.3. Objectives of this study

As the very title of this study indicates, the fundamental objective of this study is to make the political economy of sustainable development of the Kerala coast explicit. 'Sustainable development' as defined by the FAO (Committee on Fisheries) 'is the management and conservation of the natural resource base, and the orientation of technological and institutional change in such a manner as to ensure the attainment and continued satisfaction of human needs for present and future generations. Such development conserves land, water, plant and genetic resources, is environmentally non-degrading, technologically appropriate, economically viable and socially acceptable' (Caddy and Griffiths, 1995, p.3).

As outlined in chapter three of this study, one of the major programme areas included in chapter 17 of agenda 21 of the UNCED (1992) was integrated management and sustainable development of coastal and marine areas, including exclusive economic zones. Sustainable development of the coast demanded integrated coastal zone management (ICZM) which is a continuous and dynamic process by which decisions are made for the sustainable use, development, and protection of coastal and marine areas and resources (Cicin-Sain and Knecht, 1998, p. 39). This process is designed to 'overcome the fragmentation inherent in both the sectoral management approach and the splits in jurisdiction among levels of government at the land-water interface. This is done by ensuring that the decisions of all sectors (e.g., fisheries, oil and gas production, water quality) and all levels of government are harmonised and consistent with the coastal policies of the nation in question. A key part of ICM is the design of institutional processes to accomplish this harmonisation in a politically acceptable manner' (ibid, p. 39).

Keeping in view of this approach to integrated coastal zone management and sustainable development, the fundamental objective of this study is to examine the need for an ICM programme in Kerala and to prescribe an ICM framework for Kerala. The study also cautions against the pitfalls of this approach to sustainable development.

1.4. Hypotheses

The following hypotheses were put forward to give some perspective to the study.

1. It holds that sustainable development of the coast demands fulfillment of ecological, economic and social criteria of sustainable development.
2. Sustainable development of the coast is possible with ICM efforts which will help in harmonising the ecological, economic and social basis of development,
3. Presently the developments in the Kerala coast is not sustainable.
4. Currently, the state is lacking in any serious ICM initiative.
5. Sustainable development of Kerala coast needs strong ICM initiatives and more precautions.

1.5. Methodology

The methodology followed in this study is analytical based on the epistemology of coastal zone management and sustainable development. The epistemology of coastal zone management combines the coastal bio-geophysical 'processes' with the economic and socio-cultural processes and directs the institutional mechanism to modify its programmes to suit the sustainability requirements of society. In this effort it merges with the received doctrine of sustainable development, whose cardinal principles are the commitment by society to fulfil the ecological, economic and social criteria of sustainability.

Following this approach, this study examined the coastal resource base of Kerala, the coastal landuse pattern, coastal zone activities, coastal issues and coastal zone management efforts in the past. From the emerging trend in coastal issues, it prescribed an ICZM programme for the sustainable development of the coast. The epistemology of ICZM, however, suggested precaution in this approach and the need for a more radical concept of 'sustainable development' with its roots in deep ecology and 'stationary' state with 'zero growth' in population and consumption.

1.6. Data base

The data base for the present study happened to be the global literature on coastal zone management which gives details of global initiatives, principles and practice of ICM, world wide. Data for analysing the coastal resource-base of Kerala, coastal land-use pattern, coastal zone activities of Kerala, coastal issues, coastal zone management activities in Kerala in the past, etc. were obtained from relevant publications of the Departments of Fisheries, Gazetteers, Planning, Tourism, etc. of the Government of Kerala and from the Centre for Earth Science Studies, Thiruvananthapuram, which is, at present, the nodal agency for coastal planning in Kerala.

1.7. Scope of the study

The geographic coverage of this study extends beyond the 500 metre narrow strip of coast from the high tide line, which is the legal limit of the defined CRZ of Kerala. This study generally considered the whole coastal districts of Kerala and sometimes the entire state covering the hinterland and the economy having forward and backward linkages with the 'coast' as the sphere of coastal zone management. This approach was taken primarily because of statistical requirements of the study and the non-availability of micro-level data for the 500 metre strip of the legally notified Coastal Regulation Zone (CRZ). Such an approach to ICM with wide ambience is well found in the literature (Cicin-Sain and Knecht, 1998, p.49).

1.8. Limitations of the study

One major limitation of this study is that it could not work out the net benefits of ICM as envisaged in the project proposal earlier, by taking hypothetical situations of 'with' and 'without' ICM efforts, for want of time and personnel for such an exercise. Another, apparent limitation of this study is that it could not make an 'in-situ' appraisal of the need for ICM in Kerala. In fact the participatory rural appraisal technique which it adopted failed to bring any useful information from the stakeholders on the ICM initiatives in Kerala. It only helped us in convincing ourselves of the general apathy and ignorance of the major stakeholders of the coast about the need for ICM and the failure of government machinery in creating a constituency for ICM efforts in Kerala. Notwithstanding these, this study has drawn extensively from local news reports and technical studies to highlight the coastal issues and the need for ICM in Kerala and its pitfalls.

1.9. Prospects

Notwithstanding the above limitations, the present study is a pioneering attempt to understand and present the need for ICM effort in Kerala and to prescribe the ICM strategy to resolve the coastal problems. In this attempt it has also posed doubts about ICM as a western liberal concept legitimising maximisation of production and consumption with no real control on population growth and 'consumerism' both of which lead to the global hunt for natural resources and to unsustainable development. The 'harmonisation' principle is then presumed to be a mere lullaby for 'growth'.

2
Review of Literature

2.1. Introduction

The objective of this chapter is to scan the inventory of literature relating to coastal zone management in India and abroad. This will help us in understanding the diversity of the coastal zone management issues and the evolving thrust in dealing with the problems. However, considering the complexity of the task at hand and the gargantuan nature of the literature on the subject, the attempt in this chapter is merely to briefly touch upon the more general and less technical studies and to identify the broad areas of global concern for coastal zone management. Keeping in view the national concern for coastal zone management and to discern it, the present review has classified the domestic literature separately and that of the rest of the world as another group.

2.2. Domestic literature

The domestic literature relating to coastal zone management is quite undeveloped. This is probably due to the lack of awareness among the scientific community about the need for coastal zone management in the country during the last couple of decades. This, however, sounds quite anomalous when a large section of the academic and scientistic community specialising in marine biology, fisheries and oceanography are thronging in the national academic and scientific environment. Quite a few of the Indian studies reported are, however, noted below.

Bose, *et. al.* (1989) wrote about the coastal zone management issues of West Bengal.

The National Conference on Coastal Zone Management, Cochin (1989) published its report in the same year.

Jhingran and Chakrabarti (1990) prepared an approach paper on coastal zone management in West Bengal.

Government of India (1991) issued the Coastal Regulation Zone Notification.

Nayak, *et. al.* (1992) gave a perspective for planning and management of the Coastal Zone of India.

Wafar (1992) pointed out the management and conservation options for Indian Coral Reefs.

Baba, *et. al.* (1993) reported about coastal erosion and sustainable management.

Harish (1993) reported about the impact of sea-level rise due to green-house effect, along the West Coast of India.

Kurien, *et. al.* (1993) reported the results of the land-use mapping of the Kerala coast for brackish water aquaculture site selection.

Swaminathan and Ramesh (1993) edited a compendium on sustainable management of coastal ecosystems.

Untawale (1993) wrote on the significance of mangroves for the coastal communities of India.

Neelakantan (1994) prepared a management plan for the Gulf of Mannar marine biosphere reserve in Tamil Nadu.

Zingde and Anand (1994) gave an account of the implications of coastal refineries to the ecology of the Gulf of Kachchh.

Baba, *et. al.* (1995) prepared the coastal zone management plan (map) of Kerala for the Government of Kerala.

Balchand, *et. al.* (1995) wrote about training, education and information services in developing countries on coastal zone management.

Baba, *et. al.* (1996) prepared a revised coastal zone management plan (map) of Kerala.

Sahasranaman (1996) compiled the laws relating to protection of coastal areas in India.

Desai (1997) reported on the bench mark survey of coastal marine environment of Gujarat.

Korakandy (1997) wrote on the need for coastal zone management in Kerala.

Nayak (1997) presented a paper on coastal zone management at the second Indian National Conference on Harbour and Ocean Engineering.

Singh (1997) outlined the issues and problems involved in managing marine protected areas with particular reference to the Marine National Park, Jamnagar.

Baba, *et. al.* (1998) prepared the final report of the coastal zone management plan (map) of Kerala in three volumes, the first dealing with coastal landuse and resources, the second with the coastal zone management of Iravipuram Panchayat and the third with the coastal landuse map of Kerala.

Nandakumar and Muralikrishna (1998) reported on the extent of coastal regulation zone violations of the Indian coast.

Zingde (1998) reported about the quality of coastal waters of India.

Ghosh, *et al.* (1999) outlined the scenario in India with respect to port development and coastal zone management.

Joseph and Balchand (2000) made an appraisal of the application of coastal regulation zones in coastal management in India.

Sengupta and Deshmukh (2000) outlined the ecology and economics of the coastal and marine environments of Gujarat.

Sharma, *et. al.*(2000) gave an account of the environmental problems of coastal areas in India.

As already noted, it is apparent from the above that the domestic literature on the subject is quite underdeveloped. Much of the above works reported are quite general and lacking in both theoretical and empirical content. It is appalling that the country with its considerable coastline and advancements in the fields of marine biology, oceanography and fisheries has not come to grip with the contemporary realities of the coastal environment and its study.

2.3. International literature

Much in contrast with the domestic literature, the international literature relating to coastal zone management is quite extensive and pretty well developed. This literature has evolved from isolated national efforts by countries and finally from concerted international efforts to study and promote global coastal zone management. In order to make this section tidy, only general and non-technical works of theoretical or empirical importance have been included here. To some extent this will help in limiting the scope of this review.

The global literature on coastal zone management is now approximately three decades old. One of the earliest works highlighting the significance of the sea and the coast was made by the U.S. Commission on Marine Sciences (1969).This study in fact led to the final passage of the U.S. Coastal Zone Management Act in 1972.

Hood (1971) showed convincingly the impingement of man on the oceans and the need for managing human activities in the ocean and the coastal environments.

Hite and Stepp (1971) indicated the need for coastal zone resource management.

The U.S. Army Corps of Engineers (1971) completed the national shoreline study relating to the North Atlantic.

The need for coastal zone management with multiple uses and conservation priorities was brought out by Brahtz (1972).

The critical problems of the coastal zone were highlighted by Ketchum (1972).

The U.S. Congress (1972) passed the Coastal Zone Management Act of 1972.

Bascom (1974) wrote about the critical issue of disposal of waste in the ocean.

The legislative political history of the Coastal Zone Management Act of 1972 of the United States was brought out by Zile (1974).

The California Coastal Zone Conservation Commission (1975) prepared the California Coastal Plan.

Hildreth (1975) reported about the coastal land use control in Sweden.

A revised edition of the shore protection manual was brought out by the U.S. Army Coastal Engineering Research Centre (1975).

Heikoff (1976) made clear the politics of shore erosion in the Westampton beach of New York State.

Clark (1977) gave an account of the coastal ecosystem management issue.

The relationship between coastal zone management and off-shore economic development was highlighted by Clark (1977).

Englander, *et. al.* (1977) outlined the basis for evaluation of coastal zone problems.

Sorensen (1978) reported about state-local collaborative planning, which was a growing trend in coastal zone management in the U.S.

The British experience in saving the coast was reported by Steers (1978).

Knecht (1979) discussed the working of the first five years of the U.S. Coastal Zone Management Act of 1972 and looked beyond that period.

Sorensen (1979) reviewed the working of state-local relations in coastal zone management in the U.S. and noted the implications for change.

Valencia (1979) edited the proceedings of the workshop on coastal area development and management in the Pacific.

Clark (1980) prepared the guidelines for coastal environmental management with special reference to conservation of resources and protection against storm hazards.

Heikoff (1980) gave a critical review of marine and shoreland resource management in the New York State of the US of both prior to and after the enactment of the Coastal Zone Management Act of 1972.

Burbridge and Keesoebiono (1981) gave a description of coastal zone management in South East Asia.

Cicim-Sain (1982) gave a perspective and retrospective account of managing the ocean commons by the U.S. in the 1970s and 1980s.

An account of coastal zone management in Australia was given by Cullen (1982).

An overall strategy in designing wetland restoration was put forward by Sorensen (1982).

A coastal area management and development plan was put forward by the U.N. (1982).

Amarsinghe and Wikremeratne (1983) gave an account of the evolution and implementation of legislation for coastal zone management in Sri Lanka.

A technical manual for the conservation of coastal zone resources was prepared by Clark (1983).

Geoghegan (1983) prepared the guidelines for integrated marine resource management in the Eastern Caribbean.

Ogden and Gladfelter (1983) gave an account of the coral reefs, seagrass beds and mangroves and their interactions in the coastal zone of the Caribbean.

Squires (1983) wrote about the ocean dumping quandary.

Knecht, *et. al.* (1984) made an assessment of the management of ocean and coastal resources in Colombia.

Sorensen, *et. al.* (1984) outlined the institutional arrangement for management of coastal resources.

A revised shore protection manual was prepared by the U.S. Army Corps of Engineers (1984).

An over-view of coastal zone management in six east Caribbean Islands was given by Cambers (1985).

Clark (1985) brought out extensive case studies of developments in coastal zone management practices.

Dubois and Towle (1985) wrote about coral harvesting and sand mining management practices in the U.S.

Joliffe and Patman (1985) delineated the challenges of the coastal zone.

Ruddle and Johannes (1985) wrote about traditional knowledge base and management of coastal systems in Asia and the Pacific.

Chua (1986) wrote about managing ASEAN coastal resources.

Amarasinghe, *et. al.* (1987) reported on the working of coastal zone management in Sri Lanka during 1978 - 86.

The role of citizen participation in coastal area planning and management was noted by Renard (1986).

The economic considerations in the management of coastal resources were noted by Burbridge (1987).

Cambers (1987) outlined the coastal zone management programmes in Barbados and Grenada.

Ching (1987) noted the issues in coastal zone management in Malaysia, and the possible solutions.

Edwards (1987) gave an introductory treatment of coastal zone economics with focus on concepts, methods and case studies.

Eichenberg and Archer (1987) outlined the federal consistency doctrine and their application in coastal zone management in the U.S.

Koekebakker and Peet (1987) gave an account of coastal zone planning and management in the Netherlands.

The Sri Lanka Coast Conservation Department (1987) reported about the coastal zone management plan for Sri Lanka.

Vallego (1987) gave an outline of the international perspective on development and management of coastal marine areas.

The World Commission on Environment and Development (1987) highlighted our dependence on ocean and coastal resources in our common future.

Archer (1988) gave a selective review and summary of coastal zone management in the United States.

Hodgson and Dixon (1988) gave an account of measuring economic losses due to sediment pollution and the interaction with logging, tourism and fisheries.

Levy (1988) highlighted the need for an integrated marine policy in developing countries.

Lowry and Wickremeratne (1988) gave an account of coastal area management in Sri Lanka.

O'Brien (1988) made an evaluation of Western Australia's non-statutory approach to coastal zone management.

Turner (1988) wrote about the economics and ethics of wetland conversion.

The role of marine parks and reserves in the management of coastal environments in South East Asia was highlighted by White (1988).

The economic value of tropical wetland ecosystems was highlighted by Barbier (1989).

The need for multiple use assessment for coastal management was indicated by Burbridge, *et. al.* (1989).

Carter (1989) gave an introduction to the physical, ecological and cultural systems of the coast lines.

Chaverri (1989) gave an account of the Coasta Rica experience in coastal management.

Chua (1989) gave a framework for developing coastal area management plans in the Southeast Asian region.

Chua and Pauly (1989) outlined the policies and management strategies for coastal area management in Southeast Asia alongwith some case studies.

The Coastal Area Management and Planning Network (CAMPNET) of the University of Miami (1989) made a global assessment of the status of integrated coastal zone management.

Degong (1989) wrote about coastal zone development, utilisation, legislation and management in China.

Dobias (1989) reported about beaches and tourism in Thailand.

Herz (1989) outlined the working of coastal and ocean space management in Brazil.

Hildebrand (1989) gave an account of Canada's experience with coastal zone management.

The Institution of Civil Engineers of England (1989) published the proceedings of a conference on Coastal Management.

A comparative analysis of national programmes for coastal zone management was made by Mitchell (1989).

Prescott (1989) outlined the current concerns of coastal planning.

Salam and Clark (1989) brought out a guide for planners and managers of marine and coastal protected areas.

An outline of coastal tourism and environmental management in Fiji was given by Chape (1990).

The Coast Conservation Department of Sri Lanka (1990) brought out the coastal zone management plan of Sri Lanka.

The relevance of sea-level rise in coastal zone management was highlighted by Eid and Hulbergen (1990).

Gubbay (1990) prepared the proposals for a coastal zone management plan for the U.K.

The Hawaii Office of State Planning (1990) prepared the Hawaii coastal zone management programme.

The Inter-Governmental Panel on Climate Change (1990) prepared the strategies for adaption to sea level rise.

Kenchington (1990) wrote about managing marine environments.

Mitchell (1990) gave an outline of the evolution of integrated resource management.

Sorensen and McCreary (1990) outlined the institutional arrangements for managing coastal resources and environments.

Thoraugh (1990) outlined the economic benefits of restoration of mangroves and sea-grass for fisheries and mariculture.

Zhijie and Cote (1990) gave an account of management approaches and institutions in the coastal zones of the People's Republic of China.

Chancharaswat (1991) outlined the role of environmental protection and coastal resource management in national development planning in Thailand.

Chua (1991 a) edited the proceedings of the ICLARM Conference on 'Coastal Area Management Education in ASEAN Region'.

Chua (1991 b) gave an account of the ASEAN's initiative in managing coastal resources for sustainable development.

Chua and Scura (1991) edited the proceedings of the ICLARM conference on 'Managing ASEAN's Coastal Resources for Sustainable Development: Role of Policy Makers, Scientists, Donors, Media and Communities'.

Chou, *et.al.* (1991) edited the proceedings of the ICLARM conference on 'Towards an Integrated Management of Tropical Coastal Resources'.

Clark (1991) made a global assessment of the status of integrated coastal management.

The importance of public participation in coastal management was noted by Coetzee (1991).

The need for integrated coastal resource management was stressed by Dahuri (1991).

Factoran, Jr. (1991) highlighted the need for integrated coastal zone management in the Philippines.

FAO (1991) published its research paper No.4 on 'Development of Coastal Areas and Enclosed Seas'.

An assessment of the coastal zone issues in the Republic of Korea was made by Hong (1991).

The role and involvement of non-governmental organisations in the sustainable development of coastal resources was highlighted by Kalaw, Jr. (1991).

Leekpai (1991) noted the value of coastal resources in national economic development in the ASEAN region.

Lohani (1991) focused on the Asian Development Bank's efforts in sustainable development of coastal resources.

Macaraig (1991) recognised the challenge and the choice existing for sustainable development of coastal resources.

Mathews (1991) noted the role of local press in creating public awareness of coastal resource management.

The Mediterranean Environmental Technical Assistance Programme (1991) prepared its report on 'Coastal Zone Management (CZM) in Turkey'.

Msangi (1991) reported about the integrated utilisation of the sea coast off the coast of Tanzania.

Needham (1991) edited case studies of experience in coastal management in the United States.

Ohta (1991) reported about the developments in coastal management in Hawaii.

The OECD (1991) published its report on coastal zone management with integrated policies and draft recommendations of the Council on ICZM.

Patterson, *et. al.* (1991) raised the issue of sewering the coast and its impact on marine water quality.

Paw and Chua (1991) gave an assessment of the ecological and economic impacts of mangrove conversion in South Asia.

Premaratne (1991) reported about the difficulties of coastal resource management in Sri Lanka.

Chua (1992) outlined the phases of initiation, implementation and management of the ASEAN/US Coastal Resource Management Project.

Chua and Scura (1992) edited the proceedings of the ICLARM Conference on 'Integrative Framework and Methods for Coastal Area Management'.

Cicin-Sain (1992) highlighted the multiple use conflicts and their resolution and proposed an agenda for comparative research.

Clark (1992) outlined the principles for integrated management of coastal zones.

The Department of Fisheries of Brunei (1992) published the integrated management plan for the coastal zone of Brunei Darussalam.

Diegues (1992) outlined the contribution of research amid the realities of politics in managing Brazil's coastal wetlands.

Edward, *et.al.* (1992) published the 'Economics of Coastal Management - A Manual of Benefit Assessment Techniques'.

Fabbri (1992) edited the work on Ocean Management in Global Change.

Godschalk (1992) made a review of implementation of coastal zone management in the U.S. during 1972-90.

The Institution of Civil Engineers of U.K. (1992) published its report on integrating coastal zone planning and management in the next century.

The Inter-Coast Net Work of USA (1992) conducted feasibility studies of pilot programmes for integrated coastal area management.

The use of remote sensing and geographic information systems in coastal zone management was highlighted by Kam, *et. al.* (1992).

A critique of the national ocean policy in the United States was offered by Knecht (1992).

A summary of the workshop on Integrated Coastal Management and Sea-Level Rise, held at Caracas in January 1992 was reported by Knecht, *et.al.* (1992).

The Malaysian Coastal Resource Study Team (1992) prepared the coastal resource management plan for south Johore, Malaysia.

The National Economic Development Authority of Philippines (1992) prepared the Lingayen Gulf Coastal Area management plan.

The National Environment Board of Thailand (1992) prepared the integrated management plan for Ban Don Bay and Phanganga Bay of Thailand.

Pernetta and Elder (1992) discussed the effects of climate change and sea level rise and the need for coastal zone management and planning.

Pido and Chua (1992) gave a framework for rapid appraisal of coastal environments.

Pomeroy (1992) outlined the available methods for economic valuation in coastal area management.

Scura, *et.al.* (1992) discussed the ASEAN experience in coastal zone management.

Smith (1992) outlined the conflicting trend of beach resort development in Malaysia.

The legal and organisational considerations in the management of coastal areas were brought out by Tobin (1992).

The U.K. Department of Environment (1992) brought out the Government's response to coastal zone protection and planning.

The concern for changing the waterfront in coastal area management was highlighted by Vallega (1992).

Wang (1992) outlined the working of coastal management in China.

The Australian Bureau of Agricultural and Resource Economics (1993) outlined the use of economic instruments in integrated coastal zone management.

Burbridge and Burbridge (1993) reported the experiences of IUCN, WWF and UNEP with integrated coastal management.

Chua (1993 a) gave a brief description of the regional efforts in the management of coastal and marine environments in the ASEAN region.

Chua (1993 b) outlined the essential elements of integrated coastal zone management.

Cicin-Sain (1993 a) gave an introduction to the special issue of Ocean and Coastal Management, dealing with 'integrated coastal management: concepts, issues and methods'.

Cicin-Sain (1993 b) outlined the linkage between sustainable development and integrated coastal management.

Cicin-Sain (1993 c) gave a brief account of the activities of Marine Affairs and Policy Associations (MAPA) for education and training in ocean and coastal management.

Cicin-Sain and Knecht (1993 a) edited the special issue of Ocean and Coastal Management, dealing with 'integrated coastal management'.

Cicin-Sain and Knecht (1993 b) outlined the implications of the Earth Summit for ocean and coastal governance.

Coughanowr and Kullenberg (1993) gave the Inter-Governmental Oceanographic Commission's perspective on integrated coastal management and noted the need for scientific input on an international scale.

Cordell (1993) wrote about indigenous people's coastal marine domains and some matters of cultural documentation.

Crawford, *et. al.* (1993) outlined the need for building capacity for integrated coastal management in developing countries.

The Department of Environment and the Welsh Office (1993) made a review of regulations relating to development below low water mark in England and Wales.

Griffith and Ashe (1993) discussed sustainable development of coastal and marine areas in small island developing states as a basis for integrated coastal management.

Guochen (1993) gave an account of coastal zone management in China.

Herz and Mascarenhas (1993) outlined the interplay of political and planning action on the Brazilian coastal management programme.

Jull (1993) noted the 'sea changes' taking place in indigenous-overseas government relations in the coastal zones.

Kahawita (1993) gave an account of coastal zone management in Sri Lanka.

Kenchington and Crawford (1993) clarified the meaning of integration in coastal zone management.

Knecht (1993) gave a perspective on the relationship between the local and national levels of government in coastal zone management.

Knecht and Archer (1993) discussed the level of integration in the U.S. coastal zone management programme.

Lee, *et. al.* (1993) gave an account of coastal zone utilisation in the Republic of Korea and its prospects.

Lei (1993) gave an account of coastal zone management in Malaysia.

A brief outline of coastal zone management in Sri Lanka was given by Lowry (1993).

Lewry, *et. al.* (1993) made an assessment of the federal consistency provision of the Coastal Zone Management Act of the U.S. and noted the need for federal-state coordination in coastal management.

Olsen (1993) raised the 'constituency' problem affecting the sustainability of integrated coastal zone management programmes.

The OECD (1993 a) published the document on coastal zone management and integrated policies.

The OECD (1993 b) also published selected case studies in coastal zone management.

Pernetta and Elder (1993) prepared the guidelines and principles for coastal area development with focus on cross-sectoral integrated coastal area planning.

An account of national coastal resources management in Thailand was given by Pintukanok and Borothanarat (1993).

Rais (1993) gave an account of marine resource evaluation and planning project for integrated coastal zone planning and management in Indonesia.

The Resource Assessment Commission of Australia (1993) published the final report of the Coastal Zone Enquiry.

Rizvi (1993) gave an over-view of coastal zone management issues in Pakistan.

Schroder (1993) outlined the need for international training in coastal management.

Sorensen (1993 a) gave a conceptual framework for coastal zone management.

Sorensen (1993 b) reviewed the international proliferation of integrated coastal zone management efforts

The U.K. Department of Environment (1993) gave a review of coastal management plans in England and Wales and the powers supporting them.

The U.S. Department of Commerce (1993) prepared the biennial report to Congress on the administration of the U.S. Coastal Zone Management Act,

A conceptual approach to integrated coastal management was given by Vallega (1993),

The need for integration of coastal zone management into national development planning was highlighted by Vallejo (1993).

A systems view of integrated coastal management was given by Vanderweide (1993).

Vellinga and Klein (1993) reported about climate change, sea level rise and integrated coastal management.

The World Bank (1993) published the guidelines for integrated coastal zone management.

The World Coast Conference (1993) published the report 'Preparing to Meet the Coastal Challenges of the 21st Century'.

Alder, *et. al.* (1994) reported the advances in marine protected area management in Indonesia during 1988-93.

Archer, *et. al.* (1994) wrote on the public trust doctrine and the management of America's coast.

Ballinger, *et. al.* (1994) gave an account of the management of coastal zones of Europe.

Barston (1994) outlined the international dimensions of coastal zone management.

Beatly, *et. al.* (1994) published the book 'An Introduction to Coastal Zone Management'.

Beck (1994) gave an account of the movement in the United States for the restoration and creation of wetlands.

Boelaert-Suomimen and Cullinan (1994) highlighted the legal and institutional aspects of integrated coastal area management in national legislation.

Borgese (1994) noted the regional and global aspects of training and education in ocean management for the 2lst century.

Bower, *et. al.* (1994) gave a framework for planning for integrated coastal zone management.

Coombs (1994) brought to light the issues and strategies relating to aboriginal autonomy.

FAO (1994) produced the guidelines for the management of mangrove forests.

Donalson (1994) gave a practitioner's perspective of working with coastal communities and found the element of an unholy alliance.

Hildebrand (1994) outlined the need for cooperation in coastal zone.

The Inter-Governmental Panel on Climate Change (1994) brought out the World Coast Conference report 'Preparing to Meet the Coastal Challenges of the 21st Century'.

The Swedish Agency for Research and Cooperation with Developing Countries (1994) published the 'Technical Recommendations of the Workshop on Integrated Coastal Zone Management in Eastern Africa including Island States'.

Lonardi (1995) gave a description of the utilisation and management of the coastal zone in Latin America and the Caribbean.

Caddy and Griffith (1995) gave the environmental and institutional perspectives of living marine resources and their sustainable development.

Cicin-Sain and Knecht (1995 a) edited 'Earth Summit Implementation: Progress Achieved on Ocean and Coasts'.

Cicin-Sain and Knecht (1995 b) gave an account of progress on UNCED implementation on ocean and coasts.

Cicin-Sain, *et. al.* (1995) gave the international perspective in growth in capacity for integrated coastal management since UNCED.

Cobb (1995) reported about building capacity for coastal management at universities.

Crawford, *et. al.* (1995) edited the proceedings of the Rhode Island workshop on 'Educating Coastal Managers'.

Ehler (1995) outlined the challenges in coastal ocean space management in the next decade.

Fuavo (1995) discussed the issue of coastal management in small island states.

Gagliano (1995) noted the role of public-private partnership in the governance of coastline.

Gilbert (1995) wrote about action on the coast.

Grigalunas and Congar (1995) edited the report on environmental economic valuation methods and policy instruments for integrated coastal area management.

Gubbay (1995) outlined the opportunity for Scotland for integrated coastal zone management.

A comparative analysis of the implementation of UNCED agenda 21, chapter. 17 in Australia and Canada was made by Haward and Vanderswaag (1995).

Hong and Huh (1995) gave an account of coastal zone development in the Republic of Korea.

The issues and approaches to coastal management in the Asia Pacific region were outlined by Hotta and Dutton (1995).

Kinball (1995) suggested an international regime for managing land based activities that degrade marine and coastal environments.

The socio-economic aspects of insular coastal management were noted by Micaleff (l995).

Olsen (1995) identified the skills, knowledge and attitudes of an ideal coastal manager.

Ozhan and Culhaogie (1995) gave an account of the MED COAST Institute training programme on coastal zone management in the Mediterranean and Black Sea.

Robadue Jr. (1995) edited 'Eight Years in Euqador: The Road to Integrated Coastal Management'.

The South Pacific Regional Environment Programme (1995) gave an outline of the coastal area management programme in the Pacific Island nations.

Turner and Bower (1995) discussed the benefits of integrated coastal zone management.

The United Nations Environmental Programme (1995 a) outlined the global programme of action for the protection of the marine environment from land based activities.

The United Nations Environmental Programme (1995 b) discussed the guidelines for integrated management of coastal and marine areas with special reference to the Mediterranean Basin.

The U.S. Department of Commerce (1995) published the Hand Book for Coastal Resource Policy Makers with focus on economic valuation of natural resources.

The coastal use-framework as a methodological tool for coastal area management was noted by Vellega (1995 a).

Vallega (1995 b) gave an outline of the regional level implementation of Chapter 17 in the Mediterranean.

Waterman (1995) noted the significance of integrated coastal policy via building with nature.

Williams and Davis (1995) pointed out the need for regulating land-based activities.

Winsamius (1995) suggested integration in policies as a requirement for coastal zone management.

The World Bank (1995) gave a framework for integrated coastal zone management of Africa.

The World Wide Fund for Nature (1995) outlined the U.K. and European initiatives for integrated coastal zone management.

Alcala (1996) gave an account of coastal resource management in the Philippines.

Anutha and Johnson (1996) gave a description of aquaculture planning and coastal management in Tasmania.

Anutha and Kriwoken (1996) gave an introduction to the special issue of 'Ocean and Coastal Management' dealing with ocean and coastal management problems in Australia and New Zealand.

Bateman (1996) noted the environmental issues with Australian ports.

Bergin (1996) gave a description of the Royal Australian Navy and the marine environment.

Brown (1996) noted the role of universities in capacity building for coastal resource management, especially in view of the inter-disciplinary, multi-disciplinary and trans-disciplinary knowledge involved.

The status of coastal area management in the Pacific Island nations was reported oy Chalapan (1996).

Chua (1996) reported the working of integrated coastal management in tropical developing countries and noted the lessons learned from successes and failures.

Chua and Paw (1996) wrote about the dichotomy of the planning process used in the ASEAN-US Project on coastal resource management.

Chua and Yu (1996) reported the findings of a case study in coastal management in Xiamen in China and noted the shift in approach from sectoral to integrated management.

An international perspective on growth in capacity for integrated coastal management since UNCED was given by Cicin-Sain, *et. al.* (1996).

Clark (1996) brought out an extensive handbook on Coastal Zone Management.

Dahuri (1996) drew attention to the problem of transmigration in the context of coastal zone management in Indonesia.

Davis (1996) gave an overview of contemporary ocean and coastal management issues in Australia and New Zealand.

The Department of Fisheries and Oceans of Canada (1996) prepared the Canadian retrospective and update of integrated coastal area management.

El-Sabh, *et. al.* (1996) edited the abstracts of the international conference, 'Coastal Zone Canada' titled as 'Integrated Management and Sustainable Development in Coastal Zone'.

Fisk (1996) made a case study of integrated coastal management in Australia.

FAO (1996 a) brought out the technical guidelines for integration of fisheries into coastal area management.

FAO (1996 b) released the 'Report of the Task Force on Integrated Coastal Management'.

Frihy (1996) presented some proposals for coastal management of the Nile delta coast.

The role of indigenous participation in coastal management in the Northern Territory of Australia and the issues and options before it were noted by Gantor (1996).

An outline of the contribution of science to integrated coastal management was given by GESAMP (1996).

Haward (1996) outlined the institutional framework for ocean and coastal management in Australia.

The Canadian experience with coastal zone management was outlined by Hildebrand (1996).

The integrated coastal and marine areas management (ICAM) programme in the Mediterranean Action Plan of UNEP was outlined by Jeftic (1996).

Knecht, *et. al.* (1996) gave an account of the perceptions of the performance of state coastal zone management programmes in the United States.

Kusuma-Atmadja and Purwaka (1996) described the legal and institutional aspects of coastal zone management in Indonesia.

Ozhan (1996 a) edited the special issue of 'Ocean and Coastal Management' dealing with coastal zone management in the Mediterranean.

An account of coastal zone management in Turkey was given by Ozhan (1996 b).

Post and Lundin (1996) gave the guidelines for integrated coastal zone management.

Rosier and Hastie (1996) presented an issue-based approach to New Zealand coastal planning.

Rothwell (1996) outlined the legal framework for ocean and coastal management in Australia.

The problems and plans of action for integrated coastal zone management in Indonesia were reported by Soegiarto (1996).

Tol *et. al.* (1996) presented some of the economic considerations to show the importance of pro-active integrated coastal zone management.

Turner, *et. al.* (1996) noted the pressures, trends and impacts in coastal zones and the interactions between socio-economic and natural systems.

The UN Environmental Programme (1996) gave the guidelines for integrated planning and management of coastal and marine areas in the wider Caribbean region.

An online data base of world-wide efforts for integrated coastal resources management is provided by the University of Rhode Island (1996).

Williams (1996) reported the Australian initiatives in combating marine pollution from land-based activities.

The World Bank (1996) recommended the shift from plans to markets.

Zann (1996) reviewed the 'State of Marine Environment Report for Australia' (SOMER) and outlined the process, findings and perspectives.

Arico and Rakotoary (1997) gave a sketch of the beginning of integrated coastal management efforts in Madagascar.

Burbridge (1997) gave a generic framework for measuring success in integrated coastal management.

The need for application of integrated coastal management system for sustaining coastal fishery development was noted by Chua (1997 a).

Chua (1997 b) gave an introduction to the special issue of 'Ocean and Coastal Management' dealing with lessons learned in integrated coastal management.

Chua, *et. al.* (1997) reported the move from sectoral to integrated coastal management in Xiamen,China.

Cicin-Sain, *et. al.* (1997) gave the guidelines for integrating coastal management programmes and national climate change action plans.

Clark (1997) highlighted the role of coastal zone management in the new century.

Dahl (1997) gave an account of integrated coastal resource management and community participation in a small island setting.

Edwards, *et. al.* (1997) reviewed the level of participation in coastal zone management initiatives by analysing the examples from the U.K.

Ellsworth, *et. al.* (1997) gave an account of the community based approach to collective governance in Canada's Atlantic coastal action programme.

Ha, *et. al.* (1997) outlined the imperatives for coastal zone management in maritime developing nations.

Hatziolos (1997) outlined the World Bank frame-work for ICZM with special emphasis on Africa.

Hatziolos and Trumbic (1997) reported the preliminary results of an assessment of coastal zone management initiatives in the Mediterranean.

Hegarty (1997) gave a community based approach to integrated coastal management and appealed to start with what the people know of it.

Hershman, *et.al.* (1997) reported the findings and recommendations of the national CZM effectiveness study.

Hildebrand (1997) gave an introduction to the special issue of 'Ocean and Coastal Management' dealing with community based coastal management.

Jacoby, *et. al.* (1997) reported on three recent initiatives for monitoring of Australian coasts by the community.

Jorge (1997) reported about developing capacity for coastal management in the absence of the public sector in the Dominican Republic.

Mckoloweka and Schurcliff (1997) discussed the decentralised community based approach to coastal management in Tanga, Tanzania.

Ngoile and Lindon (1997)reported the development of policy on ICZM at the national and regional levels and the lessons learned from Eastern Africa.

Okemwa, *et. al.* (1997) gave an account of the initial experiences and progress in integrated coastal zone management in Kenya.

Olsen, *et. al.* (1997) presented a common framework for learning from ICM experience.

Rivera and Nowkirk (1997) gave a documentation of NGO experience in community based coastal resource management in the Philippines.

Sorensen (1997) outlined the national and international efforts at integrated coastal management with focus on definitions, achievements and lessons.

Talaue McManus and Chua (1997) gave an account of the Lingayen Gulf (Philippines) experience in coastal management.

A brief account of the working of coastal zone planning in Denmark was given by Worm (1997).

Alcala (1998) reported on the working of community based coastal resource management in the Philippines.

Basiron (1998) outlined the challenges and opportunities in the implementation of Chapter 17 of Agenda 21 in Malaysia.

Bower and Turner (1998) commented about characterising and analysing benefits from integrated coastal management.

Chiau (1998) gave a review of coastal zone management in Taiwan.

Chua (1998) reported on the lessons from practising integrated coastal management in South East Asia.

Cicin-Sain and Knecht (1998) brought out an extensive treatise on integrated coastal and ocean management with focus on concepts and practices.

Deb (1998) outlined the environmental and socio-economic impacts of shrimp culture in the coastal areas of Bangladesh.

El-Sabh, *et al.* (1998) reviewed the changes in coastal management and sustainable development from Stockholm Conference to Rimouski Conference.

Fabbri (1998) offered a methodology for supporting decision making in integrated coastal zone management.

The role of inter-governmental organisations in coastal zone management was outlined by Holland (1998).

Hugget (1998) discussed the role of federal government intervention in coastal zone planning and management in the U.S.

Huming and Chua (1998) recommended ICM training for marine pollution prevention and management.

The Independent World Commission on the Oceans (1998) linked the oceans with our future.

Kay and Alder (1998) wrote on coastal planning and management.

Nadia (1998) edited the FAO guidelines on integrated coastal area management, agriculture, forestry and fisheries.

Needharn (1998) suggested an innovative approach to training and capacity building for integrated coastal management.

A manual for self-assessment of coastal management planning and implementation was prepared by Olsen, *et. al.* (1998).

Plink (1998) gave a brief account of training and education in integrated coastal zone management.

Ranjith and Silva (1998) gave an account of the coastal resource management programme in Brunei Darussalam.

The institutional arrangement and implementation of coastal management in Singapore was reported by Sien (1998).

South and Veitayaki (1998) gave an account of capacity building in the South Pacific and the role of the marine studies programme at the University of the South Pacific.

Vandermeulen (1998) wrote on the development of marine indicators for coastal zone management.

Wong (1998) outlined the development of coastal tourism in Southeast Asia and the relevance and lessons for coastal zone management.

The 'beneficial uses' approach in coastal management as a compromise between rapid urban development and sustainability was discussed by Wu, *et. al.* (1998).

Ali Mohammed (1999) gave an account of coastal zone management in Egypt.

Ballinger (1999) noted the evolving organisational framework for integrated coastal zone management in England and Wales.

Ducrotoy and Pullen (1999) gave an account of integrated coastal zone management commitments and developments from an international, national and U.K. perspective.

Hershman, *et. al.* (1999) traced the effectiveness of coastal zone management in the United States.

Lowry, *et. al.* (1999 a) reviewed the role of donor evaluations of ICM initiatives and noted what can be learned from them.

Lowry, *et. al.* (1999 b) gave a policy relevant assessment of community level coastal management projects in Sri Lanka.

Sudara (1999) outlined who and what is to be involved in successful coastal management and cited the example of Thailand.

The World Bank (1999) prepared a strategic agenda for integrated coastal management in sub-Saharan Africa.

Ballinger and Lalwani (2000) outlined the role of internships in marine policy and integrated coastal management higher education.

Cicin-Sain, *et. al.* (2000) noted the role of education and training in integrated coastal management and the lessons from the international arena.

Ducrotoy, *et. al.* (2000) reported on the need for networking in higher education in coastal sciences and management.

Hewawasam (2000) wrote on advancing knowledge as a key element of the World Bank's integrated coastal zone management strategic agenda in sub-Saharan Africa.

Jentoft (2000) wrote on co-management of the coastal zone.

Johnson, *et. al.* (2000) reported on integrated coastal management education in the Russian Federation through academic partnership.

Olsen (2000) outlined the dimensions of the challenge of education for the governance of coastal ecosystem.

Ozhan (2000) noted an NGO role in enhancing integrated coastal management in the Mediterranean and the Black Sea.

Smith (2000) pointed out the role of the University system in the education and training for integrated coastal area management.

Snoussi and Aoul (2000) outlined the working of integrated coastal zone management programme in the north west African region.

Vallega (2000) gave an introduction to the special issue of 'Ocean and Coastal Management' dealing with education and training in coastal management.

It is apparent from the above scanning of the global literature that it is quite extensive and growing. It has evolved and moved from a U.S. concern for coastal zone management which has its first expression in the U.S. Coastal Zone Management Act of 1972 to a global concern and movement which is assisted by the U.S., the U.N. and other national and international organisations. This is reflected in the many national, regional and global initiatives, and the proceedings of many conferences, some of which are noted in the above review.

Remarkably, the global literature has benefitted from the USAID, ASEAN, ICLARM, UNEP, UNCED, World Bank and many UN consultations held for coastal zone management in the Asia-Pacific, African, Mediterranean, European and Latin American regions.

Interestingly, the global literature is now sustained by an exclusive international journal, 'Ocean and Coastal Management', which continuously monitors and reports the developments in the field of ocean and coastal management. Quite a large number of the publications noted above were published in this journal.

An outstanding feature of the global literature which is evident but not explicitly stated above is the fact that the global literature which has evolved from an over all concern for protecting the coastal environment in particular countries and climates has since become a global mission, finding itself embedded in the spirit of agenda 21 of the UNCED now proliferating into specific means and areas for accomplishing the goal of sustainable development of the coast by capacity building, NGO participation, global networking, academic partnerships and by other means. Much of the current literature noted above focus on the new and emerging areas of capacity building, co-management and networking for coastal zone management, using internet services. Details of such programmes and agencies promoting these are discussed in the following chapters.

2.4. Conclusion

The review of literature made above makes two things clear. First, it reveals that the domestic literature is quite underdeveloped and this probably was due to the lack of awareness among the scientific community about the need for coastal zone management. This is, however, considered to be quite anomalous when a large section of the academic and scientific community specialising in marine biology, fisheries and oceanography are thronging the national academic and scientific environment.

The second point emerging from the review is that the global literature on coastal zone management is quite extensive and fast growing. It has evolved from national and regional concern for protecting the coastal environment and has grown into a global concern for sustainable development of the coastal zone. The global literature has benefitted from regional and global programmes for coastal zone management, promoted by the US, UN, World Bank and other national and international organisations. The global literature is now nurtured by an exclusive journal, 'Ocean and Coastal Management'. It is also being sustained by many 'intercoast' networks.

3

Coastal Zone Management—A Conceptual Framework

3.1. Introduction

In the current literature on coastal zone management, phrases like Integrated Coastal Zone Management (ICZM), Integrated Coastal and Ocean Zone Management (ICOZM), Integrated Coastal Area Management (ICAM), Integrated Coastal Management (ICM), Coastal Resource Management (CRM), Integrated Marine and Coastal Area Management (IMCAM) and Community Based Coastal Resource Management (CBCRM) are all used frequently to denote the strategies and programmes for the careful and planned use of the coastal environment and its resources. It, nevertheless, appears that these phrases have evolved in different geo-political and economic contexts and have specific meaning and content attached to them.

The objective of this chapter is to make the conceptual framework of coastal zone management clear. This is considered important for understanding the 'process' of coastal zone management. More precisely, it should help in understanding the coastal issues and their resolution. As a starting point, this Chapter seeks to present some of the definitions of coastal zone management and the evolution of the concept over the last three decades.

3.2. Definitions

An early idea of the concept (theory) and practice of coastal zone management was given by the U.S. Congress when it passed the Federal Coastal Zone Management Act of 1972, as amended in 1976. It noted 'the congress finds and declares that it is the national policy (a) to preserve, protect, develop, and where possible, to restore or enhance, the resources of the nation's coastal zone for this and succeeding generations, (b) to encourage and assist the states to exercise effectively their responsibilities in the coastal zone through the development and implementation of management programmes to achieve wise use of the land and water resources of the coastal zone' (U.S. Congress, 1972).

Heikoff gives a general definition of coastal zone management. He notes that 'in its most general sense the phrase 'coastal zone managemnt' could signify the public interest in managing anything and everything that goes on in the coastal zone, however, that area may be defined. In these terms coastal zone management overlaps and includes everything that all governments already do or will do in the area' (Heikoff, 1980), p.5). Heikoff recognises that 'this most comprehensive definition of the phrase is too broad to give it operational meaning, particularly as it may be applied to public policies and programmes' (ibid, p.5).

The CAMPNET defined the ICZM as 'a dynamic process in which a coordinated strategy is developed and implemented for the allocation of environmental, socio-cultural, and institutional resources to achieve the conservation and sustainable multiple use of the coastal zone' (CAMPNET, 1989). The CAMPNET also noted that an ICZM programme should have all of the following five attributes:

1. It is a process that continues over considerable time. ICZM is a dynamic programme that usually requires continual updating and amendments.ICZM is not a one-time project.
2. There is a governance arrangement to establish the policies for making allocation decisions,and if the programme is implemented, a governance arrangement for making allocation decisions.
3. The governance arrangement uses one or more management strategies to rationalise and systematise the allocation decisions.
4. The management strategies selected are based on a systems perspective which recognises the interconnections among coastal systems. The systems perspective usually requires that a multisectoral approach be used in the design and implementation of the management strategy.The coastal zone is characterised by an aggregation of natural and infrastructure systems.These include coastal watersheds, estuary circulation

systems, the longshore movement of sediments within littoral cells, populations of species that are harvested for their commercial or recreational value, and water supply, sewage treatment and highway systems.

5. It has a geographic boundary that defines a space which extends from the ocean environment across the transitional shore environments to some inland limit.

A systems perspective and multi-sectoral approach are the two key characteristics that serve to distinguish ICZM from other types of environmental planning and management programmes which occur in coastal areas.

Mitchell writes that 'the underlying intent of integrated resource management is to share and coordinate the values and interests of a broad range of interests when conceiving, designing and implementing policies, programmes or projects' (Mitchell, 1990).

Macaraig while speaking on managing the ASEAN's coastal resources notes that 'one of the most promising and creative options now available to us is the concept of integrated coastal resources management (CRM), which pursues an interdisciplinary and multisectoral approach. Affected communities are consulted and the socio-cultural disruptions that are likely to accompany economic and technological changes are considered in the planning process. As opposed to the unisectoral approach currently being practised (in the ASEAN region), integrated management tackles the resource utilisation—conservation dilemma from various aspects and angles, linking engineers, scientists, resource managers, economists, government officials, policy makers, sociologists and local communities in a complex but rational strategy of data-gathering, consultation, planning and decision making' (Macaraig, 1991, p.11). Macaraig adds that 'integrated management aims development plans primarily towards long-term sustainability, more than short-term economic benefits. It recognises the linkages and inter-dependence between upland ecosystems and lowland coastal and marine ecosystems and considers the two as one large system in the building of management models' (ibid, p.12).

Barcena, while outlining the role of UNCED in ocean and coastal management, notes that 'management refers to the attempt to provide order for a directed balance between and among the various uses of ocean space, as well as to protecting the environmental viability of the ocean. It encompasses several steps which include: collection, organisation and analysis of data; setting of priorities; making choices related to policy directives, laws and regulations; implementation of policies; surveillance and enforcement of rules and evaluation of results ... The overall objective for future ocean management lies in utilising the environmental and economic goods and services provided by marine and coastal ecosystems to meet development objectives whilst at the same time ensuring the long-term maintenance of marine environmental health, resource quality and ecological integrity' (Barcena, 1992, p. 22).

Barcena further observes that 'integrated coastal zone management (ICZM) is both a concept and a tool for inter-sectoral coordination, following modern principles of natural resource management, involving inter-disciplinary processes and requiring adequate information bases and people's participation ... A viable ICZM programme needs to be comprehensive but its content and complexity will vary from area to area according to development trends, conservation needs, traditions, norms, governmental systems and current critical issues and conflicts. A minimum programme would encompass: policy, enforcement mechanisms, an institutional arrangement for coordination and the assigning of responsibilities for approval of permits and performance of Environmental Impact Assessment procedures (EIA). In reactive policies, crises tend to shape the programme, making however, corrective measures more expensive and difficult to apply. In a procative mode, ICZM is part of development planning and may help achieve lower cost solutions, may anticipate problems early in the process and may better reconcile developmental and environmental concerns ... The ICZM process starts with a strategic plan stating the objectives of the programme in broad terms, indicating how these objectives would be met, assigning responsibilities, identifying funding, organising collaboration, and defining timeframes. The Master Plan provides a detailed description of the coastal zone, an inventory of the resources and of critical areas in terms of protection or potential for development, and an identification of permissible uses. It elaborates the procedures for permit approval, monitoring and enforcement' (ibid, pp. 26-27).

Scura *et. al.* while speaking on the lessons for integrated coastal zone management and the ASEAN experience observe that 'the purpose of integrated management is to allow multisectoral development to progress with the fewest unintended setbacks and the least possible imposition of long-run social costs. In contrast to a sectoral development plan, the focus of an integrated management plan is on mitigating measures to reduce social costs associated with sectoral activities accruing both inside and outside the sector in question. To be effective, management plans should be integrated with development plans, and implemented in a coordinated fashion' (Secura, *et. al.* 1992, p.22). These writers further emphasised that 'CAM employs an integrated, multisectoral, strategic approach for the efficient allocation of scarce resources among competing uses, and minimising unintended natural resources and environmental effects. The policy options and management strategies formulated within this framework are well founded on information on the natural function of ecosystems, the assimilative capability of the environment, the motivations of and incentives faced by people using the resources, the economic setting, and the ways and means to bring private behaviour in line with social goals' (ibid, p. 22).

Clark notes that 'ICZM refers to a special type of governmental programme established for the purpose of conserving coastal resources or environments ... through control of development. Use of the term implies that the governmental unit administering the programme has distinguished a special coastal zone as a geographic area combining both ocean and terrestrial domains. A coastal programme includes several types of resources and environments as well as the interests of the various economic sectors that are stakeholders in coastal resources. This latter aspect - the involvement of all parties of interest - is what distinguishes 'integrated coastal zone management'. The sectors may include shipping, housing, manufacturing, fisheries, agriculture, electric power, transport, nature conservation, or tourism' (Clark, 1992, p.8).

Clark further reports that 'ICZM is interdisciplinary. It considers, coordinates, and integrates the interests of all appropriate sectors ... It is needed in order to cope with special conditions of coastal resource conservation and economic development. It is particularly useful in solving problems that exist between the various sectors; for example, in resolving conflicts among fisheries, tourism, oil and gas development, and public works where these sectors are all attempting to use the coastal zone simultaneously. The above needs are accomplished by managing the coastal area as a unit and by integrating the management process with all appropriate economic sectors (shipping, mining, housing, transportation, etc.). An integrated coastal zone management programme must address coastal waters and shorelands, low lands, intertidal areas, lagoons, and open waters as a single interacting and indivisible resource unit that lies between the hinterlands and the open sea and whose future must be planned and managed as a unified whole' (ibid, p.10).

Knecht *et. al.*, defined ICM as follows: 'Integrated coastal management is a dynamic process by which decisions are taken for the use, development, and protection of coastal areas and resources to achieve goals established in cooperation with user groups and national, regional and local authorities. Integrated coastal management recognises the distinctive character of the coastal zone - itself a valuable resource - for current and future generations. Integrated coastal management is multiple purpose oriented; it analyses implications of development, conflicting uses, and interrelationships between physical processes and human activities, and it promotes linkages and harmonisation between sectoral coastal and ocean activities' (Knecht *et. al.* 1992)

Bower writes of ICM as 'at minimum, any definition should include the integration of programmes and plans for economic development and environmental quality management and more specifically the integration of cross-sectoral plans for fisheries, energy, transportation, waste disposal, tourism, etc. ICM should also include the vertical integration of responsibilities for management actions among various levels of government - international, national, state and local or between the public and private sectors. It should include all the components of management - from the planning tasks of analysis and design, to the implementation tasks of installation, operation and maintenance, monitoring and evaluation of strategies overtime. ICM should be cross-disciplinary among the sciences, engineering (technology), economics, political science (institutions), and law. In practice, it is all of the above' (Bower, 1992).

Cicin-Sain observes that 'there appears to be clear consensus that integrated coastal management represents a continuous and dynamic decision-making process. Integrated coastal management is a dynamic process by which decisions are taken for the use,development, and protection of coastal/marine areas and resources. Integrated coastal management is a process that recognises the distinctive character of the coastal zone, itself a valuable resource - for current and future generation ... The goals of integrated coastal management are to attain sustainable development of coastal/marine areas, to reduce vulnerability of coastal areas to natural hazards, and to maintain essential ecological processes, life support systems and biological diversity in marine/coastal areas. Integrated coastal management is multi-purpose-oriented, it analyses implications of development, conflicting uses, and interrelationships between physical processes and human activities, and it promotes linkages and harmonisation between sectoral, coastal and ocean activities' (Cicin-Sain, 1993, pp. 29-30).

Chua states that 'ICZM is a resource management system which employs an integrative, holistic approach and an interactive planning process in addressing the complex management issues in the coastal area. It could serve as the blueprint for attaining the goals and objectives of sustainable development by: maintaining the functional integrity of the coastal resource systems; reducing resource-use conflicts; maintaining the health of the environment; facilitating the progress of multisectoral development' (Chua, 1993, p. 84).

The OECD described integrated coastal zone management as 'management of the coastal zone as a whole in relation to local, regional, national and international goals. It implies a particular focus on the interactions between the various activities and resource demands that occur within the coastal zone and between coastal zone activities, and activities in other regions. In practical terms this might mean the integration of environmental protection goals into economic and technical decision making processes, the management of the impacts agricultural runoff is having on coastal zone water quality, the coordination of tourism policies with nature conservation policies, the coordination of pollution control policies within different parts of a particular coastal zone, or (most probably in practice) all of these and more simultaneously. The concept involves combining, coordinating or integrating, at a number of scales, values, interests and goals, many of which are in competition' (OECD, 1993, p. 25).

Pernetta and Elder called it as 'holistic coastal management' and defined it as 'the process of combining all aspects of the human, physical and biological aspects of the coastal zone within a single management framework' (Pernetta and Elder, 1993).

According to Kenchington and Crawford, it is 'the integration of environmental protection goals into economic and technical decision making process' (Kenchington and Crawford, 1993, p.111).

Quoting William Eichbaum of the World Wildlife Fund, Knecht and Archer wrote that 'integrated coastal management is a framework of principles and methodology for identification of important environmental priorities and allocation of scarce resources' (Knecht and Archer, 1993, p.187). The authors also noted the following five principles suggested by Eichbaum—(1) maintenance of ecological process while meeting human needs for services (sustainable development), (2) comparative assessment of risks and management, (3) integration of different disciplines, (4) responsive to high degree of scientific uncertainty, and (5) driven both by science and public expectations (ibid, p.187).

The Intergovernmental Panel on Climate Change considers it as 'the most appropriate process to address current and long-term coastal management issues, including habitat loss, degradation of water quality, changes in hydrographical cycles, depletion of coastal resources, and adaptation to sea level rise and other impacts of global climate change' (IPCC, 1994, p. 25).

UNEP defines it as 'an adaptive process of resource management for environmentally sustainable development in coastal areas. It is not a substitute for sectoral planning, but focuses on the linkages between sectoral activities to achieve more comprehensive goals' (UNEP, 1995, p.16).

The FAO Technical Guidelines for Responsible Fisheries describes it as 'the process of resources management in the interface between the sea and the land, which principle also apply to the water/land interface of large inland water bodies' (FAO, 1996). It also noted that 'the fundamental problem in coastal area management is one of resource allocation. Coastal resources are becoming increasingly scarce due to a combination of economic development and increased population in coastal areas. In common with other resources, the scarcity of coastal resources requires that choices be made between different uses. Coastal area management involves establishing a framework within which such choices might be made and the resultant policies implemented' (ibid, p. 3).

Clark, while writing on the integrated approach to ICM states that 'the ICZM approach can be expressed in a variety of forms of comprehensive, integrated coastal management, whether the focus is on management of privately owned shorelands or of the waters of the coastal 'commons' (the areas held for use of all citizens). In purpose, ICZM programmes are intended to address all resources in a defined coastal zone and to integrate the interests of a variety of economic sectors in conservation. ICZM type programmes, while distinctive in purpose, are rooted in such well-known and standard approaches as regional development planning, resource conservation and water-shed management. While the main purpose of ICZM is to manage development so as not to harm environmental resources, it does not directly manage use of the resources. The resources themselves would usually continue to be managed by sectorally oriented resource agencies, such as forestry, fisheries, wildlife and water pollution. But the development process would be managed by ICZM, which in this way would assist in conserving environmental resources by serving a multi-sectoral and multi-agency coordinative purpose, a function that would not otherwise be filled' (Clark, 1996, p. 20). Clark also notes that 'the overall purpose of the ICZM-type programme is to provide for the best long-term sustainable use of coastal natural resources and for perpetual maintenance of the most beneficial natural environment. In practical terms, the ICZM programme is intended to support the management goals and purpose ... by providing the basis for sustainable use of the resources, bio-diversity preservation, protection against natural hazards, pollution control, enhancement of welfare, development of sustainable economy, and optimum multiple use' (ibid, p. 25).

The GESAMP defines ICM as a continuous and dynamic process that unites government and the community, science and management, sectoral and public interests in preparing and implementing an integrated plan for the protection and development of coastal ecosystems and resources' (GESAMP, 1996, p. 1). The GESAMP further noted that the goal of ICM is 'to improve the quality of life of human communities who depend on coastal resources while maintaining the biological diversity and productivity of coastal eco-systems' (ibid, p.159).

According to Jeftic 'the ICAM is a dynamic process of achieving aims of environmentally sustainable development within the limitations of the physical, social and economic conditions of the development, and within the limitations of the legal, financial and administrative system. It has to be understood as an adaptable process of resource management capable of reacting to all expected and unexpected changes and phenomena. It is not a replacement for sectoral planning; its objective is rather to establish connections and understanding among various sectoral activities ... ICAM should not be seen as an additional burdensome layer of bureaucratic machinery. Rather, it should be seen as a process, within the broader framework of a long term national development plan, by which the required integration, coordination, and harmonisation occurs between and among various coastal and ocean sectorial activities in order to ensure, that the very substantial benefits of a nation's coastal and ocean resources be secured in perpetuity for this generation and those generations to follow' (Jeftic, 1996, p. 96).

The FAO Guidelines for Integrated Coastal Area Management notes that 'ICAM offers a means of balancing the competing demands of different users of the same resources and of managing the resources to optimise the benefits to be derived on a sustainable basis that is consistent with a country's goals' (FAO, 1996, p.vii). It also states that 'integrated management refers to management of sectoral components as parts of a functional whole, with resource users, not stocks of natural resources, as the focus of management. This focus highlights the need for the active participation of communities. Relevant line agencies must be involved so as to mitigate cross-sectoral impacts and adjust sectoral development portfolios to make them consistent with integrated coastal management goals' (ibid, p. 24). The Guidelines further note that 'coastal resource management includes a wide array of management practices such as: land-use planning; legal, administrative and institutional execution; demarcation on the ground; inspection and control of adherence to decisions; solution of land tenure issues; settling of water rights; issuing of concessions for plant, animal and mineral extraction; and safeguarding the rights of different interest groups (e.g., traditional and indigenous people, women...") (ibid, p.23).

While writing on the role of coastal zone management for the new century, Clark noted thus: 'ICZM is a system for resource management operated by governments at the local/regional level with central government assistance. ICZM focuses on sustaining coastal resources, conserving biodiversity, protecting the littoral environment, and countering natural hazards. It does so by influencing the form of shoreline development through education, resource management, regulations, and environmental assessment.

The main tools of the ICZM are (1) governmental regulations which protect bio-diversity and control the harvest and use of natural resources and (2) environmental assessments which can predict the impacts of various economic development schemes. ICZM encourages broad civic participation, coordinates actions of the various government agencies and the private sector, and spreads knowledge about coastal conservation.

In its planning mode, ICZM examines the consequences of various development actions and proposes necessary safeguards, constraints, and development alternatives that will guarantee sustainable development and the sustainable use of coastal natural resources at the most productive levels possible.

In its management mode, ICZM guides development in the coastal zone to promote resource conservation and biodiversity protection, using a variety of approaches. For example, ICZM assesses the environmental and socio-economic impacts of development projects and through environmental impact assessment (EIA) recommends changes necessary to conserve resources and protect biodiversity. ICZM coordinates economic sectors to ensure that advances in one sector do not bring reverses in another; for example, that port development does not diminish local fisheries or tourism' (Clark, 1997, p.199).

According to Bower and Turner 'ICM is a continuous, adaptive, day-to-day process which consists of a set of tasks, typically carried out by several or many public and private entities. The tasks together produce a mix of products and services from the available coastal resources. ICM involves continuous interactions between human systems and natural systems, among human systems and among natural systems, as these systems 'coevolve' over time'(Bower and Turner, 1998, pp.41-42). These writers also reported that 'the objective of coastal zone management is to produce overtime a 'socially desirable' mix of coastal zone products and services. This mix is likely to change over time with changing demands, changing knowledge and changing pressures. Fulfilment of this objective will require the mitigation of current market and intervention failures, continuous monitoring of performance and of coastal zone conditions and application of research findings overtime. The desired social mix can be most effectively and efficiently provided by an integrated approach to coastal zone management. The analysis required for ICM performs an overall resource management auditing role; it forces decision makers to ask relevant questions relating to coastal ecosystems and processes, coastal zone pressure trends, trade-offs, environmental impacts and various aspects of response strategies, including sources of finance and human/institutional capital resource potential. In macro-policy terms, ICM can be seen as a component of sustainable resource management within a regional/national economic development strategy' (ibid, p. 45).

Cicin-Sain and Knecht defined integrated coastal management 'as a continuous and dynamic process by which decisions are made for the sustainable use, development, and protection of coastal and marine areas and resources. First and foremost, the process is designed to overcome the fragmentation inherent in both the sectoral management approach and the splits in jurisdiction among levels of government at the land-water interface. This is done by ensuring that the decisions of all sectors (e.g., fisheries, oil and gas production, water quality) and all levels of government are harmonised and consistent with the coastal policies of the nation in question. A key part of ICM is the design of institutional processes to accomplish this harmonisation in a politically acceptable manner' (Cicin-Sain and Knecht, 1998, p. 39).

According to Fabbri, 'ICZM deals with the management of the coastal zone as a whole in relation to local, regional, national and international goals. It implies interactions between various activities, sectors and resource demands. ICZM is an inherently dynamic process which involves decision-making under uncertainty where uncertainty includes socio-economic, demographic, ecological, physical, climatic and technological conditions. Ideally ICZM considers both short-term as well as long-term impacts and it is therefore difficult to say for certain which activities, trends and processes will prevail in the future. The combination of uncertainty and the possibility of irreversible decisions emphasises the importance of a certain-risk-averse behaviour if a goal of society is to achieve sustainability' (Fabbri, 1998, pp. 53-54).

Vandermeulen states that 'coastal zone management is essentially the gathering of a complex set of social, economic and environmental information and making decisions (hopefully in an atmosphere of open consultation with all interested parties) based upon that information which lead to sustainable development. The availability of relevant, reliable data and its judicious assessment is central to this outcome' (Vandermeulen, 1998, p. 63).

According to Ducrotoy, *et. al.*, 'ICZM involves an ecosystem approach to environmental issues in opposition to a limited pollution approach, which only focuses on curbing the introduction of pollutants to the marine environment. In this case, management is based on the expected response of the whole ecosystem, i.e., on a more complex understanding of casual relationships ... These developments are of the cutting edge of marine environmental policy because approaching environmental management at ecosystem level involves not only an understanding of food chains and food webs but also social and political issues. When referring to the coast, management can be integrated in several ways. The coast needs to be understood as an interface where human activities and their impacts have to be considered in synergy among levels of governments in one nation and between nations and also between the various strata of society. Integration reguires interdisciplinarity among sciences and a thorough dissemination of their findings. In particular it relies on cross-fertilisation between the pure sciences and the social sciences ... Integrated coastal management is clearly about the sustainable use of the world's coastal resources' (Ducrotoy, *et. al.* 2000, p.428).

What is apparent from the above, many long and short, definitions and descriptions of coastal zone management is that they all invariably focus on the objective, mode and arena of management programme. The objective in general is to promote harmonious (multiple) use of the coastal resources for sustainable development of the coast, and the means in common is the integrated approach to planning at all levels of resource use and allocation in the coastal zone. It is significant to note here that there has indeed been a progressive enlargement of the spectrum of goals (objectives), methods and the sphere of management functioning since the ICZM idea began to grow. This is further highlighted in the next section which presents the evolution of the concept of coastal zone management.

3.3. Evolution of the concept

The concept of integrated coastal zone management has evolved through a series of national and international efforts which made it the guiding principle for sustaining the global coastal environment and its management. One of the few attempts to visualise and classify this evolutionary model (process) of development of the concept was made by Vallega (1993). Vallega gave a four-stage-based model of coastal management which is shown in table 3.1.

Table 3.1
Stage-based model of coastal management

Stage		*Features*
Stage-1		The Preparation for take-off
	Time	Late 1960s
	Objective	Use development
	Uses Under Management	Single use or a few uses
	Management area	The near-shore or a narrow land-sea interface
Stage-2		Take-off
	Time	1970s
	Objective	Partial use management and environmental protection
	Uses under management	Multiple Uses
	Management area	Delimited through administrative or arbitrary criteria
Stage-3		Drive to maturity
	Time	1980s
	Objective	Comprehensive coastal use management, environmental protection and the conservation of special and fragile areas
	Uses under management	Generally all uses
	Management area	Landward : delimited by various criteria; seaward : coincident with the extent of national maritime jurisdictional zones
Stage 4		Maturity
	Time	1990s
	Objective	Integrated coastal management, involving both uses and the ecosystem
	User under management	All
	Management area	Landward: delimited by various criteria; seaward: coincident with national maritime jurisdictional zones, generally the exclusive economic zone

Source: Vallega, 1993, p.152,

This model, perhaps created after Rostow's stages of economic growth (Rostow, 1960), shows four stages in the evolution of coastal management. These four stages coinciding with the last four decades of the last century in succession marks 'a progression from a developmental to a more mature concept of management' (Vallega, 1993, p. 151). Vallega notes that this stage based model, 'though presented in very general terms, points out how profound the evolution of coastal area management has been and how many steps were needed to lead to the integrated management concept' (ibid, p. 151). It is also pointed out that over this period (of four stages), the 'management goals, the spectrum of coastal uses to be managed, the extent of the coastal area, and its subsequent environmental implications have expanded and evolved contextually and so intensively that effective management involves an increasing number of disciplines which were called on to make progress in building up multi-disciplinary, integrated views' (ibid, pp. 151-152). Notwithstanding this general recognition, this model fails to give a concrete picture of the development of the ICM concept or the processes which led to it.

In this context it is interesting to note what Vallejo, a U.N. based writer says. Vallejo states that 'there have been three major stages in the world-wide recognition of the importance of CZM in national economies and social development. During the decade of the 1970's concern of developed countries over the quality of their coastal and marine environments prompted enactments such as the U.S. Coastal Zone Management Act of 1972, and some specific measures in various European countries. These experiences, although not formally replicated in the developing world, had a profound impact there, and later became the basis for concepts and approaches developed to tackle the problems encountered in the coastal areas of developing countries. International organisations started a number of research and training programmes in this field. The decade of the 1980s found strong advocates in both developed and developing countries, and international organisations continued to expand their work programmes in support of the initiatives of various countries ... The decade of the 1990s has witnessed a further development of CZM efforts ...' (Vallejo, 1993, pp.168-169). It is worth probing this evolutionary process in some detail.

It is now generally agreed that the idea of coastal zone management as a national or government sponsored programme has its beginning in the United States where the Congress passed the Coastal Zone Management Act in 1972 (Knecht and Archer, 1993, p.183). Prior to this, scholars like Donald, W. Hood and Peter McRoy had expressed deep concern for the management of the ocean and coastal resources. Hood and McRoy wrote that 'the great variety of present and future uses of the sea impose stresses on the oceans of such kind and magnitude that the most dedicated and intelligent efforts of reasonable people of the world must now attempt to resolve the many conflicts of interest that have and will occur. Historically, the oceans have been used mainly for fisheries, limited mineral extraction, transportation, warfare, recreation, and waste disposal. These are not vastly different uses than those of the present or expected future; however, the intensity has increased and consequently their use for waste disposal, whether direct (dumping) or indirect ... has now reached an alarming level. It is now time that we stop triffling with the world ocean contamination problem and learn to detail the processes involved to assure ourselves that the many uses of the ocean's resources for the benefit of man will be possible for our and future generations' (Hood and McRoy, 1971, p.667).

Hood, in fact, called upon the world saying that 'the time has come for knowledgeable individuals to set down the current status of the present level of damage, evaluate the ultimate effects of our present trends, develop guidelines for an international ethic concerning the ocean, and stimulate action to correct hazardous activities as needed to protect the ocean for multiple and proper use to mankind' (Hood, 1971, p. 3).

It is significant to note here that the two centuries of development and the accentuated boom following the Second World War had led to unprecedented expansion of economic activities in the coast and this coupled with the land grab movement by the private sector had despoiled the coast and alienated the public from the beach. This has reportedly led to mass protests against the despoliation forcing many county and district administration to take protective measures. Some of the coastal states like California and New York were reported to be pioneers in introducing protective legislations. It,however, took some time for the federal government to act finally in 1972, when the Coastal Zone Management Act was passed.

The attempt in this section is to present in some detail the various stages and events (processes) that finally led to the present state of coastal zone management concept. In this regard four major turning points or initiatives for ICM are identified and discussed. They are (1) the U.S. beginning, (2) the U.S. AID—led ICM programmes, (3) the European initiatives and (4) the international efforts.

3.3.1. The U.S. beginning

The Coastal Zone Management Act of the U.S. was passed in 1972, largely in response to the recommendations of the U.S. Commission on Marine Science, Engineering and Resources (1969), popularly known as the 'Stratton Commission' which submitted its report 'Our Nation and the Sea', in January 1969. Following the recommendation of the 'Stratton Commission', the National Oceanic and Atmospheric Administration (NOAA) was also created in 1970. Since 1972, the NOAA has been charged with the responsibility of administering the CZM Act.

The U.S. concern for the coastal environment is reflected in the language of the Coastal Zone Management Act. Section 302 of the Act states that 'the coastal zone is rich in a variety of natural, commercial, recreational, ecological, industrial and esthetic resources of immediate and potential value to the present and future well-being of the nation; the increasing and competing demands upon the lands and waters of our coastal zone occasioned by population growth and economic development ... have resulted in the loss of living marine resources, wildlife, nutrient-rich areas, permanent and adverse changes to ecological systems, decreasing open space for public use, and shoreline erosion.

The coastal zone, and the fish, shellfish, other living marine resources, and wild-life therein are ecologically fragile and consequently extremely vulnerable to destruction by man's alterations.

In light of competing demands and the urgent need to protect and to give high priority to natural systems in the coastal zone, present state and local institutional arrangements ... are inadequate.

The key to more effective protection and use of land and water resources of the coastal zone is to encourage the states to exercise their full authority' (Heikoff, 1980, p. 6).

Pursuing this logic, section 303 of the Act states that 'the Congress finds and declares that it is the national policy (a) to preserve, protect, develop, and where possible, to restore or enhance, the resources of the nation's coastal zone for this and succeeding generations, (b) to encourage and assist the states to exercise effectively their responsibilities in the coastal zone through the development and implementation of management programmes to achieve wise use of land and water resources of the coastal zone ...' (ibid, p.6).

Contrary to some of the current interpretations and insinuations on the U.S. Act as focussing predominantly on environmental protection, it may be noted here that the U.S. concern was not narrowly protective but more comprehensive. As Heikoff puts it, 'consideration and protection of the natural environment is not the exclusive concern of the Coastal Zone Management Act. Congress recognised also that much of the nation's economic activity has concentrated along the marine and Great Lakes coasts. Increasing the prosperity and potential for growth of the national economy is also an objective of coastal management ... The congressional declaration of policy in Sec. 303 of the Act favours the promotion of both environmental and economic values. Coastal programmes for the wise use of land and water resources are to give full consideration to ecological, cultural, historic, and esthetic values as well as to needs for economic development ...' (Heikoff, 1980, p. 6). The economic and non-economic value of the coast is very much in the ambit of the U.S. law. This has been maintained in the 1976, 1980 and 1990 amendments to the Act as well. Here, it is enough to note that the U.S. initiative has given sufficient conceptual clarity and vision for coastal zone management to evolve in the ensuing period.

3.3.2. The U.S.A.I.D. - led ICM programmes

The U.S. initiative in coastal zone management had its impact in many developing countries and that has led to a quick expansion of interest in developing country participation in coastal zone management. As noted by Sorensen, the 'awareness of prospects for ICZM has been stimulated by the international travel of government, industry, and academic representatives to national as well as international conferences' (Sorensen, 1993, p. 59). This seems to have worked very much in the case of the Southeast Asian nations, where a pioneering programme for coastal zone management was initiated with US support.

The ASEAN/US CRMP was initiated in 1984 by the Working Group on Marine Science (WGMS) of the ASEAN Committee on Science and Technology (COST) and jointly funded by the United States Agency for International Development (USAID). Referring to the genesis of this programme, Chua writes, 'the possibility that USAID would cofinance a marine resource management project spurred some marine scientists of the region to submit the relevant country proposals through the appropriate ASEAN channel - WGMS-COST Standing Committee for funding support during the ASEAN/US dialogue. The approval led to a series of preparatory meetings involving experts recruited by USAID and those from the region ... The International Centre for Living Aquatic Resources Management (ICLARM) was appointed to execute the project and provide technical and administrative support ... Initially, Indonesia, the Philippines, Singapore and Thailand participated in the project; a year later, Brunei Darussalam and Malaysia joined too ... The project was officially launched in January 1986 ...' (Chua, 1992, p.72).

The ASEAN/USAID-CRMP was a novel attempt. It was the first regional effort in coastal area management (CAM). As noted by Scura, *et. al.*, it was against the backdrop of serious resource over-exploitation, environmental degradation and escalating resource-use conflicts resulting from the sectoral orientation of development and management in coastal areas, the six members of the ASEAN ... began a collaborative effort to develop integrated coastal resource management (CRM) plans in their respective countries' (Scura, *et. al.* 1992, p. 2). The primary purpose of the plan was to provide financial and technical assistance and encourage the improvement of domestic abilities in technical, institutional and organisational approaches for managing coastal areas in the participants' countries. The CRMP was divided into two complementary components; component-1 focussed on management plan preparation and component-2 emphasised human resource development and creating a constituency for change through public education and information dissemination. As noted by Chua 'the goal of CRMP was to increase national capabilities within ASEAN for developing and implementing comprehensive, multi-disciplinary and environmentally sustainable CRM strategies through analysing, documenting and disseminating information on trends in coastal resource development; increasing awareness of the importance of CRM policies and identifying and where possible, strengthening existing management capabilities; providing technical solutions to coastal resource-use conflicts; and promoting institutional and organisational arrangements that bring multisectoral planning to coastal resource development' (Chua, 1992, pp.72-73).

The project focused on the following areas:

1. Human resource development— by undertaking short term and academic training to strengthen existing capabilities;

2. Public Awareness—by producing educational materials on the ecological and socio-economic contributions of the natural resources and the consequences of unsustainable exploitation;
3. Political Will—by organising policy workshops involving relevant policy makers and law makers to increase their understanding of and commitment to the sustainable use of natural resources and appropriate actions to arrest further destruction of the resource base;
4. ICZM programme—by establishing case studies in pilot sites of the six countries.

The first three activities were executed through the project office of the ICLARM. The ICZM programmes were developed by participating countries.

The planning process for the development of ICZM programmes followed a general scheme covering a number of essential phases. The first phase (profiling) included the compilation and analysis of secondary data and reconnaissance surveys and interviews to determine the management issues, community perception of the environment and information gaps. The second phase involved specific issue-oriented research to generate information crucial to management planning and policy reforms. The third phase dealt with the synthesis of data bases for formulating resource management policy, management strategies and action plans. This phase required close interaction between various tasks teams and the planning team for appropriate technical inputs, verifying and integrating of findings for resource-use conflict resolution, strengthening sectoral management. formulating environmental conservation measures, raising public awareness, involving public consultation, assessing the impacts of plan implementation and finally integrating the ICZM plan into the national development plan. There were about 49 agencies and 200 researchers and resource managers participating in the ASEAN/USAID CRMP during 1986-92. Details of participating organisations are given in appendix 3.1.

Among the achievements of the plan, Scura, *et. al.*, note that 'pilot coastal sites were selected in the six countries and intensive, interdisciplinary planning programmes were conducted, involving over 200 resource and scientific personnel from 49 institutions including universities, government agencies and non-governmental organisations (NGOs). In addition, training courses, workshops and conferences were held, and publications and educational materials were disseminated as part of CRMP. Approximately 120 nationals from ASEAN have been trained in subjects relevant to CAM as part of CRMP. This include young scientists who obtained masters' degrees from U.S. Universities, nationals who received on-the-job training in areas related to CAM, and numerous participants in six regional short-term training courses conducted by CRMP. Also as part of CRMP, five regional workshops were conducted to address specific issues pertaining to CAM and two major conferences were organised. Through these forums, CRMP was extremely successful in promoting awareness among policy makers and general public in the region, as well as among the donor community and the media, of the rationale for the efficacy of CAM. The first multinational commitment to CAM—the Baguio Resolution was adopted by participants at a project-sponsored policy conference, comprised of key policy makers from each ASEAN member, as well as extra-regional participants including technical experts, and representatives of the media and donor agencies' (Scura, *et. al.* 1992, pp.3-4) (See Baguio Resolution in appendix 3.2).

A gleaning of the lessons learnt from the ASEAN/USAID CRMP will be further helpful in understanding its contribution to the CZM principles. The lessons learned from the ASEAN experiment have been outlined by Scura, *et. al.* (See appendix 3.3). Broadly they are grouped into three categories: (1) process related lessons, (2) development stage related lessons and (3) institutional setting related lessons. Among the process-related lessons noted are, the desirable characteristics of the planning phase of the management process, essential features of a coastal area management plan, essential mechanisms of integration and essential mechanisms of coordination. Among the development stage related lessons are the basic management issues considered. Institutional setting related lesson correspond to the specific resource focus, the bottom-up vs. top-down issue, and the choice of information techniques.

The outstanding characteristics of the planning phase of the management process noted are:

1. Management should be viewed as a long-term, iterative and continuous process.
2. It should be perceived as originating from within rather than from outside.
3. Integration with local, regional and national development agenda should be pursued.

4. Local participation by government and communities in policy making, monitoring and enforcement should be encouraged.
5. Existing institutional and organisational arrangements must be fully considered.
6. Research should be oriented toward improved information and analysis useful for the identification of management priorities and formulation of management strategies.
7. Management actions must be matched with issues and goals.

The ultimate impact of the ASEAN CRMP are noted by Chua. The main impacts noted by Chua are:

1. The ASEAN has developed a pool of resource persons and a network of organisations with the knowledge and experience in ICZM to assist national governments within or outside the region to undertake the programme. The ASEAN can therefore play a leading role in Agenda 21 of the United Nations Conference on Environment and Development.
2. The knowledge and experience acquired through CRMP shaped an ICZM typological frame-work applicable to other developing nations. The lessons learned helped formulate the 'Technical Guidelines' for the application of ICZM in developing nations jointly sponsored by the World Bank, United Nations Environment Programme, and Food and Agriculture Organisation.
3. The CRMP has 'sensitised' policy makers in ASEAN on the importance of sustainable coastal area management that has contributed to a greater commitment of political will and national resources to ICZM in almost all countries of the region.
4. The ICZM plans have been integrated, fully or partly, into the national or local economic development plans of Brunei Darussalam, the Philippines, Indonesia, Malaysia and Thailand.
5. The CRMP has made substantial documentation on the environment and development of the coastal areas. The information generated makes useful data bases that could be enriched for future planning and management of the coastal resources (Chua, 1992, pp. 89-90).

Referring to the role of ASEAN/CRMP in promoting organisational networking and information exchange on CRM, Chua notes that 'the 49 organisations participating in the project were linked and collectively undertook research, training and information exchange activities related to ICZM. The project served as a focal point for regional collaboration and cooperation. Its newsletter, Tropical

Coastal Area Management, was primarily produced as a source of information on ICZM activities undertaken in the region as well as in other parts of the world. The newsletter also contributed significantly to the dissemination of concepts, experiences and methods used for tropical ICZM to more than 75 nations. The project published a number of technical reports, conference/workshop proceedings, educational materials and the management plans of the six countries ... These publications were distributed to members of the project and major libraries in the world ...' (Chua, 1992, p.87).

The U.S.A.I.D. has also provided support for ICZM efforts in Sri Lanka and Equador and the apparent success of the ICZM projects in these areas has reportedly led the agency's decision to initiate a regional ICZM project with the Organisation of Eastern Caribbean States (Sorensen, 1993, p.56).

As already noted, one of the most outstanding achievements of the ASEAN/USAID-CRMP has been the compilation of a wast array of documents and reports highlighting the coastal issues, un-sustainability of the development path followed and the need for integrated approach in coastal development planning. It is gratifying to note that some of the reports produced by Chua and Scura (1991,1992, etc.) and by many others from the ASEAN are standing testimony to the integration of the growing knowledge of the inter-dependence of the economy and environment of the region and the need for integrated planning and management of the coastal zone for sustainable development of the region. It is also significant to note here that the ASEAN/USAID-ICZM had prepared several ICZM plans for specific sites in the region incorporating the sustainability criteria. It was precisely with this experience and knowledge that the ASEAN assisted the UN in the preparation of Agenda 21, Chapter 17 of the UNCED as noted by Chua, earlier. In view of all these it can be stated that the USAID-led-ICM Programme in the ASEAN was a major turning point in the evolution of the concept and practice of coastal zone management, world-wide.

3.3.3. European initiatives

Another source which contributed to the development of the concept and practice of coastal zone management is the European initiatives. This is, however, one of the least recognised and barely documented source of development. The attempt here is to point out some of the notable sources which contributed to the contemporary knowledge and understanding of the concept of ICZM

Huggett notes that 'coastal zone management (CZM) has been on both national and European Union (EU) political agendas now for at least 25 years. As early as 1970, changes to the way the coastline of England and Wales was managed were recommended whilst soon after that the Council of Europe began promoting integrated coastal planning to help ensure wildlife conservation in coastal areas' (Huggett, 1998, pp.33-34). One of the most important results of the initiative was the establishment of 'Heritage Coast' in England and Wales by the Country Side Commission.

The prolonged interest in CZM is considered as an acknowledgement of the socio-economic and wild-life importance of the coastal zone. However, it is also viewed as an indictment of the continuing loss of European coastal biodiversity as a result of ineffective action. A significant contributory factor to the continuing degradation of coastal habitats in Europe is said to be the fact that action was focused at the local level whilst many of the issues to be addressed were transboundary. The issues were mainly related to navigation and communication, waste disposal and pollution control, nature and landscape conservation, recreation and tourism, fisheries, minerals and energy exploitation, and coastal engineering. In response to this, the European Council of Environment Ministers had adopted a resolution calling for the production of a European Community strategy for integrated coastal zone management and the incorporation of the strategy into the 5th Environmental Action Programme (EAP).

Progress towards the production of the strategy was considered to be slow. However, by the end of 1995, the European Union Commission published a Communication on ICM proposing the establishment of a demonstration programme which aims to show how to achieve better coordination between sectors using existing mechanisms.

The EU Commission considered that there is justification for community action with regard to the development of a coastal zone programme. The reasons given for the Commission's interest in the fate of the coastal zone are the existence of problems of a European dimension which cannot be solved by the countries separately, the influence of EU policies and actions on the development of coastal zones and the need for an exchange of experience and know-how in a field where successes are still rare and where there is sustained public and political demand for the conservation of the coastal zones and their sustainable development.

The 'scoping study' on integrated environmental assessment of coastal zones produced by the European Topic Centre on Marine and Coastal Environment and presented to the European Environment Agency identified how the Topic Centre could assist in the development of a European Wide Coastal Zone Management Strategy. As Huggett reports it, 'the European Topic Centre should:

(1) Identify the main aims and objectives for CZM throughout the European Union,

(2) Review EU directives and policies with a potential impact on activities in the coastal zone with a view to:

   (2.1) Identify the relative importance of these instruments for the state of the environment of the coastal zone in the long term; and

   (2.2) Assess these instruments through which the CZM strategy could be structured,

(3) Identify the mechanisms needed to coordinate the development and implementation of coastal zone policies, both within the Commission and between member states,

(4) Identify means to assess progress in reaching the objectives of CZM,

(5) Identify actions that would be required by the Commission and by member states to implement the strategy, including the financial implications' (Huggett, 1998, p.37).

While looking at the contribution of European sources to the development of coastal zone management principles, it is significant to note that some of the EU regional studies are path-breaking. The AMBER report 'Economic Development and Environmental Protection in Coastal Areas - A Guide to Good Practice' and the 'Scoping Study on Integrated Environmental Assessment of Coastal Zones, Final Report' published by the European Topic Centre on Marine and Coastal Environment, in 1994 and 1995, respectively are quite noteworthy.

The EU published a Communication on the Wise Use of Wetlands in 1995 and a Communication on Integrated Management of Coastal Zones (Ducrotoy, 1999, p.10). These followed a Council Resolution in 1994 on a Community Strategy for Integrated Coastal Zone Management and the publication of a guide to good practice on economic development and environmental protection in coastal areas (ibid, p.10). Ducrotoy notes that 'the communications recognise the continuing deterioration of the environment and natural resources in many of Europe's coastal regions and admits a long recognised need to conserve coastal zones as an element of the Community's natural and cultural heritage and as an essential basis for economic and social development. The main problem is recognised to be an absence of mechanisms allowing the complex relationship between human activities and the environment to be taken into account into decision-making processes. The communications recognise the need for joint action by the Union and the Member states in order to accelerate implementation at all levels of sustainable development, by improving the effectiveness of legislation and of the existing financial and planning tools' (ibid, p.10).

Even prior to the EU becoming quite active in the conservation and management of the coast in the region, the OECD had been concentrating its efforts for the preservation of the coast and the promotion of environmentally sound practices. In 1991, it published the 'Report on CZM: Integrated Policies and Draft Recommendations of the Council on Integrated Coastal Zone Management (OECD, 1991). This called on member countries to develop and implement strategic planning and integrated management of coastal zones in order to achieve ecologically sustainable development and integrated resource management. In 1993, the OECD published the results of a three-year study into the experiences, issues and problems faced by the OECD member countries in their coastal zones (OECD, 1993). It focused on identifying the resources required for better integration of economic and environmental considerations. The assessment of the policies identified a number of environmental problems that need to be addressed. It recognised that environmentally sensitive areas are being lost, not only on the coast but also in the catchment areas and hinterland. Losses of wetlands, coastal forests, dune systems and the reclamation of bays and estuaries are highlighted as particular problem, as is the fact that insufficient action has been taken to reduce pollution through the construction of appropriate waste treatment or disposal facilities. Issues such as hard coastal defences, water abstraction, fisheries, disturbance from recreation activities, development of tourism and industry also were identified for attention.

The study recognised that environmental standards are to be laid down for coastal areas and adequately enforced. Standards were suggested for development set-back, beach-front construction, noice levels, protection of dunes, bathing beaches and general coastal quality, construction of beach protection structures and importantly, habitat protection. The OECD also recognised that national legislation for coastal conservation and preservation objectives is needed. Such legislations should cover coastal wetlands, forests, coral reefs, access to beaches, native species (flora and fauna), management of sensitive beach features such as dunes, spits, archaeological and spiritual/cultural sites, etc. There was a clear recognition that within ICZM there is a requirement for integrated protected areas, i.e., zones for protection that are considered in relation to other activity zones.

The European contribution to the concept of coastal zone management is further reflected in the presence of the Oslo and Paris conventions, which seek to prevent marine pollution by dumping from ships and aircrafts and from land based sources, respectively (later replaced by the 1992 Convention for the Protection of the Marine Environment of the North-east Atlantic, known as OSPAR), the MARPOL-Annex which prohibit tankers washing out oil tanks at sea, the London Convention of 1982 introducing a formal ban on dumping in the sea, and the 1993 agreement on dumping of radio-active wastes at sea.

Referring to the European contribution to the theory and practice of ICM, it may be said that the EU and the OECD together with other organisational arrangements have helped in focusing on the diverse issues of coastal land-use planning and the need to protect the coast and its environment with proper national and international arrangements. In this regard, the European effort is only another link in the long chain of initiatives that lead to the goal of sustainable development via ICM.

3.3.4. International efforts

The international efforts considered here are the global initiatives that have come mainly from the impetus given by the United Nations and its various affiliates. The main efforts noted under this category are the initiatives from (1) United Nations Conference on the Human Environment (Stockholm 1972), (2) Third United Nations Conference on the Law of the Sea (1973-1982) and subsequent actions, (3) United Nations Conference on Environment and Development (UNCED), and (4) Post-UNCED efforts.

3.3.4.1. The United Nations Conference on the Human Environment, Stockholm, 1972

The UN Conference on the Human Environment was held in Stockholm, Sweden in 1972, at the peak of wave of environmental concern triggered by incidents such as the January 1969 oil spill offshore from Santa Barbara, California in the United States and when there was a growing realisation that environmental degradation was becoming a serious problem in many parts of the world. One of the most significant actions of the conference was the creation of a new institution to coordinate environmental activities within the United Nations system - the United Nations Environment Programme (UNEP) and its governing council. The UNEP has since been an important player in the international arena, organising such activities as the Regional Seas Programme and performing important roles in ozone depletion and biodiversity issues, among others.

The Stockholm declaration of principles and its accompanying 109 - item action plan represented the first effort by the international community to deal with environmental problems on a comprehensive basis. It also acted as a catalyst in accelerating the adoption of several pending international agreements dealing with ocean dumping, vessel source pollution, and trade in endangered species. Although the Stockholm agenda and resulting action plan spanned the entire spectrum of environmental issues, in many respects ocean and coastal issues were emphasised throughout the conference.

Some of the most important impacts of the Stockholm conference occurred in the ocean and coastal field. The London Convention (Convention on the Prevention of Marine Pollution by Dumping of Wastes and Other Matters), establishing the first global standards to govern the dumping of wastes into the oceans, was adopted in 1972. Similarly, the first comprehensive convention on vessel source pollution, the International Convention for the Prevention of Pollution from Ships (MARPOL) was adopted shortly after the Stockholm meeting. Through the Regional Seas Programme, of the UNEP, it was also possible in creating action programmes in more than a dozen important enclosed or semi-enclosed seas around the world. The Stockholm Conference has been thus instrumental in creating a world forum for initiating measures for protecting the coastal and marine environment.

3.3.4.2. The Third United Nations Conference on the Law of the Sea (1973-1982) and subsequent actions

The Third United Nations Convention on the Law of the Sea which began in 1973 was finally concluded on 10th December 1982 when it reached agreement on a new 'constitution' of the worlds' oceans. The Convention, which entered into force on 16th November 1994, is the first comprehensive attempt by states to implement a global convention on the law of the sea. In one of the most detailed international conventions ever negotiated, it deals not only with coastal state rights over certain maritime zones, but also navigation rights, management of the deep sea bed, protection and preservation of the marine environment, marine scientific research, and the rights of archipelagic states and geographically disadvantaged and land-locked states.

The Convention also gave further content to, and recognised for the first time, a number of maritime zones. These include the territorial sea, contiguous zone, exclusive economic zone (EEZ), continental shelf, deep seabed, archipelagic waters and high seas. In the case of the territorial sea, the Convention continued to recognise that a coastal state's sovereignty extended beyond its land territory and internal waters to the outer limits of the territorial seas. Importantly, the Convention also for the first time recognised that the outer limit of the territorial sea can extend upto 12 nautical miles. This was a most important development as previously there had been no uniformity in territorial sea claims. Similarly, it also extended the outer limit of the contiguous zone from 12 to 24 nautical miles. It did not, however, modify the extent of a coastal state's jurisdiction within the contiguous zone, but rather, extended the ability to exercise jurisdiction for certain purposes in regard to offences committed within the territorial sea. In the case of the continental shelf, the Convention sought to give more definition to what constituted that area. At a minimum, it provided that the continental shelf of a coastal state extended beyond the territorial sea to a distance of 200 nautical miles. In some instances, it is possible for the continental shelf to extend beyond this limit to the outer edge of the continental margin. When reliance is placed upon the continental margin as being the limit of the continental shelf, the outer limit shall not be in excess of 350 miles from the territorial sea base lines or 100 miles from the 2500 metre isobath. The extent of a coastal state's sovereign right to explore and exploit the natural resources of the continental shelf were not altered by the convention.

The recognition of Coastal State rights to an exclusive economic zone was one of the most significant achievements of the Convention. The EEZ shall extend upto 200 miles from a coastal state's base lines. Within the zone, a coastal state is granted sovereign rights for the purposes of 'exploring and exploiting, conserving and managing the natural resources, whether living or non-living of the water superjacent to the sea-bed and of the sea-bed and the sub-soil. Coastal state jurisdiction is also conferred to establish artificial islands and installations, for the purposes of marine scientific research, and also to protect and preserve the marine environment. With the exception of exploration and exploitation of the natural resources of the continental shelf within the EEZ, coastal states do not have exclusive sovereign rights over the area. Subject to the Convention, all states enjoy traditional freedoms of navigation within the EEZ. With respect to living resources within the EEZ, coastal states have 'preferential' rights. Coastal states are however, required to promote optimum utilisation of living resources within the EEZ, and to that end if the coastal state does not have the capacity to harvest the total allowable catch within the area, other states are to be given access to the surplus.

As Barcena puts it, 'that framework (Law of the Sea) governs the further development of legal and policy instruments at global, regional, and national levels. Increasingly, it is a framework for programming in global and regional institutions, to further understanding of the ocean environment and to create cooperative efforts to build national capacities - both to benefit from marine use and to support implementation and enforcement of applicable laws and standards' (Barcena, 1992, p.48). Barcena further notes that 'the convention establishes an important balance between the rights of states and their obligations, including those relating to conservation of the marine environment and its living resources and the promotion of marine scientific research. The basic principles and rules represent prevailing international law demonstrated by state practice over the past ten years or more. The vast majority of states have adopted legislation which largely conforms with the provisions of the Convention, and most global and regional instruments drafted since the mid to late 1970s have been careful to ensure conformity with its provisions.

In both its provisions on the marine environment and on living resources, the Convention emphasises the need for a sound scientific basis for regulatory and management systems. It further calls on states to promote and facilitate the development and conduct of marine scientific research, as well as environmental assessment and monitoring. The Convention specifically calls for the continuous elaboration of international rules, standards, and recommended practices and procedures for marine environmental protection. The

Convention also seeks to promote the development and transfer of marine technology and the establishment of national and regional marine sciences and technology centres, particularly in developing countries' (ibid, p.48).

The adoption in 1982 of the UN Convention on the Law of the Sea provided a new framework for the better management of marine resources. It also gave coastal states rights and responsibilities for the management and use of the living and non-living resources. It, however, became very clear within a short time that many of the world fisheries resources could not be sustained with uncontrolled increase in exploitation. Significantly, the nineteenth session of the FAO Committee on Fisheries (COFI), held in March, 1991, recommended that new approaches to fisheries management embracing conservation and environmental, as well as social and economic considerations were urgently needed. Also, FAO was asked to develop the concept of responsible fisheries and to elaborate the Code of Conduct to foster its application. Subsequently, the Government of Mexico, in collaboration with FAO, organised an International Conference on Responsible Fishing at Cancun, in May 1992. The declaration of Cancun endorsed at the conference was then brought to the attention of the UNCED Rio Summit in June, 1992, which supported the preparation of a Code of Conduct for Responsible Fisheries. The FAO Technical Consultation on High Seas Fishing, held in September 1992, further recommended the elaboration of a code to address the issues regarding high seas fisheries.

The twentieth session of COFI, held in March 1993 examined in general the proposed framework and content for such a code, including the elaboration of guidelines, and endorsed a time frame for the further elaboration of the Code. This resulted in the FAO Conference, at its twenty-seventh session in November 1993, adopting the Agreement to Promote Compliance with International Conservation and Management Measures by Fishing Vessels on the High Seas, which according to FAO conference resolution 15/93 forms an integral part of the Code.

The Code was formulated so as to be interpreted and applied in conformity with the relevant rules of International Law, as reflected in the United Nations Convention on the Law of the Sea, 1982, as well as with the agreement for the implementation of the provisions of the United Nations Convention on the Law of the Sea of 10 December 1982 relating to the conservation and management of straddling fish stocks and highly migratory fish stocks, 1995, and in the light of *inter alia* the 1992 Declaration of Cancun, the 1992 Rio Declaration on Environment and Development, in particular Chapter 17 of Agenda 21.

The twenty-eighth session of the FAO Conference in Resolution 4/95 adopted the Code of Conduct for Responsible Fisheries, in October 1995. The same resolution requested the FAO, *inter alia*, to elaborate as appropriate technical guidelines in support of the implementation of the Code in collaboration with members and interested relevant organisations.

Article 10 of the Code of Conduct related to the integration of fisheries into coastal area management. FAO issued the Technical Guidelines for Responsible Fisheries (No.3) in 1996 dealing with the integration of fisheries into coastal area management. The Technical Guidelines noted that 'marine fisheries, as well as fisheries in large lakes, depend on the coastal area in a variety of ways. Most capture fisheries are based on coastal stocks, others exploit offshore stocks which spend part of their lives in inshore waters, e.g., in a nursery or feeding area. Fish stocks also rely on primary productivity in the coastal area as an important part of the food chain. Coastal aquaculture is also heavily dependent on the coastal area for space and resources. This dependency of the marine fisheries sector on the coastal area makes it particularly susceptible to activities which result in coastal environmental change which may have major impacts on the sector. At the same time, the fisheries sector can affect other coastal activities, e.g., through competition for space. The need is apparent, therefore, to consider the development and management of the fisheries sector within the context of the protection and management of the resources, the environment and the activities of the coastal area' (FAO, 1996, p.iv).

The main provisions of the Code relating to integration of fisheries with coastal area management are presented in four sections. They are, (1) institutional framework, (2) policy measures, (3) regional cooperation and (4) implementation.

The institutional framework required that—

(a) states should ensure that an appropriate policy, legal and institutional framework is adopted to achieve sustainable and integrated use of coastal resources, taking into account the fragility of coastal ecosystems and the finite nature of their natural resources, and the needs of coastal communities (Article 10.1.1.).

(b) in view of the multiple uses of the coastal area, states should ensure that representatives of the fisheries sector and fishing communities are consulted in the decision making processes and involved in other activities related to coastal area management planning and development (Article 10.1.2.).

(c) states should develop, as apprcpriate, institutional and legal frameworks in order to determine the possible uses of coastal resources and to govern access to them taking into account the rights of coastal fishing communities and their customary practices to the extent compatible with sustainable development (Article 10.1.3.).

(d) states should facilitate the adoption of fishing practices that avoid conflict among different fisheries resource users as well as with other users of the marine environment (Article 10.1.4.).

(e) states should promote the establishment of procedures and mechanisms at the appropriate administrative level to settle conflicts which arise within the fisheries sector and between them and other users of the coastal area (Article 10.1.5.).

Policy measures suggested required that—

(a) states should promote the creation of public awareness of the need for the protection and management of coastal resources and the participation in the management process by those affected (Article 10.2.1.).

(b) in order to assist decision-making on the allocation of coastal resources, states should promote the assessment of their respective value, taking into account economic, social and cultural factors (Article 10.2.2.).

(c) in setting policies for the management of coastal areas, states should take due account of the risks and uncertainties involved (Article 10.2.3.).

(d) states, in accordance with their capacities, should establish or promote the establishment of systems to monitor the coastal environment, as part of the coastal management process, using physical, chemical, biological, economic and social parameters (Article 10.2.4.).

(e) states should promote multidisciplinary research in support of coastal area management, in particular on its environmental, economic, social, legal and institutional aspects (Article 10.2.5.).

Regional Cooperation required that—

(a) states with neighbouring coastal areas should cooperate with one another to facilitate the sustainable use of coastal resources and the conservation of the environment (Article 10.3.1.).

(b) in case of activities that may have an adverse transboundary environmental effect on coastal areas, states should, (1) provide timely information and, if possible, prior notification to potentially affected states, (2) cooperate at the subregional and regional level in order to improve coastal area management (Article 10.3.3.).

Regarding implementation, the Code stated that—

(a) states should establish mechanisms for cooperation and coordination among agencies involved in development, planning and management of the coastal area (Article 10.4.1.).

(b) states should ensure that the authority or authorities representing the fisheries sector in the coastal management process have the appropriate technical capacities and financial resources (Article 10.4.2.).

The Third Law of the Sea Convention, although not directly concerned with coastal zone management has been instrumental in directing world public opinion in managing the ocean resources and in determining the role of coastal states and other organisations in managing the affairs of the sea. The lead which FAO gave in preparing the Code of Conduct for Responsible Fisheries and the work of elaborating the Code with respect to the integration of fisheries into coastal area management are major steps in the evolution of the concept of coastal zone management and sustainable development. The culmination of this conceptual development is found in the UNCED Declarations.

3.3.4.3. The United Nations Conference on Environment and Development (UNCED)

The United Nations Conference on Environment and Development convened at Rio de Janeiro during June 3-14, 1992, was in many respects a remarkable event as far as evolution of the concept of coastal zone management is concerned. Among others, it produced the most comprehensive document, Chapter 17 of Agenda 21, dealing with ocean and coastal management.

Chapter 17, is considered as the most complex and the longest Chapter of Agenda 21 and is titled as 'Protection of the Oceans, All Kinds of Seas, including Enclosed and Semi-Enclosed Seas, and Coastal Areas and the Protection, Rational Use and Development of Their Living Resources'.

The introduction to the Chapter (Para, 17.1) stresses both the importance of oceans and coasts in the global life support system and the positive opportunity for sustainable development that ocean and coastal areas represent. It notes that 'the marine environment forms an integrated whole that is an essential component of the global life support system. The oceans cover 70 per cent of the surface of the globe and play a dominant and decisive role in the biogeochemical processes of the planet on local, regional and global scales. The global energy, climate and weather, the hydrological and carbon cycles, atmospheric and physical processes are critically influenced by the properties of the oceanic processes. Yet our understanding of these processes is less well developed than those occurring in the terrestrial environment and atmosphere. Long-term management and sustainable development of the world's resources must be based on a sound understanding of the role of the ocean in shaping conditions on the globe and on a proper evaluation of the benefits of the marine resource base for sustainable development' (Barcena, 1992, p.15).

It is also pointed out that 'degradation of the marine environment can result form a wide range of activities on land, either from lack of, or an excess of, economic and industrial growth. Human populations, land use, agriculture, forestry, fisheries, urban development, tourism and industry all impact on the marine environment' (ibid, p.15). The introduction also noted that 'oceans have critical importance as a lead sector in international law and in providing a model for management for sustainable development. Ocean management policy must be integrated horizontally, across disciplines, departments and specialised agencies and between the public and private sector, as well as vertically, across levels of governance, national, regional and global, in a coherent system' (ibid, p.15). It also underscored that 'the Law of the Sea Convention offers the most appropriate framework which integrates effectively the protection of the environment from pollution, whether land based, oceanic or atmospheric and economic development of living and non-living resources. Its full implementation requires new approaches that are integrated in content and precautionary and anticipatory in ambit to ocean and coastal area management and development, at the national, regional and international levels' (ibid, p.16).

Chapter 17 gave prescription relating to seven major programme areas for priority attention. These are related to:

(1) Integrated management and sustainable development of coastal areas, including Exclusive Economic Zones,
(2) Marine environmental protection,
(3) Sustainable use and conservation of living resources of the high seas,
(4) Sustainable use and conservation of living marine resources under national jurisdiction,
(5) The addressing of critical uncertainties in management of the marine environment and climate change,
(6) The strengthening of international, including regional, cooperation and coordination, and
(7) Sustainable development of small islands. A brief outline of the prescriptions made in these areas is given below.

1. Integrated management and sustainable development of coastal and marine areas, including Exclusive Economic Zone

In this section, coastal nations commit themselves to 'integrated management and sustainable development of coastal areas and the marine environment under their jurisdiction' (para 17.5).

The text calls for integrated policy and decision-making processes and institutions. It says each coastal state should consider establishing, or where necessary strengthening, appropriate coordinating mechanisms (such as a high-level policy planning body) for integrated management and sustainable development of coastal and marine areas, at both the local and national levels (17.6). It also provides a series of suggested actions that coordinating institutions should consider undertaking, such as preparation of coastal and marine use plans (including profiles of coastal ecosystems and of user groups), environmental impact assessment and monitoring, contingency planning for both human-induced and natural disaster, improvement of coastal human settlements (particularly in terms of drinking water and sewage disposal), conservation and restoration of critical habitats, and integration of sectoral programmes (such as fishing and tourism) into an integrated framework (17.6). Cooperation is also called for among states in the preparation of national guidelines for integrated coastal management (17.11) and the undertaking of measures to maintain biodiversity and productivity of marine species and habitats under national jurisdiction (17.7).

This section also highlights the need for information on coastal and marine physical systems and uses, information on both natural science and social science variables (17.8), education and training in integrated coastal and marine management (17.15), and capacity building, including building of human resource capacity, support of pilot demonstration programmes and projects in integrated coastal and marine management, and establishment of centres of excellence in the area (17.17). As in other parts of Agenda 21, there is a strong affirmation in this section of the need to include traditional ecological knowledge and socio-cultural values as an input to management and of the importance of coastal areas for indigenous peoples (e.g., 17.15, 17.6,17.3). The need for international cooperation on both bilateral and multilateral basis to support efforts by coastal states in these areas is also emphasised.

2. Marine environmental protection

Chapter 17 calls for coastal nations to increase their efforts to deal with both land-based and sea-based sources of marine pollution. Although land-based sources account for as much as 70 per cent of the pollution, there is currently no global scheme to address such pollution (17.18). This section stresses the need for a precautionary and anticipatory, rather than reactive, approach to prevent degradation of the marine environment (17.21). Here, nations commit themselves to prevent, reduce and control degradation of the marine environment so as to maintain and improve its life-support and productive capacities (17.22).

The section on controlling land-based sources of pollution points to the need to relate control of land-based sources to integrated coastal and ocean management (programme area, 1), by updating, strengthening and extending the 1985 Montreal Guidelines for the Protection of the Marine Environment Against Pollution from Land-Based Sources, and by promoting new regional arrangements, where appropriate. Among other items, it also calls on UNEP to convene an intergovernmental meeting on protection of the marine environment from land-based sources of pollution (17.24, 17.25). Priority is given to the control of sewage effluent (an acute problem in many developing countries) and to other sources of pollution such as synthetic organic compounds, sediments, organohalogen compounds, and anthropogenic inputs of nitrogen and phosphorus (17.28). Watershed management practices are encouraged to prevent, control, and reduce degradation of the marine environment (17.29).

Likewise, building on the international framework already established through the International Maritime Organisation and other relevant international organisations and additional measures to reduce degradation of the marine environment from sea-based activities are called for, including control of pollution from shipping, dumping, offshore oil platforms, and ports (17.30).

More systematic observations to measure environmental quality are also called for, such as expansion of the mussel watch programme, establishment of a clearing house for marine pollution control technologies, and establishment of a global profile and data base (17.35). The section further stresses the need for technology transfer of clean or cost-effective pollution control technology (17.37) and education and training in this area (17.37, 17.38).

3. Sustainable use and conservation of living marine resources of the high seas

This section recognises that as the world has witnessed a significant expansion of fishing activity on the high seas in the past decade, a number of highseas resources have become over utilised and problems in the management of high sea fisheries have become evident.

The problems include unregulated fishing, over-capitalisation, excessive fleet size, reflagging of vessels to escape control, insufficiently selective gear, unreliable data bases, and lack of sufficient cooperation among states (17.44, 17.45). In this section, therefore, states commit themselves to the conservation and sustainable use of marine living resources on the high seas (17.46) and to the development of fisheries to meet nutritional needs as well as social, economic, and development goals. The protection of endangered marine species at levels that can produce maximum sustainable yield as qualified by relevant environmental and economic facts taking into account relationships among species is also considered (17.46). Regarding marine mammals, this section defers the question of management of cataceans to the appropriate International organisations (17.47), recognising the competence of the International Whaling Commission and its scientific work on large whales and other cetaceans, as well as the work of other international organisations (17.62).

Nations are called on to give full effect to the provisions of the Law of the Sea with regard to the management of fish populations whose ranges lie both within and beyond the exclusive economic zones (straddling stocks and highly migratory species) (17.49). They are also called on to convene an inter-governmental conference under the auspices of the United Nations to promote effective implementation of the provisions of the Law of the Sea treaty on these species (17.50). Other measures that nations are called on to implement include resisting the reflagging of vessels as a means of avoiding compliance with applicable conservation and management rules; prohibiting destructive fishing practices, fully implementing general Assembly Resolution 46/215, on large-scale pelagic driftnet fishing and reducing waste, post-harvest losses, and discards (17.54-17.56). This section also underscored the importance of international cooperation in fisheries management, particularly in enclosed and semi-enclosed seas and within global or regional fisheries bodies.

4. Sustainable use and conservation of living marine resources under national jurisdiction

This section addresses management issues related to fisheries in Exclusive Economic Zones and other areas under national jurisdiction, reaffirming that the Law of the Sea convention provides the basic framework of management of these areas (17.70). Fisheries management problems discussed in this section include local overfishing, unauthorised incursions by foreign fleets, eco-system degradation, over capitalisation and excessive fleet sizes, under valuation of catch, insufficiently selective gear, unreliable data bases, and increasing competition between artisanal and large-scale fishing and between fishing and other activities (17.72). In addition to fisheries-related problems, problems related to coral reefs and other marine and coastal habitats, such as estuaries and mangrove forests, are highlighted (17.73). States therefore commit themselves to a number of objectives of both a development and a conservation nature, such as to develop fisheries to meet nutritional needs, taking into account traditional knowledge and small-scale fisheries; to use selective fishing gear to minimise by–catch of non-target species, and to protect endangered marine species and ecologically sensitive areas (17.75).

Among the major management activities called for in this section are development of fisheries and marine aquaculture, with special emphasis on small-scale artisanal fisheries (17.79,17.82); strengthening of legal and regulatory frameworks for fisheries management; use of selective gear to reduce waste, post-harvest losses and discards; use of environmentally sound technology, including assessment of the environmental effects of major new fisheries practices (17.79); encouragement of recreational and tourism activities based on marine living resources (17.81); and protection of marine ecosystems exhibiting high levels of diversity and productivity, such as coral reefs, estuaries, wetlands, seagrass beds, and the like (17.86).

This section also calls for a transfer of environmentally sound technologies to develop fisheries and aquaculture, particularly to developing countries (17.93), and for a number of measures designed to raise capacity for fisheries management, such as support to local fishing communities (17.95).

5. Addressing critical uncertainties for the management of the marine environment and climate change

This section calls for long-term cooperative research commitment to provide the data required for global climate models and to reduce uncertainty.

Meanwhile precautionary measures are to be undertaken to diminish the risks and effects of global climate change, particularly on small islands and in low-lying and coastal areas of the world (17.97,17.98).

Accordingly nations agree to commit themselves to improve understanding of the marine environment and its role in global processes by promoting scientific research and systematic observation, exchange of data and information (from both scientific and traditional ecological knowledge sources), and development of standard intercalibrated procedures, measuring techniques, data storage, and management capabilities (17.100).

This section also asked the states to consider the following activities: improved forecasts of marine conditions; development of methodologies for coastal vulnerability assessment; research on the effects of marine systems of increased ultra-violet radiation caused by ozone depletion (17.17.101); utilisation of studies by the

Intergovernmental Oceanographic Commission (IOC) and others on the role of the oceans as a carbon sink (17.102); support of the role of the IOC and others in collection, analysis, and distribution of ocean data (including data from the proposed Global Ocean Observing System (17.103); improvement of regional and global data bases (17.106 and elsewhere); capacity building in the marine sciences for coastal and island states (17.104, 17.113 and elsewhere) and strengthening (or establishment, where necessary) of national oceanographic commissions (17.114).

Another call in this section is that research conducted in the Antarctic be made freely available to the international community and widely disseminated (17.105).

6. Strengthening international, including regional cooperation and coordination

This section underlines the proposition that the role of international cooperation is to support and supplement national efforts and that given the existence of numerous national and international organisations with competence in marine issues, there is a need to improve coordination and to strengthen links among them so that a multisectoral approach to marine issues is also developed (17.116).

Nations are therefore to commit themselves to promote institutional arrangements necessary to support the implementation of the programme areas in this chapter for purposes of integrating sectoral activities; exchanging information and improving linkages among bilateral and multilateral, national, regional, and other organisations; promoting regular intergovernmental review within the United Nations system of ocean and coastal issues; and promoting effective cooperation among UN agencies (17.117).

This section also called for management related activities at the global level including requesting the UN Secretary General and executive heads of UN entities to improve coordination among relevant UN agencies dealing with oceans and coasts, other specialised UN agencies, and other international, subregional, and regional coastal and marine programmes, and also developing a centralised system to provide information and advice on implementing of legal arrangements on oceans and coasts (17.118).

At the regional and sub-regional levels, it called for strengthening and extending, where necessary, intergovernmental regional cooperation, the Regional Seas Programme of UNEP, regional and sub-regional fisheries organisations and regional commissions, and other measures to improve coordination among UN entities and other multilateral organisations at regional and sub-regional levels, including consideration of allocation of their staff (17.120).

Regarding the practice of establishing trade sanctions for environmental reasons (as practised by the US), this section emphasises that unilateral trade policy measures for environmental protection outside the jurisdiction of the importing country should be avoided (17.119). Trade policy measures addressing international environmental problems should, as far as possible, be based on an international consensus and be guided by certain suggested principles, such as non-discrimination, transparency and consideration of the special circumstances of developing countries.

7. Sustainable development of small islands

Small island states, because of their special characteristics (e.g., small size, limited resources, geographical dispersion and isolation from markets, ecological fragility and vulnerability, and high degree of biodiversity) present a special challenge in integrating environment and development in coastal zone management. For small island developing states, oceans and coasts are of paramount importance as an avenue for developments both for strategic reasons and for the environmental challenges facing their coastal zones (e.g., storms, sealevel rise) (17.124-17.126). This section recognises that for meeting the challenges of planning and implementing sustainable development, small-island developing states will need the cooperation and assistance of the international community (17.127).

As per this section, states commit themselves to address the problems of sustainable development of small-island developing states and, *inter alia*, to adopt measures that will enable these states to address environmental change, mitigate adverse environmental effects, and reduce threats posed to marine and coastal resources (17.128).

Small-island developing states, with the assistance of the international community, are called onto conduct studies of island environments; determine carrying capacity; prepare plans for sustainable development; adapt coastal area management techniques to the special characteristics of small islands; review and, where appropriate, reform existing institutional arrangements to provide for effective implementation of sustainable development plans; design and implement responses to effects to climate change; and promote environmentally sound technology for sustainable development (17.129). International organisations are called onto recognise the special development requirements of small-island developing states and to give them adequate priority in providing assistance (17.132). Inter-island and inter-regional cooperation and information exchange are also to be strengthened. A call was made to convene a first global conference on sustainable development of small-island developing states in 1993 (17.131). To build scientific and management capacity, the section calls for the creation (or strengthening) of centres on coastal ocean science, technology, and management on a regional basis (17.134); training programme in integrated coastal area management and development (17.135) and public awareness programmes (17.135).

The most significant achievement of Chapter 17 of Agenda 21 of UNCED as far as coastal zone management is concerned is that it produced a broad international consensus on major problems, in the ocean and coastal arenas and on principles to guide concerted action to address these problems. It also gave political legitimacy to the concept of integrated ocean and coastal management, underscoring the importance of 'integration' in the process. Cicin-Sain and Knecht identified three major developments since the UNCED that are contributing or are likely to contribute to the implementation of the concept of integrated coastal management. They are: (1) The ICM concept has come to be embraced as a central organising concept in a number of UNCED related conferences and in international agreements formerly lacking a coast and ocean emphasis, such as the Conference on Biological Diversity, (2) The ICM concept has been further interpreted and operationalised in several efforts by international entities to develop ICM guidelines to assist national governments and others in formulating and implementing ICM programmes, (3) There have been a number of efforts by international organisations and others to build capacity in ICM by establishing new teaching and training programmes (Cicin-Sain and Knecht, 1998, pp.96-97).

Among the international agreements and pronouncements which embrace ICM as an appropriate and even necessary means of addressing the coastal sustainability issues are,

(1) Framework Convention on Climate Change,

(2) Convention on Biological Diversity,

(3) Global Programme of Action on Protection of the Marine Environment from Land-Based Activities,

(4) Programme of Action for the Sustainable Development of Small Island Developing States and

(5) International Coral Reef Initiative.

The Framework Convention on Climate Change (FCCC) was negotiated between January 1991 and June 1992 by an Intergovernmental Negotiating Committee (INC) appointed by the UN General Assembly. The work of the INC was closely supported by the Intergovernmental Panel on Climate Change (IPCC) established in 1988 by the World Meteorological Organisation (WMO) and the UN Environment Programme (UNEP). The IPCC's position on the key role of ICM was incorporated into the text of the Framework Convention on Climate Change by the negotiators. In Article 4 of the Convention, nations commit themselves, *inter alia*, 'to develop integrated plans for coastal zone management'. The Framework Convention on Climate Change thus reinforces the ICM prescriptions contained in Chapter 17 of Agenda 21.

The Convention on Biological Diversity (CBD) entered into force in December 1994 and at the first meeting of the Conference of Parties held in the Bahamas in November-December 1994, it was decided that priority attention should be given to coastal and marine ecosystems, given their dominant contribution to global biodiversity. The second Conference of Parties held at Jakarta on November 6-17, 1995 resolved and reported that it encourages the use of integrated marine and coastal area management as the most suitable framework for addressing human impacts on marine and coastal biological diversity and for promoting conservation and sustainable use of this biodiversity and encourages parties to establish and/or strengthen, where appropriate, institutional, administrative, and legislative arrangements for the development of integrated management of marine and coastal areas, and their integration within national development plans (UNEP, 1995, c).

The Global Programme of Action for Protection of the Marine Environment from Land Based Activities was adopted by the Inter-Governmental Meeting on Protection of the Marine Environment from Land-Based Activities held at Washington D.C. in October-November 1995. The text emerging from the conference makes clear that integrated coastal zone management is seen as an important tool in accomplishing the goals of the programme at the national level. It noted that 'states should ... focus on sustainable, pragmatic and integrated environmental management approaches and processes such as integrated coastal area management, harmonised, as appropriate, with river basin management and land use plans' (UNEP, 1995, b).

The Programme of Action for the Sustainable Development of Small Island Developing States was evolved at the Global Conference on the Sustainable Development of Small Island Developing States, held at Barbados in April-May 1994. Three of the nine substantive issues addressed in the Programme of Action (climate change and sea-level rise, coastal and marine resources, and tourism resources) call for the formulation of new policies and programmes in the context of integrated coastal area management. An improvement in the capacity for integration of economic and environmental policy in national planning and across sectors was also called for in the section dealing with national institutions and administrative capacity. Besides this, international organisations and donor nations were asked to support small island developing states in responding to the call by the IPCC for vulnerable coastal nations to develop integrated coastal zone management plans including the development of adaptive response measures to the impacts of climate change and sea level rise.

The International Coral Reef Initiative (ICRI) combines national and international efforts to conserve and manage coral reefs and their related ecosystems, including mangrove forests and seagrass beds. It was announced at the first conference of parties of the Convention on Biological Diversity in December 1994 and at the high level segment of the April 1995 session of the UN Commission on Sustainable Development. The ICRI sponsored a major Global Workshop in Philippines from May 29 to June 2, 1995, where it endorsed integrated coastal management as a framework for achieving the sustainable use of and maintaining the health of coral reef, and associated environments. In fact, one of the six principles contained in the Framework for Action noted that 'integrated coastal management, with its special emphasis on community participation and benefit, provides a framework for effective coral reef and related ecosystem management' (ICRI, 1995, p.4).

3.3.4.4. Post UNCED efforts

A number of efforts have been made by other international organisations to further define, interpret and operationalise the concept of ICM during the last decade. Cicin-Sain and Knecht identified five major efforts to develop international guidelines for integrated coastal management. They are led by World Bank, World Coast Conference (WCC), OECD, UNEP and IUCN (Cicin-Sain and Knecht, 1998, p.102). Some of these efforts, such as those by OECD and UNEP were only a continuation of their previous efforts.

The World Bank's guidelines were the result of a joint effort initiated by the World Bank, UNEP and FAO in 1992 in response to mandates from UNCED. A technical workshop on guidelines for coastal zone management was held at the World Bank's headquarters in November of that year. Subsequent to that meeting, the World Bank prepared the guidelines which were then tabled at the World Coast Conference (WCC), held in the Netherlands in November 1993. The Conference statement representing the views of ninety or more participant nations, contains a 'strong statement' about the urgency and the benefits of integrated coastal zone management. The statement also lists the key elements of ICZM and outlines the obstacles nations often encounter as they endeavour to implement the concept.

The OECD guidelines, developed prior to UNCED and evolved from an analysis of seventeen country reports and sixteen case studies, were aimed specifically at identifying measures to achieve better integration in coastal zone management and, especially, integration of economic and environmental considerations.

The UNEP guidelines, on the other hand, emerged from experience gained in administering the Mediterranean Action Plan (MAP) for the Mediterranean Regional Seas Programme. The guidelines were initially drafted by the Priority Action Programme of

MAP, since integrated management of coastal areas was recognised by countries bordering the Mediterranean as having the highest priority.

The guidelines of the IUCN (International Union for the Conservation of Nature and Natural Resources, now the World Conservation Union) produced by the IUCN's Marine and Coastal Areas Programme as a contribution to the deliberations on coastal zone management emphasise ecological and planning considerations in sustainable coastal development.

Two additional sets of guidelines have also since emerged. A guide to good ICM practices is contained in the report of an International Workshop on Lessons Learned in ICM held in Xiamen, People's Republic of China, in May 1996 (Chua, 1996). Similarly, draft guidelines addressing climate change within the framework of ICM were developed at an International Workshop on Climate Change and ICM held in Taipei, Taiwan, China, in February 1997 (Cicin-Sain, *et. al.* 1997).

After making a review of the previous five major efforts and the guidelines for ICM prepared by these initiatives, Cicin-Sain and Knecht identified ten variables which are considered very important in the design and implementation of ICM programme. They are: (1) scope and purpose (major aspects covered), (2) principles, (3) definition of the management area, (4) functions and goals of ICM, (5) legal basis for ICM, (6) horizontal integration (mechanisms for intersectoral coordination), (7) vertical integration (mechanisms for intergovernmental integration), (8) financial arrangements, (9) prescriptions for the use of science, and (10) capacity building. Further details of these guidelines are given in appendix 3.4.

Following an examination of the common features of the above five sets of guidelines, Cicin-Sain and Knecht concluded that 'it is possible to distil, a set of guidelines that would generally be consistent with all five' (Cicin-Sain and Knecht, 1998, p.104). Table 3.2 shows the 'consensus set of guidelines' which is considered to be a 'reasonable characterisation of the ICM concept as it is understood today' (ibid, p.104).

Table 3.2
A consensus set of ICM guidelines

Purpose of ICM	The purpose of ICM is to guide coastal area development in an ecologically sustainable fashion.
Principles	ICM is guided by principles in the Rio Declaration on Environment and Development with special emphasis on the principles of inter-generational equity, the precautionary principle, and the polluter-pay-principle. ICM is holistic and inter-disciplinary in nature, especially with regard to science and policy.
Functions	ICM strengthens and harmonises sectoral management in the coastal zone. It preserves and protects the productivity and biological diversity of coastal ecosystems and maintains amenity values. ICM promotes the rational economic development and sustainable utilisation of coastal and ocean resources and facilitates conflict resolution in the coastal zone.
Spatial Integration	An ICM programme embraces all coastal and upland areas whose use can affect coastal waters and the resources therein and extends seaward to include that part of the ocean that can affect the land of the coastal zone. An ICM programme may also include the entire ocean area under national jurisdiction (exclusive economic zone) over which national governments have stewardship responsibilities under both the Law of the Sea Convention and UNCED.
Horizontal and Vertical Integration	Overcoming the sectoral and inter-governmental fragmentation that exists in today's coastal management efforts is a prime goal of ICM. Institutional mechanisms for effective co-ordination among various sectors active in the coastal zone and among the various levels of government operating in the coastal zone are fundamental to the strengthening and rationalisation of the coastal management process. From the variety of available options, the coordination and harmonisation of mechanisms must be tailored to fit the unique aspects of each particular national government setting.
The Use of Science	Given the complexities and uncertainties that exist in the coastal zone, ICM must be built on the best science (both natural and social) available. Techniques such as risk assessment, economic valuation, vulnerability assessment, resource accounting, cost-benefit analysis, and outcome based monitoring should be built into the ICM process, as appropriate.

Source: Cicin-Sain and Knecht, 1998, p.108.

As noted by Cicin-Sain and Knecht, the 'consensus guidelines' given above, represent the core of the ICM concept as it is understood today at the international level.

One of the three major developments noted earlier and following the UNCED, which needs further highlighting is the growing capacity building exercise that is taking place internationally. This has manifested in two ways. They are, (1) the major UN entities involved in oceans and coasts have expanded their own capacities in integrated coastal and ocean management and have also sponsored efforts to build capacity at national, regional, and subnational levels, and (2) a number of new training efforts in integrated coastal and ocean management have been created at the international level, and examples of similar efforts at regional and national levels are also in evidence.

The major UN entities that have made substantial contribution to the development of ICM are, (1) The Intergovernmental Oceanographic Commission (IOC), (2) United Nations Division for Ocean Affairs and the Law of the Sea (UNDOALOS), (3) Food and Agriculture Organisation of the United Nations (FAO), (4) United Nations Environment Programme (UNEP), (5) United Nations Development Programme (UNDP), (6) International Maritime Organisation (IMO), (7) GESAMP, (8) World Bank and (9) Global Environmental Facility (GEF).

Among the new ICM training initiatives at the international level are, (I) The Train-Sea-Coast Programme of UNDOALOS, (2) The International Ocean Institute Network, (3) UNEP's NETLAP Programme, (4) CANADA/ASEAN marine science programme and, (5) MEDCOAST training programmes. Many other institutions, including Universities, in developed and developing countries are also now involved in ICM training.

It should be noted here that the major international initiatives at developing ICM, starting from the United Nations Conference on the Human Environment (Stockholm 1972) and progressing through the UN Conference on the Law of the Sea (1973-1982), the UN Conference on Environment and Development (UNCED 1992) and Post-UNCED efforts have made it a global movement for sustainable development. In this course it has progressed into a multidisciplinary or transdisciplinary subject having its own language, concepts and techniques.

3.4. Summary

This chapter attempted to make the conceptual framework of coastal zone management clear. As a starting point it recognised the plurality of phrases like Integrated Coastal Zone Management (ICZM), Integrated Coastal and Ocean Zone Management (ICOZM), Integrated Coastal Area Management (ICAM), Integrated Coastal Management (ICM), Coastal Resource Management (CRM), Integrated Marine and Coastal Area Management (IMCAM) and Community Based Coastal Resource Management (CBCRM). It then scanned through the many definitions of coastal zone management available in the literature and found the commonality of their approach with regard to objectives, mode and sphere (arena) of management functions. It noted a progressive widening of the spectrum of goals, methods and sphere of management actions contemplated in the literature.

A review of the evolution of the concept of coastal zone management made in this chapter led to the identification of four stages (sources) viz. (l) The U.S. beginning, (2) The USAID led ICM programmes, (3) The European initiatives and (4)International efforts. The U.S. initiative, though considered primarily as an environmental protection measure provided the basic framework for further evolution of the ICM concept and through USAID led ICM programmes in the ASEAN and the European and International efforts (predominantly supported by the UN) has culminated in the present concept and practice of ICZM for sustainable development of the coast. The concept of ICZM is now a complex concept with multidimensional features combining ecological, economic, social and cultural aspects of development transcending and integrating the spatial, horizontal and vertical dimensions of planning and administration of coastal activities. In this process, it now calls upon nations to use the knowledge of science including social science and to build capacity for that on a global scale.

4
Rationale of Coastal Zone Management

4.1. Introduction

The objective of this chapter is to make clear the rationale of coastal zone management. This is important because an explicit understanding of the need, objective and basis of coastal zone management can help us in assessing or evaluating the coastal issues in Kerala in later chapters. Accordingly, this chapter presents the ecological, economic, social, political and other arguments generally put forward in the literature in support of coastal zone management. A holistic view of the need for coastal zone management is also presented in this chapter.

4.2. Ecological basis

Understanding the ecological basis of coastal zone management pre-supposes some familiarity with the coastal ecology, coastal processes and coastal environment, However, since a detailed explanation of the coastal ecology, process and environment is not in the scope of this study and in the reach of this scholar, the attempt here is only to focus on the outstanding features of the coastal (natural) resource system and the transition taking place in it, leading to its damage as a result of natural and economic development processes. Sustaining the ecology and ecological processes of the coast are important in so far as they provide the natural and environmental resource base for all human activities on the coast.

Prior to an explanation of the coastal resource base and the transformations taking place therein, it is essential to note the boundaries of the coastal zone.

4.2.1. Boundary of the coastal zone

Defining the coastal zone or setting a boundary for the coastal zone is considered to be quite difficult. Cicin-Sain and Knecht, for example, noted that 'one of the thorniest questions in integrated coastal management is how far inland and how far offshore an ICM regime should extend' (Cicin-Sain and Knecht, 1998, p. 50). Sorensen and McCreary defined the coastal zone or the coastal area as the interface or transition zone and especially 'that part of the land affected by its proximity to the sea and that part of the ocean affected by its proximity to the land ... an area in which processes depending on the interaction between land and sea are most intense' (Sorensen and McCreary, 1990).

Clark, however, finds some problem with this definition. He noted that 'the border between land and sea is not fixed - it changes daily with the tides, with the moon stages, seasonally with astronomic forces and sporadically with sea storms and great river floods' (Clark, 1996, p.1). In spite of this difficulty, Clark observes that 'the coastal zone may be drawn wide or narrow in order to meet programme goals. For example, it could embrace a wide band of shorelands or a quite narrow strip. It can include coastal islands and the shallower nearshore coastal waters, but it could in some cases extend to the outer edge of the continental shelf' (ibid, p. 1). This author, however, insists that 'the coastal zone always includes the inter tidal and supra tidal zones of the water's edge that include flood plains, mangroves, marshes, and tide flats, as well as beaches and dunes and fringing coral reefs' (ibid, p. 1). It is also recognised that 'this is the place where agency authority changes abruptly, where storms hit, where water front development locates, where boats make their landfalls, and where some of the richest aquatic habitat is found. It is also the place where terrestrial type planning and resource management programmes are at their weakest' (ibid, pp.1-2). It is considered as the 'core of the coastal zone'. This zone is considered as belonging to the 'wetside' of the coast which is in the realm of the 'common property resources'. The 'dry side' of the coast, which is frequently, under 'private property' regime also form part of the coastal zone (Clark, 1992, p.11).

Cicin-Sain and Knecht have identified five main zones within the coastal marine spectrum. They are: (1) inland areas, which affect the oceans mainly via rivers and non-point sources of pollution, (2) coastal lands-wetlands, marshes, and the like-where human activity is concentrated and directly affects adjacent waters, (3) coastal waters - generally estuaries, lagoons, and shallow waters - where the effects of land-based activities are dominant, (4) offshore waters, mainly out to the edge of national jurisdiction (200 nautical miles offshore), and (5) high seas, beyond the limit of national jurisdiction (Cicin-Sain and Knecht, 1998, p.43).

The boundaries of the coastal zone are likely to depend on political, administrative, legal, ecological and pragmatic considerations and also because of the presence of broad array of possible coastal issues and the effects of remote activities (Clark, 1992, p.11). The prevalence of a wide range of coastal demarkation is reflected in the shoreland exclusion or restriction setbacks made by countries (states) as shown in Table 4.1

Table 4.1

Shoreland exclusion or restriction setbacks

Countries	*Distance inland from shoreline**
Equador	8 m*
Hawaii	40 ft
Philippines (mangrove green belt)	20 m
Mexico	20 m
Brazil	20 m
New Zealand	33 m
Oregon	66 ft
Colombia	Permanent vegetative line (variable)
Costa Rica (public zone)	50 m
Costa Rica (restricted zone)	50 m
Indonesia **	50 to 200 m
Indonesia (mangrove green belt)	50 m
Venezula	400 m
Chile	50 m
France	80 m
Norway (no buildings)	100 m
Sweden (no buildings)	100 m (in some places 300 m)
Spain	100 to 200 m
Uruguay	250 m
Greece	500 m
Denmark (no summer homes)	1-3 km
U.S.S.R. (preporistroiska-Black-Sea Coast-exclusion of new factories)	3 km

* Definition of shoreline varies, but it is usually the mean high tide. Most nations and states exempt coastal dependent installations such as harbour development and marinas.

** Indonesia has both a 50 m setback for forest cutting and a 400 m. 'green belt' for fishing support purpose.

Source: Clark, 1992, p.138.

A similar approach to fixing the boundaries of the coastal zone seems to have been taken by the ASEAN/USCRMP. Table 4.2. gives the description of coastal area boundaries under the ASEAN/ USCRMP.

Table 4.2
Description of coastal area boundaries under ASEAN/USCRMP

Country	*Landward boundary*		*Seaward boundary*	
	Description	*Type*	*Description*	*Type*
Brunei Darussalam	All land and water areas 1 km inland from MHWST and areas inundated by tides any time of the year	AD/SEU	From MHWST level of the shore to 200m isobath	PL/C
Indonesia	Municipal boundary of Cilacap (east), border between Cilacap and Ciamis districts (west), north point where there is no tidal influence or rivers and streams	AB/SEU	From shore upto 60 km isobath (south)	PL/C
Malaysia	District boundaries of Pontian, Johore Bahru and Kota Tinggi	AB	Upto 20 km from the shore to include some islets in East Johore (Mersing district)	AD, PL
Philippines	Boundaries of 17 coastal municipalities along Lingayen Gulf and 5 non-coastal municipalities with brackish water fishponds	AB, PL/C	100 fathom isobath with straight lines connecting the 2 coastal municipal boundaries Bolinao and San Fernando	PL/C
Singapore	Whole island of Singapore	PB	Territorial water and offshore islands	PB
Thailand	Boundaries of all coastal districts of Phangnga and Ban Don bays, Upper South	AB	Shoreline of Ban Den and Phangnga Bays into shallow continental shelf to include major islands within	PL/C

AB— Administration boundaries.
AD— Arbitrary distance.
MHWST— Mean high water at spring tide.
PB— Political boundaries.
PL/C— Physical landmark/criteria.
SEU— Selected environmental units.
Source: Scura, *et. al.* 1992, p.33.

Referring to a possible inland boundary for the coastal zone, Cicin-Sain and Knecht note that 'in terms of the inland boundary, a watershed (containment area) approach permits better control of pollutants coming into a particular marine environment. However, watersheds often span large distances and encompasses multiple jurisdictions. Hence if too wide an area is included under the aegis of integrated coastal management, attention and resources may well be directed away from the area constituting the heart of the land-sea interface. Thus, a watershed-based inland boundary may be appropriate for the specific purposes of controlling land-based sources of marine pollution and freshwater inflows but not for ICM purposes' (Cicin-Sain and Knecht, 1998, p.50).

The FAO observed that 'coastal areas are commonly defined as the interface or transition area between land and sea, including large inland lakes. Coastal areas are diverse in function and form, dynamic, and do not lend themselves well to definition, by strict spatial boundaries. Unlike watersheds, there are no exact natural boundaries that unambiguously delineate coastal areas ... coastal areas are therefore characterised by the vertical accretion of near-shore land. This depends on several factors: sediment supply from rivers or from the sea, the width of the shelf, or the proximity of a submarine canyon through which currents remove sediments, and the strength of longshore currents and incidence of cyclones, both of which transport and redistribute sediments along the coast. Sedimentation is the major geological activity that shapes coasts, but human induced land subsidence is having an increasing impact on coastal morphology' (FAO, 1998, pp.3-4).

It nevertheless notes that 'for management purposes, a variety of landwards and seawards boundaries, ranging from fairly narrow and precise ones to much broader and more nebulous ones, have been utilised around the world. Management boundaries are pragmatic, being influenced by the geographic scope of relevant management concerns, including biophysical, economic, social, institutional and organisational aspects. Therefore, the boundaries of a coastal area may change over time for management purpose, as the issues to be faced become more extensive or complex and require more far-ranging solutions' (ibid, p.4).

The FAO has also suggested that a distinction be made between the terms 'coastal zone' and 'coastal area'.

The former is to refer to the geographic area defined by the enabling legislation for coastal management, while the latter would refer to more broadly to the geographic area along the coast that has not yet been defined as a zone for management purposes.

The World Resources Institute has defined the coastal zone as including the land area within 60 km of adjacent nearshore waters (FAO, 1998, p.10).

The National Oceanic and Atmospheric Administration (NOAA) defines the 'coastal areas' from a natural systems viewpoint as 'at minimum, the coastal watersheds that drain directly into estuaries, other coastal land areas that drain directly into other coastal waters and the adjacent coastal waters and sediment out to the edge of the continental shelf or 200 mile exclusive economic zone' (Ehler, 1995, p.175).

The practical difficulties of setting an offshore boundary for integrated coastal management are also noted by Cicin-Sain and Knecht. They observed that 'living marine resources do not respect human made boundaries in coastal waters, nor do ocean processess. Nevertheless, ... different governmental units will be involved and somewhat different interests will be at stake as one goes farther offshore. How far from the coast an ICM regime ought to extend will depend in part on the character of the physical system offshore, especially the continental shelf system, as well as on the relations between national and provincial governments in a particular nation' (Cicin-Sain and Knecht, p. 51).

Based on their 1996 survey of ICM practice in selected developed, middle developing and developing countries, Cicin-Sain and Knecht reported that in more than half (57 per cent) of the countries the landward boundary of the coastal zone either varied according to use or was not yet determined. The same situation was reported with respect to the seaward boundaries by 38 per cent of the countries. Twenty-one per cent of the respondent countries was reported to have the boundaries established at the 12 nautical mile territorial limit, with the greatest proportion of respondents from developed countries (36 per cent). Eight per cent of the respondent countries reported boundaries at the edge of the 200 nautical-mile EEZ, with the greatest number of respondents from middle developing countries (21 per cent). Table 4.3 shows the details of land-ward and sea-ward boundaries of ICM in selected countries as reported by Cicin-Sain and Knecht.

Table 4.3
Details of landward and seaward boundaries of ICM in selected countries

Boundary	*Countries*			
	All per cent (N=48)	*Developed per cent (N = 14)*	*Middle developing per cent (N = 14)*	*Developing per cent (N = 20)*
Landward Boundary				
Upto 100 m (0.062 mi.)	4	0	14	0
100-500 m (0.062-0.311 mi.)	8	7	0	10
500 m to 1 km (0.311-0.62 mi.)	4	0	0	10
1-10 km (0.62-6.21 mi.)	10	0	7	15
Extent of local government jurisdiction (e.g., coastal city or county)	4	7	0	5
Water shed	4	7	0	5
Varies according to use	6	0	14	10
Not yet determined	38	50	36	30
Uncertain	19	21	29	15
Seaward Boundary	6	14	0	5
Mean low tide or mean high tide	2	7	0	0
Arbitrary offshore distance from tidal mark	17	0	14	30
3 nautical miles territorial sea boundary	6	7	7	5
12 nautical miles territorial sea boundary	21	36	14	15
Edge of continental shelf	2	0	0	5
Limit of national jurisdiction 200-nautical mile EEZ or fisheries zone	8	7	21	0
Varies according to use	23	21	21	25
Not yet determined	15	14	14	15
Uncertain	6	7	7	5

Source: Cicin-Sain and Knecht, 1998, pp 51-52.

4.2.2. Natural resources of the coastal zone

As noted by Clark, 'the transitional strip of land and sea that straddles the coastline contains some of the most productive and valuable habitats of the biosphere, including estuaries, lagoons, coastal wetlands, and fringing coral reefs. It is also a place of natural dynamism where huge amounts of natural energy are released and a great abundance of life is nurtured. It is a place of high priority interest to people, to commerce, to the military and to a variety of industries. Because it contains dense populations, the coast undergoes great environmental modification and deterioration through land fill, dredging and pollution caused by urban, industrial, and agricultural development', (Clark, 1996, p. 1).

Coastal zones are also credited for their unique features. 'Such things as daily tides, mangrove forests, coral reefs, tidal flats, sea beaches and barrier islands are found only at the coast. Because of these features and because coastal enterprise is also distinctive, most countries recognise the coastal zone as a distinct region with resources that require special attention. In all but the larger coastal settlements, the coastal location creates distinctively maritime cultures' (ibid, p. 1).

Referring to tropical countries, Clark noted the following 'critical habitat' resources: mangrove forests (including wet lands and other inter-tidal areas), coral reefs, submerged seagrass meadows, beach-dune systems, lagoon/estuaries (including embayments) and other habitats. All these systems are known to be especially valuable.

4.2.2.1. Mangrove forests, wetlands and other intertidal systems

Clark reports that some 24 million hectares of mangrove forests occur in coastal areas of subtropical and tropical countries of the world. The geographic distribution of mangroves is given in appendix table 4.1. Mangroves are found along sheltered coastlines where wave activity tends to be minimal. The term mangrove refer to any of dozens of species of trees capable of living in saltwater and salty soil regimes.

Ecologically, mangrove communities are reported to have a variety of recognised roles in the areas where they occur. A prominent role is the production of leaf litter and detrital matter which is exported to lagoons and the nearshore coastal environment. The organic matter exported from the mangrove habitat is utilised in one form or another by the inhabitants of estuaries/ lagoons, near coast waters, seagrass meadows, and coral reefs which may occur in the area. Most tropical commercial shrimps and many fish species are supported by this food source.

Mangrove ecosystems are also said to 'provide a valuable physical habitat for a variety of important coastal species. Waterfowl and shorebirds are well known and highly valued inhabitants of wetlands, as are alligators and musk-rats. Less evident, but equally important inhabitants are crabs, shrimp, and the important juvenile stages of commercial and sport fishes, alongwith numerous forage species of fish and invertebrates' (Clark, 1992, p.15).

Mangroves found along the coast (shoreline) are recognised as a buffer against storm-tide surges that would otherwise have a more damaging effect on low-lying land areas. Clark reported that the littoral strip mangroves planted by the Bangladesh Government in the 1980s are credited with saving thousands of lives and millions of dollars worth property during the cyclone of 29 April 1991 that ravaged the south-east coast of the country (Clark, 1992, p.17). Mangroves are also noted for their ability to stabilise coastal shoreline that would otherwise be subject to erosion and loss.

The value of mangrove resources in terms of its marketed products can be expressed in economic terms. However, the 'free' or 'non-marketed' services provided by mangroves are more difficult to measure and are consequently often ignored. In view of this the total value of the mangrove resource is quite significantly underestimated. The real value of mangrove resources can be understood from the assemblage of uses and products that they provide to the community. Table 4.4 presents the products of the mangrove ecosystem as reported by Saenger and others.

Table 4.4

Products of mangrove-ecosystems

Users	*Products*
A. Mangrove forest products	
Fuel	Firewood (cooking, heating), charcoal, alcohol
Construction	Timber (scafolds), heavy construction (e.g., bridges), rail road ties, mining pit props, boat building, dock piling, beams and poles for buildings, flooring (pannelling), thatch or netting, fence posts, water pipes, chip boards, glues.
Fishing	Poles for fish traps, fishing floats, wood for smoking fish, fish poison, tanning for net and line preservation, fish attracting shelters.
Textiles, leathers	Synthetic fibres (e.g., rayon), dye for cloth, tanning for leather preservation.
Food, drugs and beverages	Sugar, alcohol, cooking oil, vinegar, tea substitute, fermented drinks, dissert topping, condiments from bark, sweetmeat from propagules, vegetables from propagules, fruit or leaves, cigar substitutes.
Household items	Furniture, glue, hair dressing oil, tool handles, rice mortar, toys, match sticks, incense.
Agriculture	Fodder and green manure
Paper products	Paper of various kinds
Other products	Packing boxes, wood for smoking, sheet rubber, wood for burning bricks, medicines from bark, leaves and fruits.
B. Other natural products	
	Fish, crustaceans, shellfish, honey, wax, birds, mamals, reptiles and reptile skins, other fauna (amphibians, insects).

Source: Saenger, *et. al.* (1983), as reported by Clark, 1992, p.40.

In order to understand fully the value of mangrove resources, the on-site and off-site value and the marketed and non-marketed value of the resources are also to be recognised. This is indicated in the form of a matrice in table 4.5.

Table 4.5

Relation between location and type of mangrove goods and services and traditional economic analysis

Type of goods and services	*Location of Goods and Services*	
	On-site	*Off-site*
Marketed	Usually included in an economic analysis (e.g., poles, charcoal, wood, chips, mangrove crabs)	May be included (e.g., fish or shellfish caught in adjacent waters)
Non-marketed	Seldom included (e.g., medicinal uses of mangrove, domestic fuelwood, food in times of famine, nursery area for juvenile fish, feeding ground for estuarine fish and shrimp, viewing and studying wildlife.	Usually ignored (e.g., nutrient flows to estuaries, buffer to storm damage)

Source: Hamilton and Snedaker, 1984, as reported by Clark, 1992, p. 90.

When the onsite and offsite marketed and non-rnarketed values of mangrove resources are taken, their total value will be immense.

The mangrove eco-system is generally believed to be fairly resistant to many kinds of environmental perturbations and stresses. However, mangroves are sensitive to excessive siltation or sedimentation, stagnation, surface water impoundment, and major oil spills. These actions reduce the uptake of oxygen for respiration which results in rapid mangrove mortality. Salinity high enough to kill mangroves (+90 ppt.) result from reductions in the freshwater inflow and alterations in flushing patterns from dams, dredging, and bulkheading. Lowered salinities from seawalls and coastal structures and restrictions of tidal flow also kill mangroves. On the other hand mangrove forests help maintain coastal water quality by extracting chemical pollutants from the water.

Clark notes that 'a major problem that affects mangrove habitat results from man's desire to convert mangrove areas to residential, commercial, industrial, and agricultural real estate by land filling. In addition, there is an increasing demand for forest wood products that results in the exploitative clear-felling of the forests' (Clark, 1992, p.17).

4.2.2.2. Coral reef systems

As noted by Clark 'coral reefs occur along shallow, tropical coastlines where the marine waters are clean, clear, and warm. They are one of the most productive ecosystems in the world. The basis for the high productivity of the coral reef ecosystem is a combination of the production of the reef with support from its surrounding environments' (ibid, p.18).

Generally, three types of reef structures are noted. They are 'fringing' reefs, 'patch' reefs and 'barrier' reefs. Fringing reefs are contiguous with the shore and are most common and widespread of the reef structural types. They are most frequently found below the low tide level. Their inshore distribution tends to make them more susceptible to degradation from coastal activities than other types of reefs. One of the largest fringing reef formation is found along the Saudi Arabian, 1100-mile Red Sea Coast which is noted for an absence of freshwater and sediment runoff. Patch reefs are said to be isolated and discontinuous bits of coral reef, often lying shoreward of offshore reef structures. Barrier reefs are linear, offshore reef structures that run parallel to coastlines and arise from submerged shelf platforms; the water area between the shore and reef is often termed a 'lagoon'.

Coral reefs have important economic outputs. They contribute to fisheries of three types: fishing directly on the reef; fishing in shallow coastal waters where coral reefs support food webs, life cycles, and productivity; and fishing in offshore waters where the reef's great productivity may contribute to support of 'high sea' fishes. Approximately one-third of the world's fish species are said to live on coral reefs.

Coral reefs also support booming tourist industries in many countries, catering for snorklars, divers, underwater photographers, sight seers, and fishermen. Reef tourism is said to produce thousands of millions of dollars of foreign exchange earnings annually. Coral reefs are also known to serve as natural protective barriers, deterring beach erosion, retarding storm waves, allowing mangroves to prosper and providing safe landing sites for boats.

Unfortunately, however, coral reefs are reported as being degraded at a rapid rate. In many countries, reefs are heavily exploited for corals which are harvested for sale as souvenirs or decorations. The market for coral is often quite lucrative and usually export-oriented. Other damaging activities noted are: (1) siltation and sedimentation created by dredging, filling, and related construction activities and increased soil erosion, (2) pollutants, including spilled oil, industrial waste water and domestic sewage, (3) discharge of large volumes of freshwater as may result from diversions and stormwater outfalls, (4) destructive fishing practices, including dynamite, (5) collection of young fishes for sale in the aquarium trade and (6) tourist visits to reefs which result in breakage from boat anchors and from hand and foot damage.

In addition, damages from natural causes are also reported. They include:

(1) outbreaks of reef destroying animals such as crown-of-thorns starfish,
(2) diseases like whitehead (which kills elkhorn coral) and blackband (which kills large structural corals),
(3) hurricanes that smash the coral and 'sand blast' away the living tissue,
(4) coral disablement and death from 'bleaching' episodes, and
(5) die-off or depletion of essential symbionts, such as parrot fish and sea urchins that clean the reef of algae.

Coral reef degradation has serious consequences for tourism, fishing, beach stability and particularly for coastal/marine parks. When serious, coral reef degradation can ruin a park and cut severely into tourism.

4.2.2.3. Seagrass systems

Submerged seagrasses are often abundant in the shallow water temperate and tropical coastal environments of the world. Seagrass beds, or meadows, are highly productive and valuable resources which enrich the sea and provide shelter and food for some of the most important and valued species of fish and shellfish.

Clark notes that 'seagrasses grow best in the quiet, protected waters of healthy estuaries and lagoons, often in beds, or meadows, that are easily delineated for classification as critical habitat areas. They are normally found in shallow areas where light can readily penetrate and enable photosynthesis to occur. Seagrass beds extend shoreward to the point where wave action prevents them from rooting' (ibid, p.17).

Seagrasses are reported to intermingle with both mangrove and reef communities at their respective seaward and landward boundaries. Submarine meadows of seagrass usually provide the link between mangrove and coral reef ecotypes.

Referring to the importance of seagrass, Clark observes: 'seagrass meadows are essential elements of coastal ecosystems.

Although seagrasses are little used for commercial purposes, they play an important ecological role, providing a substantial amount of nourishment, nutrients and habitat. These meadows provide vital places of refuge not found in the open ocean. They attract a diverse and prolific biota and serve as essential nursery area to some important marine species. Seagrass meadows are also known to trap and bind sediments, thereby reducing particulate pollutants' (ibid, p.18).

Seagrasses, though considered a relatively hardy group of plants, can be damaged by unfavourable conditions such as excessive siltation, turbidity, water pollution, bottom trawls which scrape and plough the meadows, and marine excavation and filling. Some pollutants in seawater are also toxic to sea grasses. Other major threats are dredging and filling operations in seagrass meadows. Clark notes that 'disappearance of seagrass communities may go unnoticed because unlike mangroves and coral reefs, seagrass communities are not visually obvious to most observers' (ibid, p.18).

4.2.2.4. Sandy beach system

Beaches are not considered as stable forms. They are dynamic landforms, constantly subject to erosion and or accretion. The condition of the beach reflects the local balance or imbalance, between deposition (gain) and erosion (loss). On a worldwide basis, erosion (natural and man-induced) is said to be stronger than deposition, partly because of the global rise in sea level. Consequently, there is a serious loss of beach and beach front in many parts of the world.

Clark reminds us that 'the key to natural protection, provided by the beach front, is the sand which is held in storage and yielded to storm waves, thereby dissipating the force of their attack. Consequently, taking sand from any part of the beach—dry beach, wetbeach, bar or the nearshore submerged zone—can lead to erosion and recession of the beach front. Therefore beach conservation should start with the premise that any removal of sand is adverse, whether for construction fill, concrete aggregate, or any other purpose, and should be prohibited' (ibid, p.21).

Ecologically, the beach is a unique environment occupied by animals that have adapted to the constant motion of the sand, gravel or shell. Many varieties of birds, reptiles, and other animals nest and breed on the berm and open beach. They, as well feed and rest there. Beaches provide a unique habitat for burrowing species such as mole crabs, coquina clams, razor clams, and others. Clark observes that 'there may also be a complex intertidal or subtidal community of crustacean organisms that attract shore birds. The shallow waters of the nearshore zone provide habitat for shellfish of many kinds and a wide variety of forage species, which in turn attract fish and birds' (ibid, p. 21).

Beaches protected by coral reefs are often considered as the best place for dwellings and villages in tropical countries. They are also the source of construction sand in many island countries. Reckless exploitation of beach sand can lead to catastrophic loss of beach. The main threat to the beach is usually from developments on the land next to it. Beach protection requires coordinated management to include both the beach and the land behind it, including action to limit construction, require reef backs, prevent excavation and control beach, harbour, and inlet construction. Clark observes that 'the general goal for a management programme should be to maintain the beach by protecting both the natural processes that supply the sand and the sand-storage capacity of the beach. Meeting this goal will require careful examination of conservation needs, natural processes, building practices, and correction engineering proposals that affect whole beach system' (ibid, p. 21).

4.2.2.5. Lagoon and estuary system

These are coastal embayments which are semi-enclosed, sheltered shallow water bodies that have special characteristics. They include such water bodies as lagoons, estuaries, small bays, sounds, fjords, esteros, etc. Estuaries, which are supplied by freshwater from rivers exist in some form throughout the tropics except on small islands and in arid and semi-arid regions where major rivers are few and discharge is sporadic. Lagoons, with limited freshwater supply and high salinity, exist widely, occupying about 10 to 15 per cent of the world's coastline.

Both estuaries and lagoons are reported to maintain exceptionally high levels of biological productivity and they perform important ecological functions. The ecological functions include

(1) exporting nutrients and organic materials to outside waters through tidal circulation,

(2) providing habitat for a number of commercially or recreationally valuable fish species and

(3) serving the needs of migratory nearshore and oceanic species which require shallow, protected habitats for breeding and/or sanctuary for their young (nursery areas).

Referring to the use of lagoons and estuaries Clark noted that 'these coastal water bodies have sustained human settlements dating back to prehistoric periods ... modern day lagoons and estuaries serve a multitude of purposes including waste disposal, mariculture, recreation, and residential development' (ibid, p.23).

The intensive use of embayments, that serve as ports and harbours are reported to create a variety of environmental impacts and severe losses of estuarine and lagunal natural resources. The increased usage of these water-bodies for transport of oil, chemicals, and other toxic materials, whether by ships, barges, pipelines, or rail roads, presents a continuous threat. This pollution is particularly damaging to estuaries and lagoons because their sluggish circulation keeps the pollutants, in high concentrations.

An increasing threat to the well-being of estuaries/ lagoons is the impoundment and/or diversion of rivers at upstream locations. Similarly, when portions of the coastal watershed system are altered or short-circuited, the natural flow pattern is disrupted and estuaries may be subject to surges of freshwater. This can not only disturb the ecosystem, but also increase flood hazards.

Another source of damage to the estuarine environment is waste disposal. Clark points out that 'a major source of degradation of shallow embayments is their continued use as pollutant discharge areas. Aside from outright fish kills and other dramatic effects, pollution causes pervasive and continuous degradation, evidenced by the gradual disappearance of fish or shellfish, or a general decline in the natural carrying capacity of the system. The most likely sources of pollution are agriculture and industrial chemicals and organic wastes. Such contaminants in high concentrations create a hostile environment that drives away fish, prevents shellfish from reproducing, or undermines the food chain' (ibid, p.24).

4.2.2.6. Other habitats

In addition to mangroves, there are inter tidal areas of the coast which include salt marshes and open tide flats. Salt marshes are reported to serve many of the same ecological purposes as mangrove forests. They assimilate nutrients and convert them into plant tissues which is broken into fine particles and swept into the coastal waters. In addition, the marsh provides a special habitat for many valuable species. Large tracts of tide flat (mud flats, sand flats, etc.) are found in estuaries and lagoons. Such flats are important in processing nutrients for the ecosystem and providing feeding areas for fish at high tide or birds at low tide. Mud flats are often important energy storage elements of the estuarine lagoon ecosystem. The mudflats serve to catch the departing nutrients and hold them until the returning tide can sweep them back into the wetlands. In many estuaries and lagoons, tide flats also produce a high yield of shellfish.

Kelp beds are reported in certain areas of the coast at higher latitudes. It often grows in thick stands, creating a submerged forest that provides an important multiple species habitat from surface to bottom for sea otters and many other valuable species. These kelp stands are vulnerable to over-harvesting, species imbalance and pollution.

4.2.3. Ecological issues of the coast

Cicin-Sain and Knecht observe that 'coastal and ocean development activities (building of structure, mining, dredging, etc.) can significantly affect the ecology of the coastal zone and the functioning of coastal and ocean processes and resources. For example, development activities in beach and dune areas can change patterns of sediment transport or alter inshore current systems, and diking for agriculture can affect the functioning of wetlands through reduced freshwater inflows and through changes in water circulation. Similarly, industrial developments in the coastal zone can decrease the productivity of wetlands by introducing pollutants, including heavy metals, and by changing water circulation and temperature patterns. Marine aquacultural activities in tropical areas often involve removal of mangrove forests to create aquacultural ponds, interfering significantly with the many functions mangrove systems perform, such as serving as buffers for coastal storms and nursery habitats for juvenile fishes. Activities such as port development and the dredging that inevitably accompanies it can significantly degrade coral-reefs through the build up of sediment. Activities farther inland such as logging, agricultural practices (e.g., burning of cane sugar), and animal husbandry practices (e.g., pollution of streams by animal waste), represent important sources of damage to estuarine and ocean areas through increased flow of sediment, pesticide, and other pollutants into riverine and estuarine systems' (Cicin-Sain and Knecht, 1998, p.19).

The damage to the coastal ecosystem and the natural resources base are attributed to three inter-related failures; market failure, policy or intervention failure and information failure (FAO, 1998, p.10).

Some of the notable ecological issues of the coast identified by Clark are (1) non-sustainable development, (2) pollution, (3) threats to biological diversity, and (4) adverse natural processes.

4.2.3.1. Non-sustainable development

The exploitation of coastal resources have reached very high levels with consequence such as biological and economic stress, loss of development opportunities, conflict, and reduced seafood security. Basic resources such as fuel, water and fertile land are in short supply and fish stocks are already heavily exploited in most parts of the coasts. Natural resource depletion, in all sectors of development, is aggravated by users concerned with short-term profits and by the absence of defined user rights. Clark observes that 'the coastal sea and transitional areas are a 'commons'. Theoretically owned by all the people the coastal commons is held in trust by the government and its uses decided by the government. Tenure systems are particularly inadequate in the aquatic coastal area and will require strong efforts to establish them explicitly or revive them formally' (Clark, 1992, p. 26).

It is now well recognised that pursuing development on a sustainable basis is an absolute necessity to sustain progress in health, food security, housing, energy and other critical areas. This, however, requires maximum efficiency in the use of natural resources and in the application of capital inputs and know-how. Such development needs 'the management and conservation of the natural resource base and the orientation of the technological and institutional change in such a manner as to ensure the attainment and continued satisfaction of human need for present and future generations. Such sutainable development in agriculture, forestry and fisheries sectors conserve land, water, plant and animal genetic resource, is environmentally non-degrading, technically appropriate, economically viable and socially acceptable' (FAO, 1998, p. 235).

4.2.3.2. Pollution

Pollution is one of the most serious indirect impacts of coastal developments. Polluted water discharges are often the most common source of adverse effects on coastal and marine ecosystems. Some of the more common sources of pollution and their impacts as discussed by Clark are given below. (1) Domestic sewage, which may result in eutrophication by overloading the marine environment with nutrients and which introduce pathogens and toxic matter, (2) Agricultural wastes (e.g., manure, fertilizers, pesticides) which contribute nutrients in the form of fertilizers as well as toxic compounds, which penetrate into the remote areas of the ecosystem, (3) Industrial wastes, which contain a variety of toxic substances including heavy metals (lead, mercury, cadmium, etc.), radioactive elements, acids and innumerable other toxic industrial chemicals and (4) Oil spills, which are becoming increasingly more common as sea traffic increases and facilities are built and the dependence on fossil fuel grows.

Some of the typical coastal water pollutants and their effects are given in table 4.6.

4.2.3.3. Threats to biological diversity

The global threat to biodiversity emanates from landuse changes, over-exploitation of resources, conversion of natural areas, pollution and effects of climate change. A large proportion of world population growth has taken place in coastal zones of developing countries which is accompanied by rapid urban development and changes in land and resource use. Increasing urbanisation, industrial development, agricultural intensification and expansion of tourism are all having profound effects on natural habitats and species.

Clark observes that 'urban sprawl has already proven to adversely affect biodiversity. Currently, about 50 per cent of the world's urban waste-water is directly discharged into or other water bodies close to the sea without any kind of treatment contributing to aquatic eutrophication and disruption of ecosystems. With intensifying demographic pressures, the sheer volume of waste products is likely to increase. Gaseous and liquid industrial emissions and solid wastes also threaten to have an increasing impact on the environment. Expanded road networks, new dams, industrial complexes and enhanced infrastructure are likely to further stress ecosystem and reduce species diversity' (Clark, 1992, p. 29).

Further increases in cultivated areas are expected to have significant impact on natural areas. This will increase the demand for water for irrigation which will change the pattern of waterflow, further altering ecosystems. Irrigation management will be vital to ensure adequate water supplies, reduce pollution from Agricultural inputs and control soil salinization. As noted by Clark, 'intensification of agriculture implies increased use of chemical inputs, which, without careful control, affect water quality, contribute towards the eutrophication of river and coastal marine areas, enter into food chains, and debilitate ecosystem' (ibid, p. 29).

Mismanagement and over use of mangrove forests are also issues of global concern. Clark pinpoints that 'over-exploitation of forests for lumber, grazing and fuelwood needs is a common practice. Deforestation not only leads to the loss of a valuable resource, but also reduces watershed protection, increases surface water run off, increases soil erosion and desertification, contributes to the siltation of dams, and results in the further loss of an already decimated habitat. The degradation of both terrestrial and marine ecosystems through over-exploitation and misuse of resources by mankind could

Table 4.6

Typical coastal water pollutants and their effects

Pollutants	*Source*	*Effects on coastal waters*
Petroleum hydrocarbons	Fuel exhausts, motor oil and grease, power plant emissions, industrial discharges, spills and dumping, leaking underground storage containers, urban runoff	Spills can kill aquatic life, damage beaches, and permanently destroy wetlandsf runoff can be toxic to marine organisms, causing death, disease and reproductive problems
Chlorine	Water treatment plants, swimming pool backwash	Kills aquatic life
Nutrients	Aquatic, forestry, and urban runofff, industrial and boat discharges, sweage treatment and package plants, septic tank, animal feed lots.	Enrichment of rivers and ponds (eutrophication) resulting in algae blooms. Blooms can alter the food chain, then decay, depleting oxygen and causing fish kills. Eutrophication is also suspected of causing some fish disease problems
Freshwater	Water running off impervious surfaces, land clearing, draining wetlands, channelisation of streams	Changes salinity patterns in estuarine habitats, causing slowed growth or death of juvenile organisms, or poor reproduction
Bacteria and viruses	Septic tanks that are special, too densely placed on porous soils, located in high water tables or that leak; sewage treatment .or package plants boat discharges,- animal feed lots, urban runoff	Contaminates shellfish waters; consumption of shellfish may cause disease. Contaminate groundwater; using for drinking or bathing may cause disease. Contaminates surface waters: swimming may cause disease or wound infections
Sediment	Land clearing, dredging erosion	Clogs marine water. Covers marine habitats, smothering some organisms. Causes turbidity in water, shading out producer organisms and altering the food chain
Temperature	Factories, electric generating plants, urban runoff	Alters reproduction of fish. Reduces dissolved oxygen which may then cause fish kills. Contaminates freshwater supplies used for drinking, irrigation and the like
Heavy metals	Fuel and exhaust of motor boats and automobiles, industrial emission and effluent sewage treatment plant, effluent landfill wastes/urban runoff, naturally in soil, hazardous waste spills and disposal	Accumulate in fish tissues and are passed onto humans, contaminate drinking water, causing brain damage, birth defects, miscarriage, and infant deaths
Synthetic organic chemicals	Forestry, urban, and agricultural runoff, industrial and municipal effluent spills or dumping	Cause cancer, birth defects, and chronic illness when consumed in contaminated water supplies or seafood

Source: NCDNR, (1986), as quoted by Clark, 1992, p. 28).

lead to further reduction in crucial global ecosystems. Amongst the measures that could contribute to the protection of these ecosystems against these impacts are various types of marine and coastal parks and reserves, managed according to carrying capacity principles' (ibid, pp.29-30).

A major global problem associated with biodiversity loss is the widespread depletion of seafood resources, caused by coastal pollution and critical habitat destruction alongwith over fishing. Clark reminds us that 'in a time of rapid increase in the global need for protein, it is necessary to conserve the productivity of coastal habitats for fisheries production (the supply), as range lands are protected for livestock, farmlands for crops, and forest lands for wood. This can be effectively managed through an ICZM programme which can help prevent pollution, regulate harmful development, and create protected areas. They should be coupled with control of destructive fishing methods' (ibid, p. 30).

4.2.3.4. Adverse natural processes

Coastal zone management issues are often complicated by natural disasters or other naturally occurring phenomena that impact environmentally sensitive areas. Clark remarks that 'tragedy is often brought by natural outbreaks of disease, like the one which caused massive die-off of the long-spined sea urchin throughout the Caribbean in the early 1980s. Other outbreaks such as black band disease, coral bleaching, etc. are also causes for increased concern' (ibid, p. 30).

The coastlines of many countries face the serious damage from certain types of natural disasters. The leading concern is loss of life and property caused by flood and hurricanes. In the many densely populated coasts, the risks of natural disasters are being increased by population growth and unmanaged development projects. Coastal people become more susceptible to natural hazards such as floods, typhoons, or sunamis when projects encourage settlement in dangerously low-lying areas or when land clearing and construction removes protective vegetation, reefs, or sand dunes.

Along with these there are also fears of global temperature rise which could be altering balances in system which may not recover from such stress and which is probably the result of a mix of natural and human causes. As noted by Clark, 'global climate change (whether natural or human induced) will affect coastal zones. They will be impacted by sea-level rise (green-house effect), changes in ocean coastal processes, modifications of river-run off patterns and sedimentation and from the expected increase in floods, storms and hurricanes. Consequences for coastal settlements are still difficult to forecast with any accuracy but could be significant' (ibid, p.30).

4.3. Economic arguments

The economic argument for coastal zone management is based on the principles of economy and efficiency. The principles of economy demands that coastal resources are used in such a way as to produce maximum economic value to the community. The efficiency principle (criterion) requires that coastal resources are exploited in such scales that they produce maximum net benefits to the society. The two principles put together aim at maximising (optimising) the value of the coastal product. It, however, needs that the value of the coastal product is to be sustained at high levels in the future as well and this calls for coastal zone management. In this regard, it encompasses the principles of sustainable development. The focus in this section is to highlight the multiple uses of the coast and its resources, which help in maximising the value (which is frequently emphasised in the literature on coastal zone management) and to present the economic argument for integration in management or the ICM approach. As a starting point, this section highlights the multiple uses of the coast and their interactions which call for ICM efforts.

4.3.1. Multiple uses of the coastal zone

As noted by Cicin-Sain and Knecht 'several efforts have been made to develop a typology of ocean and coastal uses and their interactions' (Cicin-Sain and Knecht, 1998, p. 20). A summary of these efforts was reported by Vallega as presented in table 4.7.

Commenting on this table, Cicin-Sain and Knecht noted that authors like Couper (1983) and Vallega (1992) emphasised the 'waterside' of the coastal and ocean uses while Sorensen and McCreary (1990) and Pido and Chua (1992) emphasised the 'landside' of the coastal zone. These authors also recognise that none of the typologies presented in table 4.7 includes 'non-consumptive' uses of the marine environment and its resources. The non-consumptive values not considered are the protection and promotion of the non-utilitarian values of the ocean, i.e., the value of its mere existence, its value for future generations and aesthetic uses or the human enjoyment and spiritual renewal that proximity to the ocean can provide (Cicin-Sain and Knecht, 1998, p. 21). The critical value of the oceans from the point of view of regulating the global climate is also not considered in the typology listed.

Table 4.7

Examples of ocean and coastal use in models

Couper's Global Marine Interaction Model (Couper 1983)	*Sorensen and McCreary (1990)*	*Pido and Chua (1992)*	*Vallega's Coastal Use Framework (Vallega, 1992)*	*Hawaii Ocean Resources Management (Example of CZM Approach) (1991)*
Navigation and Communication	Fisheries	Agriculture	Sea ports	Research
Mineral and energy resources	Natural area and protection systems	Fisheries and aquaculture	Shipping	Recreation
Biological resources	Water supply	Infrastructure	Sea pipelines	Harbours
Waste disposal and pollution	Recreation development	Mining	Cables	Fisheries
Strategy and defense	Tourism	Ports and harbours	Air transportation	Marine ecosystem protection
Recreation	Port development	Industry	Biological resources	Beaches and coastal erosion
Research	Energy development	Tourism	Hydrocarbons	Waste Management
Marine environmental quality	Oil and toxic spill, contingency planning	Urban development	Metalliferous renewable resources	Agriculture
	Industrial siting	Forestry	Renewable energy resources	Energy
	Agriculture	Shipping	Defence	Marine mammals
	Mariculture	Recreation	Water front structural development	
			Waste disposal	
			Research	
			Archaeology	
			Environmental protection and preservation	

Source: Vallega, 1996, as quoted in Cicin-Sain and Knecht, 1998, p. 20.

A revised list of major uses and activities of the coastal zone and ocean is given by Cicin-Sain and Knecht. Table 4.8 presents the details as given by these authors.

Table 4.8.

Details of principal coastal and ocean activities

Navigation and communications	**Coastal infrastructure development**
Shipping	Roads, bridges, other transportation infrastructure, water supply and treatment.
Port and harbour development	Reclamation or alteration of coastal waters (e.g., for building of human settlement, impoundment for aquaculture ponds, diking for recreational facilities).
Navigation aids	
Communication cables	Desalination facilities.
Living marine resources	**Waste disposal and pollution prevention**
Fishing (traditional, artisanal, industrial)	Siting of industrial facillities
Aquaculture	Sewage disposal
Gathering Seaweed	Dumping of dredged materials, disposal of other wastes.
Gathering of other marine creatures (e.g., sea cucumbers, snails, shells, corals, pearls)	Non-point sources of marine pollution (agriculture runoff, river sedimentation)
Tropical fish collection	Oil and toxic spill contingency planning.
Collection of marine mammals for consumption, display or research	**Ocean and Coastal environmental quality protection.**
Watching marine mammals (e.g., whale watching)	Protection of the ocean's global role in regulating climate
Marine biotechnology application: use of marine organisms or processes for product development	Protection of the ocean from pollution.
Mineral and energy resources	
Hydrocarbon (oil and gas) exploration and production	Protection of the oceans from transport and disposal of hazardous materials (radio active chemicals, etc.)
Offshore drilling, pipeline laying, platforms, installations	Establishment of marine and coastal protected areas, parks to protect special areas or features (e.g., coral reefs, wildlife sanctuaries)
Exploitations of sand and gravel aggregates	Marine mammal protection
Exploitation of other minerals (gold, placer deposits, polymetalic sulfides, manganese nodules)	Protection of cultural resources (e.g., religious sites, archeological sites, ship wrecks)
Other forms of ocean energy (e.g., wave energy, tidal power, ocean thermal energy.	Protection of the ocean from transfer of alien species (e.g., through ballast waters)

(Contd. Table 4.8)

(Table 4.8 Contd.)

Tourism and recreation Hotel, vacation homes, tourism infrastructure (transportation services) Swiming and diving, underwater parks, Recreational fishing, boating Non-consumptive aesthetic uses **Beach and shoreline management** Erosion control programmes Protection structures (against storms, waves) Replenishment of beaches Prevention and mitigation of coastal hazards (storms, inundation, sea-level rise). **Military activities** Transit and maneuvers by navies Military special areas (test ranges, exercise areas) Enforcement of national ocean zones.	Prevention and mitigation of harmful algal bloom phenomena **Research** Oceanography Marine geology and coastal processes Fisheries and marine mammal research. Marine biology, biodiversity, biotechnology Archaeology Studies of human uses of the ocean.

Source: Cicin-Sain and Knecht, 1998, pp.21-22

Typical economic sectors of coastal countries that have direct impacts on the coast as noted by Sorensen and McCreary are given in table 4.9.

Table 4.9

Typical economic sectors of coastal countries that impact on coasts

Sectors that are often coastal zone or ocean specific	*Sectors that are rarely coastal zone specific but have direct impacts*
Navy and other national defence operations (e.g., testing, coastguard, customs) Port and harbour development (including shipping channels) Shipping and navigation Recreational boating and harbour Commercial and recreational fishing Mariculture Tourism Marine and coastal research Shoreline erosion control	Agriculture Mariculture Forestry Fish and wildlife management Parks and recreation Education Public health- mosquito control and food Housing, Water pollution control Water supply Transportation Flood control Mining, Industrial development, Energy generation

Source: Sorensen and McCreary, 1990, as quoted by Clark, 1992, p.77.

It may be noted that many of these activities are not coastal, but will have substantial impact on the coast. The major upland activities affecting coastal and ocean activities as noted by Cicin-Sain and Knecht are given in table 4.10.

Table 4.10

Major upland activities affecting coastal and ocean activities

Agriculture
Forestry
River diversions, damming, other alterations
Industrial (point source) waste
Non-point sources of pollution
Construction of human settlement and roads
Mining

Source: Cicin-Sain and Knecht, 1998, p. 22.

It is significant to note here that the activities noted in table 4.10 are only indicative of the upland activities and almost every one of the upland or upstream activities will have its impact on the coastal zone through the geo-physical processes.

As is evident from the above tables, the typology of activities of the 'dry' side and 'wet' side of the coast noted therein do not give any indication of their impact on the coastal zone and the need for coastal zone management. The rationale for coastal zone management has to be understood from the impacts they produce in the coast and the need to maintain, mitigate or control them. This, however, necessitates a closer examination of the dominant coastal activities and their interaction within the coastal system.

As noted by Clark, 'the coastal zone is used extensively and increasingly for a large number of activities. These multiple uses are not always compatible and may result in a wide array of problems for resource users and decision-makers. Coastal land is used for human settlement, agriculture, trade, industry and amenity. The coastal area presents problems related to transport, fishing, dumping, mining, etc. stemming from an intensification and diversification of ocean uses. There is over-exploitation of fishery resources, pollution by dumping and an array of conflicts due to the interaction among user groups in congested marine areas. Coastal zones are the 'sink' for the continents; they receive and concentrate pollutants and other negative consequences of development activities taking place in the hinterlands. In particular, the flow of rivers has often been severely modified for irrigation purposes, and they carry to the coastal areas the pollutants coming from inland agricultural and industrial activities.

Because general development may result in over exploitation, pollution or alteration of natural systems, as well as conflicts between the users for limited, but highly priced coastal and shoreline space, its impacts must be understood and countered' (Clark, 1992, p. 32). The attempt in the remaining part of this section (sub-sections) is to highlight the multiple uses of the coast, their interactions and the need for ICM.

4.3.1.1. Human settlements

The coasts are considered 'home' to more than half of world's population. Two-thirds of the world's largest cities are located on coasts and populations of coastal areas are growing faster than inland populations. A World Bank estimate in 1994 showed that two-thirds of the population of developing countries would be living along coasts by the end of the last century (Cicin-Sain and Knecht, 1998, p.16).

Clark reports that 'the shoreline is in increasingly strong demand for human settlements, agriculture, trade, industry, and marine transport activities such as shipping, fishing boats and recreational marinas. This demand, which responds to essential needs for economic growth, leads to a linear approach to coastal development focusing on the exact shoreline ... with access to recreational beaches or outstanding views of the sea. Human settlements may crowd the seas with boats, over exploit resources, generate polluting industries, produce heaps of garbage, and create large amounts of chemical waste. Waterfront expansion may be necessary for coastal cities, it can be threatening to coastal resources if development interests do not respect conservation principles' (Clark, 1992, p.32)

It is further noted that 'the shoreline is an essential natural habitat (mangrove wetlands, tide flats, and seagrass beds) easily obliterated as settlements pre-empt the shallow seas by filling for real estate. Sewage treatment, water supply, electric power production and other utilities and services add strain on available resources and on natural systems' (ibid, p.32).

It must also be noted that the ocean beach front is a most hazarduous place for buildings. The berm/foredune/backdune system (where they exist) are considered high risk locations for buildings and keeping development far enough inland to avoid the high risk zone is important in natural hazard prevention efforts. Establishing a setback line at a safe distance inland and prohibiting all constructions on the water side are considered prudent here. The growth in coastal population and human settlement cause further damage to the coastal zone. As noted by Clark, 'the density of urban population creates demand for factories, power plants, warehouses, homes, docks, streets, automobiles, water supplies, resource depletion and waste disposal. It results in competition with the needs of nature, threatens the system's integrity and impinges on the sensibilities of mankind by reducing natural diversity and creating ugliness. Although impacts are an unavoidable consequence of human survival, they often can be greatly reduced by appropriate planning and management' (ibid, p. 34).

The environmental impacts of population growth on the coast have been well documented. In 1990, the Joint Group of Experts on the Marine Environment in its report on 'the State of the Marine Environment' noted that the coastal strip, encompassing the shallow-water and intertidal areas along with the immediately adjacent land, is clearly the most vulnerable as well as the most abused marine zone. Its sensitivity is directly tied to the diversity and intensity of activities which take place there, and the threat to its future is related to the increasing concentration of the world population in this area. The consequences of coastal development are thus of the highest concern' (Ehler, 1995, p.177). The need for coastal zone management is obvious.

4.3.1.2. Agriculture

The development of intensive agriculture with increased use of chemical inputs poses a serious threat to coastal environments. Excessive amount of chemical runoff the land into coastal water bodies contributing to eutrophication and toxification of rivers of coastal marine areas. Unlimited use of pesticides, herbicides and fertilizers in agriculture impacts on coastal living organisms, affecting their bio-diversity and sustainability. Conversion of coastal wetlands and low lands to rice farming and other agricultural land has potentially harmful effects on coastal environment and natural resources. The potential productivity of reclaimed wetland soils is supposed to be low because of acid-sulphate soil and waterlogging.

Moreover, the frequent flooding of coastal lowlands from rain storms and cyclonic sea storms are also likely to be exacertbated by the clearing and draining of coastal areas and uplands. Such floods also destroy property, risk lives, drown crops, and carry huge amounts of sediment silt, fertilizing substances and organic and chemical pollutants into coastal waters.

The damage that (coastal) agriculture can cause to the coastal zone is summarised by Clark. Clark observes that 'because these impacts can originate in farmlands, a long distance from the coasts, they may be difficult to identify and control for the benefit of coastal environmental resources. Yet they must be addressed, or lagoons, coral reefs, shellfish and seagrass beds, tourism, and sea fisheries may suffer', (Clark, 1996, p. 9).

4.3.1.3. Coastal aquaculture

Aquaculture is one of the fastest growing sectors of the coastal zone economy. Socially, its product is seen as a supplement to local diets and as a valuable means of earning foreign exchange through export. Financially, it is seen as a fast profit earner.

Coastal aquaculture projects are usually built near the shoreline to gain access to saltwater supplies and seed stock. They often run into direct confrontation with environmental conservation objectives requiring government intervention to balance the benefits of aquaculture development against the losses to the environment and to other economic sectors dependent on the resources of the coastal zone. As Clark observes, 'many of the environmental implications are well known: preemption of critical fishery habitat (e.g., mangrove); pollution of lagoon waters; excessive exploitation of natural stocks of larvae and juveniles ..., importation of inferior, sick or non-compatible seed stock; and geopardy from the introduction of exotic species. Also conflict over space and water supplies can be expected with coastal rice culture, nature reserves (mangrove forests), solar salt production activities, and many other enterprises ... From a worldwide viewpoint, the major coastal environmental impact of aquaculture seems to be from expansion of shrimp farms in the tropics. Shrimp culture projects often involve the conversion of massive amounts of mangrove forests to shrimp 'grow out' ponds, with all the biodiversity and ecological implications that loss of such wetland implies' (ibid, p.63).

It is further noted that 'if aquaculture expansion is not controlled, the long-term consequences may be to reduce resource values and to pollute shallow coastal waters. Aquaculture may be either a polluter or a petitioner for a clean environment. On the other hand, success in aquaculture requires a clean water supply from the environment and, on the other hand, intensive aquaculture practices themselves may pollute coastal waters and reduce biodiversity' (ibid, p.10).

In view of all these, it is suggested that an over all (ICM) plan for each coastal area is needed to meet broad regional and national needs in the various sectors such as aquaculture, agriculture, forestry, fishery, tourism and others.

4.3.1.4. Fisheries

Fisheries play a key role in the economies of many countries. With close to 100 million tons of fish production per year, the sea provides more protein worldwide than other animal meat. Fisheries also provide livelihood for fishermen and their families and for others in the fishing industry, including boat builders, trap and net makers, packers, distributors and retailers, all of which enhances social, cultural, economic, and political stability in the coastal areas. A strong domestic fishery promotes self-sufficiency and reduces the outflow of foreign exchange. Also profitable coastal fisheries reduce rural population migrations to already overcrowded cities.

Unfortunately, however, fisheries' contribution to national diets and income is diminishing partly because fisheries are not usually managed properly for sustainability. This is evident from the following observation by Clark. Clark points out that 'past and present over-fishing has led more than 25 of the world's most valuable fisheries into serious depletion ... In addition to depleting fish, crustacean, and molluscs stocks, over-fishing has greatly depleted some species of whales, sea cows, and sea turtles. Many species are under pressure because of incidental exploitation, that is, they are captured alongwith 'target' species, killed and discarded ... As the commercially valuable fisheries for fish, crustaceans and molluscs become more fully exploited, the effects of habitat destruction and pollution will become more evident particularly on those species depending on coastal wetlands and shallows or on inland wetlands and flood plains for nutrients or for spawning grounds nurturing areas' (ibid, pp.309-310).

The industry is further threatened by coastal developments. As coastal populations swell and as aspirations for economic growth remain strong, pressures to over exploit coastal resources intensify. Too many people are placing unrealistic demands on these resources, and the results are deteriorating water quality, coastal erosion, loss of mangroves, decreasing biological diversity, destruction of coral reefs, water polluted by untreated sewage and, occasionally, disastrous oilspills. And all these cause a decline in the productivity of coastal resources.

Now, it is essential that water quality and critical habitat are protected and convenient boat landing and fish processing facilities are maintained in the coasts. One of the objectives of coastal zone management is to maintain these conditions.

4.3.1.5. Coastal forests

Coastal forests are important economically as well as ecologically, as they serve as water catchment areas, providing freshwater supply and flood control.

These forests help to moderate storm flows by reducing runoff and increasing infiltration to underground aquifers. As a result erosion and sedimentation in coastal waters are also reduced.

The Malaysian Coastal Resources Study Team observe that 'coastal forests are also a potential resource for nature tourism, which includes activities such as boat tours and wild life watching. These are also valuable as scientific research and cultural sites' (The Malaysian Coastal Resources Study Team, 1992, p.44). It also noted that 'destruction of coastal woodlands could result in reduced freshwater supplies, degraded water quality, and increased sedimentation and vulnerability of neighbouring areas to floods. These could have adverse impacts on economic activities such as agriculture, aquaculture and tourism along the coastal and offshore island areas as well as on coral reefs and fisheries' (ibid, p.44).

The damage that destruction of forests cause to the coastal zone has been explicitly pointed out by Clark. Clark notes that 'the removal of forest cover in water sheds increases sediment loadings of rivers ... water quality is reduced and siltation increased ... The enhanced runoff may bring chemical pollutants of any types to the coast. A most serious effect is 'smothering' of coral reefs and submerged vegetation (seagrass and seaweed beds) of key importance as fish habitat. Sediment runoff also leads to smothering of shellfish such as oysters and clams and reduces the vigour of life in coastal systems ... Maritime forests ... coastal mangrove forests are a major ecological resource. They nurture an abundance of plants and animals (e.g., crustaceans, molluscs, fishes and birds), which form a significant part of the mangrove resource, indicating their important contribution to marine biodiversity ... Mangrove ecosystem deterioration caused by intensive human activities aimed at maximising short-term gains, and the negative economic consequences on the coastal communities, in both the short and long term, are causing increased concern in many countries and international agencies, resulting in urgent calls for conservation. The other lowland wetland forest types, such as nypa palm, hardwood hammocks, and freshwater tidal swamps, also need management attention' (Clark, 1996, pp.10-11).

4.3.1.6. Coastal/offshore sand mining

Coastal sand mining is considered as a lucrative venture in many coastal nations. With projected economic growth and the attendant buoyant local construction sector, the demand for sand aggregates is certain to increase. There is also the prospect of a growing export market for sand.

Sand mining operations, however, often cause adverse impacts on the coast, such as shoreline change as a result of altered sediment transport, lower productivity, direct loss of living aquatic resources and other problems.

The impacts of sand mining in the coast are considered to be of three types; ecological, physical and socio-economic. The ecological effects of sand mining has been summarised by the Malaysian Coastal Resources Study Team. It noted that 'offshore dredging often causes the suspension of sediments and the release of absorbed pollutants from the disturbed sediments. Dredging induced suspensions have the potential to change water quality and affect local biota. Thus, the impacts of dredging on the biological environment are determined by the operational design, scale and duration of the mining activity. While the direct environmental effects of offshore dredging are attributed to the massive displacement of the substrata and the subsequent destruction of non-motile benthic communities, its more subtle impacts may escape recognition and detection' (Malaysian Coastal Resources Study Team, 1992, pp.98-99).

The concentration of resuspended sediments and their subsequent distribution and deposition are the primary causative agents of the biological stresses. Survival under these conditions is said to depend largely on the specific living requirements of the marine communities affected and a host of extraneous factors such as depth of sediment, length of time under burial, time of year, and sediment grain size and quality.

Another cause for concern is the resulting physical reduction in habitat area, which affects the rate of repopulation in the dredged area. Sea bottom burrow pits remain intact for long periods unless back filling occurs from current-induced sediment movement. If the sediments are organic-laden, the subsequent deposition may lead to anearobic conditions and deteriorating quality of the water. Hence, the reestablishment of marine habitats at dredged areas is, again, dependent on the magnitude of the dredging operation, new sediment interface and water quality.

The Malaysian Study Team also noted the physical impacts thus: offshore mining activity normally incurs the risk of altering beach dynamics, waves and swell patterns, as well as coastal current circulation, which may lead to erosion or sedimentation. Dredging can influence the coastal physical processes through (a) erosion of beaches from drawdown due to the backfilling of the dredged pit during calm periods, (b) interception of sediment by the dredged pit, which result in sand depletion onshore or down drift, (c) removal of protection afforded fry offshore banks, which leads to bigger waves impinging on the coast, and (d) changes in the wave refraction pattern, which concentrates wave energy at a particular place.

The socio-economic impacts are felt by the fishermen whose earnings are reduced by the fall in fish catches caused by the environmental stress.

The impacts of land-based and riverine sand mining is also not positive. River dredging, which is usually conducted at the lower reaches, has the greatest potential of inducing changes in river and coastal morphology, and affecting such activities as capture fisheries and agriculture due to the resulting turbidity.

The importance of regulating coastal mining in coastal zone management is highlighted by Clark. Clark notes that 'mining for beach sand has been an important industry in many countries. Sand for construction is a valuable commodity, but it must be remembered that the key to the natural protection provided to water front properties by the beach front is sand. Quantities of sand are held in storage by the beach and then temporarily sacrificed to storm waves, thereby dissipating the force of their attack. Thus sand is later restored to the beach by waves, current, and wind. Consequently, taking sand from any part of the beach or the nearshore submerged zone can lead to erosion and recession of the beach front. Therefore, beach conservation should start with the presumption that any removal of sand is adverse and should be prohibited, unless it can be shown to be naturally replaceable ...

Coral mining also require, firm controls. It is extensively undertaken in some island countries in the Indian Ocean and Southeast Asia and leaves the shoreline exposed to erosion and storm surges, causing serious loss of beach and shoreland and damage to coastal human and marine resources habitats. In addition, loss of coral reef habitats reduces bio-diversity, depletes fisheries, and discourages tourism. 'Dryside' quarrying for rock or mining for other construction materials for coastal projects may have 'secondary impacts', including loss of environmental quality (aesthetic), reduction in downstream freshwater fisheries production, endangerment of protected species, or loss of other wildlife-related values. The stone and aggregate quarry sites that are in stream beds often flow through valleys that are quite scenic or are important to wild life. Coastal projects can reduce both species and habitats at quarry sites; therefore, when a quarry site is selected, it should be surveyed ecologically to ensure that important species and habitats will not be depleted' (Clark, 1996, p.13).

4.3.1.7. Petroleum industry

All phases of oil and gas production - extraction, transport and refining - can cause serious environmental impacts to coastal waters. In the past, important disturbance of coastal ecosystem has been caused by oil and gas operations in the coastal zone. It was indeed the oil slick caused by the petroleum industry at Port Valdez in Alaska in the US that ultimately led the US Government to enact the US Coastal Zone Management Act in 1972.

The major potential environmental disturbances in the extraction and processing of oil and gas are: (a) pollution by oil spills from blow outs, pipeline ruptures and transport accidents, (b) preemption or destructions of vital habitat areas (e.g., shellfish beds, wetlands) and energy flows, (c) general disruption of the coastal environment (e.g., from channel dredging) and (d) primary and secondary environmental and socio-economic impacts from a wide variety of associated offshore facilities.

Development of oil and gas resources is a complex industrial process that requires extensive advance planning and coordination of all phases from exploration to processing and shipment. Each of dozens of components linking development and production systems has the potential for adverse environmental effects on coastal water resources and it is necessary to understand these probable effects in sufficient detail so that methods can be devised to minimise environmental damage.

Protecting the coast from marine pollution is a difficult task. Clark notes that 'sea pollution does not usually come directly under ICZM but rather a national pollution control authority. However, when the expansion and infrastructure needs of shore facilities are addressed, they should be referred to the ICZM agency so that plans and designs can be modified for environmental protection, as is done for any industry. This can be difficult to accomplish because of the political power wielded by big oil enterprises' (ibid, pp.15-16).

4.3.1.8. Coastal industries

Coastal zones accommodate a large number of industries, big and small. They include food processing, sugar refining, pulp and paper, fertilizer, cement, tannery, pharmaceutical, steel and iron manufacture, electroplating and petrochemicals. These industries are attracted to the coastal zones for the following advantages. They are (a) they can benefit from access to low-cost marine and inland transportation systems, (b) they can use seawater for process or cooling purposes or for waste disposal, (c) utilize marine transportation, and (d) draw directly on the marine environment for raw material. Industries are also attracted by labour availability in coastal population centres. These industries, while contributing significantly to local, regional and national economic values also impact on the local, social, cultural and natural environment. The impacts on the natural environment are more acute and they affect the very sustainability of the coastal ecosystem.

The major threats to the coastal environment are caused by the extensive pollution these industries are creating in the coasts. The waste waters from these industries pollute the coastal eco-systems. Their impacts range from relatively minor disturbances (such as temporary, localised turbidity increase) to major disruptions (major water pollution caused by discharge of toxic chemicals). Thermal pollution, alongwith the uptake of large quantities of cooling water also cause disturbance to the local ecosystem. Both pose a major threat to free-floating planktonic forms of life, including larval and juvenile species of important fish and crustacean species.

Along with the major industries that pollute the coast there are also several 'spin-off' industries that grow and add to the coast's problems. As noted by Clark, 'spin-off' industries may often be attracted to the coastal zone by the development of large factories and may be environmentally damaging, imposing higher costs on the community for streets, police, fire protection, schools, and other essential services' (ibid, pp.11-12).

With regard to the management of coastal industrial pollution, Clark states that 'pollution control and location are the major management tools. As a rule, industry with high waste output, such as power plants with large estuarine water intake, chemical plants with irremediable toxic discharges, and oil transfer terminals, should not be located on estuarine water bodies and unless there is no practicable alternative - that is, the private and public costs of protection of ecological resources from pollution would be exorbitant ... Industrial facilities with difficult discharge problems, such as food processing, petro-chemical, wood pulp, and steel processing plants, should not be located on confined estuarine waters. Moreover, tidal streams, dead-end harbours, small lagoons, and similar small or poorly flushed water bodies should be completely avoided because of their extremely limited capacity to accept and assimilate even small amounts of contaminants' (ibid, p. 332).

4.3.1.9. Infrastructure

Coastal development involves development of infrastructure. Development infrastructure—electricity, water, gas, sewers, roads, etc.—is designed to serve multiple users and is usually planned and provided by government. What is typical of these systems is that they are linear and often complex—combining several systems such as roads, wires, pipes, etc.—to supply linear development corridors or commercial nuclii.

Development of infrastructure in the coast can have serious environmental consequences. As pointed out by Clark 'roadways, bridges, airports and other transportation infrastructure can create special problems along the coast unless properly designed ... These structures often pollute the sea, preempt critical intertidal habitats, and obstruct natural water flows. If they are carelessly planned, coastal environmental resources can be seriously jeopardised, sometimes more by the extra development they enjender than by the wires, pipes, or causeways that are installed' (ibid, p.13).

Electric power plants for example, cause major impacts to coastal waters via both intake and discharge of massive amounts of cooling water. Here fragile life forms are killed (e.g., planktonic shrimp larvae). Similarly, the hot water discharge causes thermal pollution, which can unbalance the ecosystem. The use of chemical additives (e.g., chlorine) also pollute coastal waters.

Sewage disposal is another difficult problem. Because secondary treatment does not remove all bacteria and is of very uncertain value in terms of virus removal, outfalls in bays and sounds can endanger recreational and shell fishing waters. Also these plants serve as 'sewage refineries', releasing large amount of mineral fertilizers, which may cause harmful algae blooms. In addition, the toxic substances, and nutrients released into such waterbodies may reach unacceptable concentrations and cause extensive ecological damage.

In view of all these, Clark notes that 'coastal infrastructure should therefore be controlled and construction initiatives always scrutinized via formal environmental assessment ... Planners and system designers can predict the type and extent of development engendered by road way routings and terminal locations and modify the plans to conserve key environmental resources' (ibid, p.13).

4.3.1.10. Ports and marinas

Ports and marinas contribute to the economic development of the coastal zones. Ports provide essential services to some major coastal industries or activities such as (a) offshore oil and gas development which requires general port facilities, oil storage capacities, refineries, land transport, and other infrastructure support, (b) the shipping industry, which requires channels, port facilities, shipyards, and extensive land areas for container storage, (c) fisheries development, which require breakwaters, channels, ports, processing plants, and other facilities for the fishing fleet, and (d) military operations, which require special port facilities, infrastructure and support services. Marinas cater to the needs of the recreational boating segment.

Ports and marinas also add to the coast's environmental problems. Clark observes that 'the major, threats from port development are preemption of fringing mangrove wetlands for development sites, dredging of channels with destructive disposal of dredge spoils, dredging and filling operations and obliteration of seagrass meadows, and spills and persistent pollution .. harbours and marinas built primarily for recreational use by small boats may disturb more of the coastal zone than commercial and industrial uses' (ibid, p.16). It is, however, noted that with proper planning, these consequences can be minimised. Quoting Clark, again, it is emphasised that 'proper site planning can help avoid or minimise many of the impacts that might otherwise result from marina development. Designing the marina to take maximum advantage of the natural attributes of a site can contribute significantly to reducing or eliminating potential environmental problems from marina construction. During marina operation and maintenance, implementation of an operations and maintenance plan can contribute significantly to the environmentally sound performance of the marina facility' (ibid, pp.350-351).

4.3.1.11. Coastal tourism

Coastal tourism is one of the fastest growing areas of international trade, particularly for smaller coastal countries and island countries with limited development options. Clark reports that 'in developing countries, rich in natural attractions, tourism is often the shortest route to broad economic growth and prosperity' (ibid, p. 442). Unfortunately, however, it is also an area where the conflicts are rising especially when it produces adverse environmental and social consequences.

The frequent environmental damage from tourism (resort) development noted is that it leaves shore bird habitat destroyed, mangrove wetlands filled for real estate, fisheries depleted, swimming beaches eroding away, coral reef tracts poisoned and harbours polluted. Sewage also top in the list of impacts from uncontrolled or poorly planned tourism development projects.

The social consequences reported are largely relating to the tourist-resident community conflict arising from uncontrolled expansion of tourism business impinging on the limited coastal environment. One of the most serious impacts from tourism development, world wide, is that of a decline in local water quality. Biodiversity reduction, resource depletion and human health problems are also reported from poorly executed tourism development projects. Resource plundering and environmental decay has led to such adverse commentary on the industry as 'mass tourism subverts the indigenous culture' and that 'economic benefits have been inflated'.

The world scenario of the usual social, economic and environmental crisis in the tourism sector is now generalised in what is called the self-destruct theory of tourism. Its standard version presents the following sequence of tourism development, the last stage showing its collapse.

1. A remote and exotic spot offers peaceful rest and relaxation and provides an escape for the rich, who live in isolation from the resident population.
2. Tourism promotion attracts persons of middle income who come as much for the rest and relaxation, as to imitate the rich. More and more hotel accommodation and tourist facilities are built to attract and accommodate more and more tourists. This transforms the original character of the place from an 'escape paradise' to a series of conurbations with several consequences. Some of the consequences of this development are
   (a) the local residents become tourism employees and earn more than ever before,
   (b) the rich tourists move on elsewhere,
   (c) the growth in tourist population makes interaction between tourism and resident population inevitable, leading to a variety of social consequences,
   (d) increased tourist accommodation capacity leads to excess supply over demand and a deterioration in product and price.
3. The country resorts to mass tourism attracting persons of lower standards of social behaviour and economic power. This leads to the social and environmental degradation of the tourist destination.
4. As the place sinks under the weight of social friction and solid waste, tourists exit, leaving behind derelict tourism facilities, littered beaches and country side, and a resident population that cannot return to its old way of life.

Coastal tourism is considered as 'very dependent on the continued healthy existence of natural resources such as forests, beaches, coral reefs, marine waters, islands and animal life. However, these very same resources are also being exploited and destroyed by other economic activities ... such as forestry, industry, aquaculture, housing and ironically, by tourist itself' (Malaysian Coastal Resource Study Team, 1992, p.195).

For sustaining tourism, preserving the environment is vital. As noted by Clark, 'for tourism, the environment is a significant part of the product which a country has to offer. A successful tourism strategy will, therefore, seek to maximise the profits while preserving the natural environment. When the situation deteriorates sufficiently, there is also loss of jobs, income, and hard currency earnings, factors that lead to socio-political instability. Such problems can be alleviated by appropriate planning mechanisms and development controls (Clark, 1997, pp. 444-445).

It is also now recognised that 'planning for tourism has traditionally been oriented to the needs of tourists, but future planning must alter its emphasis and take account of the welfare of the indigenous population. The development plan should seek to discover the most effective means whether institutional, regulatory, legislative or economic of integrating environmental and social policy not only with tourism but also with the policies of other economic sectors (ibid, p. 445). The need for ICM is apparent here.

4.3.1.12. Waste disposal

The safe disposal of human wastes is a world wide problem. In many countries, there are no modern sewage collection systems, even in urban areas. Sewage treatment facilities are often not properly designed, constructed, operated, or maintained, nor are they sited sufficiently far from water bodies. The result is serious contamination of drinking vater supplies and pollution of coastal waters important to tourism and fishing.

One of the major constituents of municipal sewage and many industrial wastes is decomposable organic material, which reduces dissolved oxygen in the water through its high BOD. The lower the concentration of dissolved oxygen, the lower the carrying capacity of the system. In addition to the depletion of dissolved oxygen, municipal waste discharges may introduce pathogenic organisms, settling materials, heavy metals and inorganic nutrients.

Since most coastal areas are vulnerable to sewage pollution, it is exceptionally important that coastal zone sewage is treated and properly disposed. This means that industry, commercial operators and households have to cooperate in a large scale programme to prevent solid and liquid wastes from entering into coastal zones.

4.3.1.13. Water supply projects

Water supply projects like dams, diversion canals, etc. can seriously upset or unbalance the river dependent ecosystems and reduce their productivity and species diversity by diverting water from the ecosystem or changing the beneficial hydro-period through use of store-and-release tactics created for irrigation, flood control, water supply, etc.

It is significant to note here that many fisheries (salmon, sciaenids, herrings, shrimp, oysters, etc.) are strongly dependent upon river flows that enter the sea. These rivers may transport beneficial nutrients to coastal ecosystems and sand to the beaches. They also establish beneficial brackish water conditions for mangrove forests and juvenile fish 'nurseries' in estuaries as well as for nesting of colonial water birds. Maintaining the quantity and seasonal cycles of water flowing to the sea is important because they are vital for sustaining coastal ecosystem. This is one of the tasks of ICM.

4.3.1.14. Shore protection works

Severe beach erosion is a common problem shared by many countries. Its severity is, however, aggravated when structural solutions are sought by the community. Clark points out that 'structural solutions to beach erosion and protection of shoreline property from the hazards of sea storms may be expensive and often temporary or counter productive. The groins, seawalls, breakwaters, and other popular protection structures often have complex and unanticipated secondary effects resulting in major 'downstream' erosion and quite often, total loss of beach. The natural forces working against the beach front are immense ... ' (ibid, p.18).

Apparently favouring a natural solution to beach erosion, Clark states that 'mobile and responsive, the beach will usually remain over the years, even if rising sea level or other natural factors cause erosion. It may shift with the seasons, yield sand temporarily to storm erosion, slowly recede landward with rising sea level, or accrete seaward with natural shifts in the flow of ocean currents which bring more sand. Major problems do not arise until hotels, houses, or other structures are placed on or near the beach and the engineering process of 'stabilisation of the shoreline' commences. If the natural movements of the sand are restrained with bulkheads or groins so as to fix the position of the beach, a complex chain reaction of problems may be started which can be solved only by the very expensive process of continuously transporting sand on to the beach (e.g., by pumping it from the ocean bottom). This remedy is so costly it is not available to most communities. Keeping development far enough inland to avoid the high risk zone is a better solution (e.g., by establishing construction setback lines)' (ibid, p. 18).

Coastal habitats, such as mangroves and other wetlands, coral reefs, and coastal carrier islands and lagoons are often recognised by natural hazards experts as the best defenses against sea storms and erosion, deflecting and absorbing much of the energy of sea storms. One of the objectives of ICM is to maintain these natural habitats for shore protection as well as for environmental conservation.

4.3.1.15. National security

As noted by Clark, 'extensive security interests exist in the coastal zone and coastal seas because they are at the frontier, the border zone, where invasion or other negative activities (smuggling) might occur. Naval ports and harbours, coastal airfields, and special bases of all kinds are sited in the coastal zone, usually with a high priority and intense security. However, with the correct approach, the military can be expected to cooperate in coastal zone conservation so long as it is not in conflict with national security needs. Therefore, the defense establishment should be included as a party to any ICZM programme' (Clark, 1992, P.46).

4.3.1.16. Marine excavation

Marine excavation is now a common practice undertaken for industrial or archaeological purposes.

It, however, physically disturbs or removes sea bottom life, suspends sediment in the water column, deposits it elsewhere on the bottom, reduces light penetration, increases turbidity, changes circulation, reduces dissolved oxygen, and increases nutrient levels in the water columns.

Referring to the possible impacts of marine excavation or dredging, Clark notes that'while direct elimination of benthic habitat may not be avoidable in dredging operations, damage to adjacent non-dredged areas, such as coral reefs, is avoidable. Many coastal ecosystems (eg. coral reef communities) are sensitive to both suspended and accumulating sediments and require long time periods for recolonisation. Reduction of dredging impacts has, in fact, been the focus of considerable attention from environmental and engineering interests. The most widespread and visible consequence of dredging and excavation is the generation of suspended sediments and turbidity. Dredged materials high in organics can generate biological oxygen demand (BOD) and depress oxygen levels. The magnitude of these effects varies considerably depending upon the type of dredging and excavation method in use' (Clark, 1996, p.19).

4.3.2. Multiple uses of the coast and their interactions

The coastal zones, as already noted, are used extensively and increasingly for a large number of activities. These multiple uses are not always compatible and may result in a wide array of problems for resource users and decision makers. Some of the coastal resource issues (conflicts) listed by USAID are given in table 4.11.

Table 4.11
Coastal resource issues listed by USAID

1. Loss of mangrove forests due to rate of exploitation above that which would sustain the resource
2. Coral reef destruction leading to reduced yield of fish species associated with reefs; reduced tourism attraction; and loss of rare ecosystems due to: dynamiting to harvest fish from the reef, harvesting of coral for construction material or, in the case of exotic coral species, for jewellery or souvenirs, siltation and smothering of coral from erosion associated with upstream deforestation, and death of coral from deleterious effluents associated with mining or oil spills.
3. Congestion and intensive use of coastal resources such as water, species, and fisheries, due to high population density and continuing growth, expansion of tourism industry, and growth of commercial and industrial activity.
4. Inadequate institutional structures to address coastal resource problems and to administer planning, management, regulation, and enforcement where it is needed.
5. Depletion of wildlife species such as turtles, crocodiles, deer, waterfowl and manatees.
6. Pollution of coastal waters which adversely affects fisheries yield and tourism revenues due to: industrial wastes, sewage, agricultural pesticide runoff, oil-spills, bilge discharges, and toxic contamination of fish/shell fish.
7. Beach and coastline erosion caused by removal of coastal mangrove forests; construction of coastal installations which alter current and wave action patterns; or mining of beaches for sand.
8. Swamp land filling that reduces fish spawning and 'nursery' habitat and reduces fisheries yields.
9. Upland deforestation leading to erosion and sedimentation.
10. Over-fishing leading to reduced fisheries yield and in some cases species extinction.
11. Salt water incursion leading to loss of coastal agricultural lands and potable water supplies.

Source: USAID, 1984, as quoted by Clark, 1992, p.33.

It is apparent from table 4.11 that the unplanned use of both the coastal as well as the upland resources are contributing to coastal resource use crisis. Inadequate institutional structures are only worsening the situation.

The complexity of issues created by the multiple uses of the coast has been reflected in the numerous citations of coastal concerns in the literature. table 4.12 gives a list of environmental and developmental concerns in coastal zone management.

The major coastal resource problems reported in Philippines are grouped into four categories (ibid, p.105). They correspond to:

1. **Natural resource degradation**: (a) beach erosion, (b) conversion of mangrove swamp lands into other land uses, (c) land fill or reclamation of foreshore areas, (d) dynamite fishing, (e) over-fishing, and (f) over-exploitation of mangrove forests.
2. **Pollution:** (a) industrial sources (industrial waste), (b) domestic sources (household wastes and solid wastes), (c) agricultural sources (pesticide and fertilizer runoff) and (d) other sources (dredging activities).
3. **Land fill conflicts**: (a) absence of access to foreshore lands due to human settlements, encroachments, (b) unusable beach areas due to excessive pollution, and (c) conservation and preservation of mangrove areas versus conversion of the same into fish ponds, or reclamation of the same for human settlements and commercial purposes.
4. **Destruction of life and property by natural hazards**: (a) flooding due to storms, (b) tropical cyclones, (c) earthquakes, and (d) tsunamis.

A summary of coastal zone problems identified by the CRMP in Thailand is given in table 4.13.

The main consequences of unmanaged coastal development recogised by the ASEAN/USCRMP are noted in table 4.14.

Efforts have been made in the literature to classify the relationship among ocean and coastal users. according to whether they are conflicting or mutually beneficial. Cicin-Sain and Knecht, quoting Couper, reported four categories of interactions among users. They are (I) harmful or conflicting, (2) potentially harmful, (3) mutually beneficial, and (4) harmful to one use but beneficial to another (Cicin-Sain and Knecht, 1998, p.22). A matrix of interaction of uses for the Mediterranean area was prepared by Vallega. Figure 4.1. presents the matrix of interaction of uses in the Mediterranean region.

Table 4.12

Environmental and developmental concerns in coastal zone management (number of citations out of a possible 1044)

Developmental concerns	*No. of citations*	*Environmental concerns*	*No. of citations*	*Environmental/ developmental interaction*	*No. of citations*
Recreation/tourism	140	Coastal resources	118	Erosion/ sedimentation	90
Petroleum industry	65	Wetlands	103	Environmental impact	38
Energy facility siting	65	Fish/fisheries	85	Conflicting uses	36
Facility siting	62	Public access	82	Floods/flooding	34
Ports/waterfronts	58	Critical area	48	Oil pollution/ effects	29
Energy	45	Vegetation	47	Energy impacts	21
Transportation	43	Marine biology	46	Pollution	17
Industry/ Commerce	42	Wildlife	46	Water pollution	13
Population	29	Water quality	44		
Dredging	29	Beach/dunes	36		
Marinas	28	Water resources	35		
Boating	25	Estuaries	34		
Growth	22	Aesthetics	28		
Shipping	18	Resource protection	22		
Agriculture	18	Living marine resources	21		
Water development project	14	Cultural/historical resources	12		
Navigation	14	Ground water	10		
Oil and gas	14	Barrier islands	8		
Marine mining	9	Open space	7		
Coal transportation/ storage	9	Preservation	5		
Energy transportation/ storage	9	Coral reefs	4		
Forestry/ logging	7	Air resources	3		
Water front development	7				
Aquaculture	6				
Total	**778**		**844**		**278**

Source: Healy and Zinn, 1985, quoted by Clark, 1992, p. 104.

Table 4.13
Summary of coatal zone problems in Thailand

General problem	*Specific problem*	*Cause and/or problem description*
Environmental quality	Water pollution	Untreated domestic/industrial sewage; dumping of waste petroleum product from boats; and sediment runoff from agriculture, logging, construction and tin mining.
	Solid waste pollution	Indiscriminate dumping from domestic/industrial sources and low handling capacity of water collection system
	Loss of wild life habitats	Forest destruction
	Loss of scenic value	Construction of buildings, fences and walls close to the shoreline
	Tourism-related problems	Destruction of natural assets and tourist overcrowding
Resource exploitation	Mangrove forest conversion	Conversion into shrimp ponds and agricultural uses; extractive uses of mangroves for construction and fuel
	Upland forest conversion	
	Improper agricultural practices	
	Over and destructive fishing	Too much fishing effort; use of small-meshed nets; blast-fishing; displacement of artisanal fishers; and indadequate enforcement of fisheries laws.
	Shoreline erosion	Sand/ gravel mining
	Coral reef damage	Illegal trawling, blast fishing, muro-ami and cyanide fishing; siltation; and tourist activities such as anchoring and collecting corals
	Illegal hunting	Demand of speciality restaurants for exotic meat
Institutional and organizational issues	Adoption of integrated management plan	Plan may not be used effectively because accelerated developments 'overshadow' planning
	Insufficient or overlapping regulations	Sectoral nature of laws on resources use in coastal areas which are geared towards short-term economic benefits and non-integration of development and environmental policies.
	Lack of interaction among government agencies	Lack of coordination and the need to transfer some functions, e.g., fish licenses, from the Harbour Department to the Department of Fisheries.
	Inadequate extension work; low public awareness	Few extension personnel in agriculture/ aquaculture; and inadequate public awareness programme.
	Ineffective law enforcement	Lack of enforcement due to scarce manpower, equipment and budget
	Socio-economic inequities	Outside entrepreneur favoured over local residents

Source: Chua and Scura (eds.), 1992, p. 47.

Table 4.14

Main consequences of unmanaged coastal development recognised by ASEAN/USCRMP

CAM Issue	*Effects on health*	*Effect on productivity*	*Effects on aesthetics*
Depletive/destructive resource over fishing use	Reduced nutrition of poor fishers	Loss of fisheries production	Loss of fish diversity
Over cutting of coastal forests	Reduced nutrition of traditional collectors of non-timber forest products	Loss of forestry products; loss of non marketed forest products	Loss of unique vista
Over pumping of water	Increased health risks due to water scarcity increased risk of injury from storms/ flooding	Irreversible loss of water supply; Salinization loss of physical assets due to erosion	Snsightly sink hole due to subsidence, loss of unique vista
Loss of habitats destruction of coral reefs/ seagrass beds	Reduced nutrition of poor fishers	Decline in fisheries; tourism, decline in storm surge protection	Loss of unique vista; loss of fish diversity
Conversion of mangrove areas	Reduced nutrition of traditional collectors; increased risk of injury from storms/ flooding	Decline in aquaculture fisheries; loss of forest products; decrease in storm damage protection	Loss of unique vista; loss of wild life diversity
Land reclamation/ draining of wetlands	Reduced nutrition of traditional collectors; increased risk of injury from storms/ flooding	Decline in fisheries; loss of marketed and non marketed wetland products; increased flooding damage	Loss of unique vista; loss of wildlife diversity.
Pollution/environmental degradation			
Water pollution	Contamination of seafood; water unsafe for recreation/bathing	Decline in aquaculture, fisheries, tourism	Offensive smell
Sedimentation	Contamination of seafood; water unsafe for recreation/ bathing	Decline in aquaculture, fisheries, tourism	Unsightly sink
Reduced freshwater inflows	Increased health risks from water borne diseases due to water scarcity	Decline in aquaculture, fisheries	
Solid waste desposal	Increased risk of disease transmission through various vectors	Decline in aquaculture fisheries, tourism	Offensive smell; unsightly sink

Source: Chua and Scura (eds.), 1992, p. 59.

Fig 4.1
Interaction of uses in the Mediterranean region

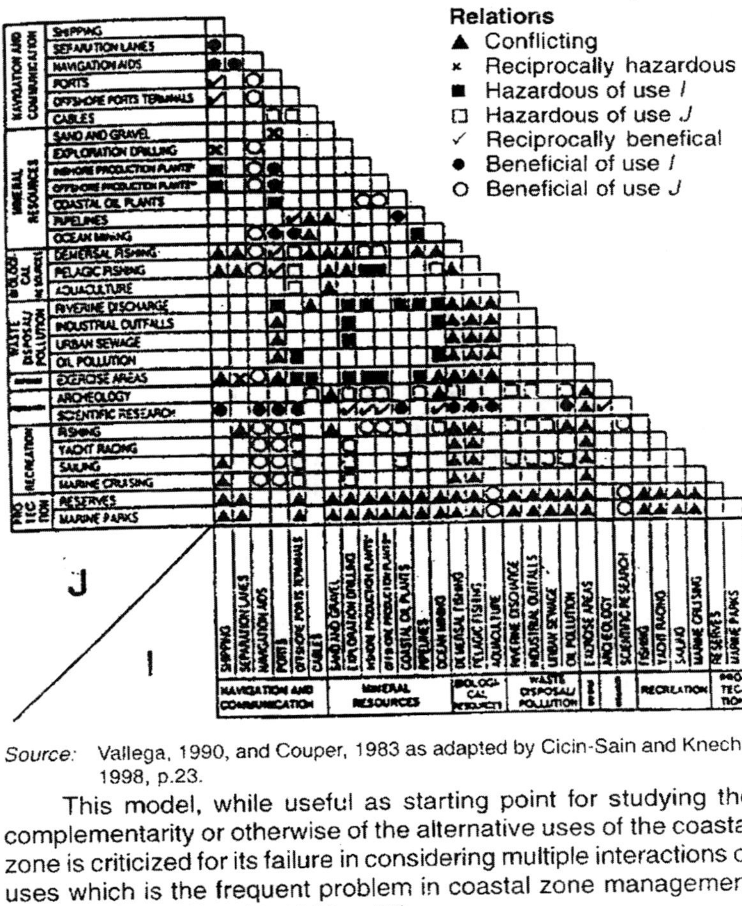

Source: Vallega, 1990, and Couper, 1983 as adapted by Cicin-Sain and Knecht, 1998, p.23.

This model, while useful as starting point for studying the complementarity or otherwise of the alternative uses of the coastal zone is criticized for its failure in considering multiple interactions of uses which is the frequent problem in coastal zone management (Cicin-Sain and Knecht, 1998, p.22).

Notwithstanding the various coastal interactions and use conflicts noted above, it is interesting to note what Cicin-Sain and Knecht (1998), Vallega (1996) and others call as 'triggers' of ICM. Cicin-Sain and Knecht observe that 'the need to establish a programme of integrated coastal management in a particular nation may arise for a number of reasons. Depletion of coastal and ocean resources (e.g., through over-fishing or exploitation of corals for building materials) typically is a powerful trigger. Another important catalyst may be an increase in pollution that endangers public health, or poses threats to water-based industries such as aquaculture, fishing, and tourism. A desire to increase the economic benefits obtained from use of the coast and ocean (as through fostering marine tourism) may also point out the need for ICM planning and management. A related catalyst may be the desire to develop uses of the coastal and marine area previously not exploited in a particular country, such as extraction of offshore oil or other minerals, marine aquaculture, or new forms of fishing for under-exploited stocks or in different areas' (Cicin-Sain and Knecht, 1998, p.41).

In their 1996 survey of ICM practices in 22 selected countries, Cicin-Sain and Knecht, had asked respondents for five reasons for initiating integrated coastal zone management in their respective countries. The reasons cited and the respondents (percentage) subscribing to these reasons are given in table 4.15.

Table 4.15

Reasons for initiating integrated coastal management in selected countries

Reasons	*Countries* All % (N = 49)	*Developed* % (N = 14)	*Middle developing* % (N = 15)	*Developing* % (N = 20)
Depletion of resources	18	0	27	25
Pollution	20	21	13	25
Ecosystem damage	18	21	13	25
Economic benefit from management	22	36	13	20
New economic opportunities on coast or in ocean	6	7	13	0
Damage from coastal hazards	10	14	7	10
Others	4	0	13	0
Uncertain	0	0	0	0

Note: Percentages do not add upto 100 per cent because reppondents were allowed to mark multiple reasons

Source: Cicin-Sain and Knecht, 1998, p.42.

Among the various reasons for initiating ICM, the majority of respondents (56 per cent) reported some kind of environmental problem, sucn as depletion of resources, pollution, or ecosystem damage. About 75 per cent of the respondents from developing countries and 53 per cent from middle developing countries designated some environaaental issue as triggering ICM. In contrast, respondents from developed countries (43 per cent) noted that some economic benefit to be the reason for initiating ICM. Cicin-Sain and Knecht considered this as 'somewhat counter intuitive', and against the prevailing assumptions that the main interest in developing nations are in seeking economic development opportunities. These authors believe that it is indicative of a 'growing realisation in developing countries, especially middle developing countries, of the environmental costs of rapid or inappropriate economic development' (ibid, p.41).

Among the catalysts noted for ICM by Cicin-Sain and Knecht in the countries studied by them, the most frequent response was 'national level government initiative' (73 per cent of all responses). Table 4.16 gives details of catalysts for initiating integrated coastal management in selected countries.

Table 4.16

Catalysts for initiating integrated coastal management in selected countries

Catalysts	*Countries*			
	All % (N = 48)	*Developed % (N = 13)*	*Middle developing % (N = 15)*	*Developing % (N = 20)*
Environmental crisis	23	8	20	35
Proposal for new coastal or marine development	42	15	67	40
National level government initiative	73	92	60	70
State or local initiative	33	23	33	40
Initiative from NGO	35	46	40	25
Initiative from international organisation	25	8	33	30
Initiative from regional entity	19	15	13	25
External funding	25	0	27	40
Earth summit prescriptions	31	23	27	40
Others	4	8	0	5
Uncertain	2	0	0	5

Note: Percentages do not add upto 100 per cent because respondents were allowed to mark multiple catalysts.

Source: Cicin-Sain and Knecht, 1998, pp.42-43.

Among the other catalysts, state or local government initiatives, external funding, Earth-Summit prescriptions, etc. were found to be noteworthy.

4.3.3. Meaning of integration in ICM

As Bower and Turner observe 'the objective of coastal zone management is to produce overtime a 'socially desirable' mix of coastal zone products and services. This mix is likely to change overtime with changing demands, changing knowledge and changing pressures. Fulfilment of this objective will require the mitigation of current market and intervention failures, continuous monitoring of performance and coastal zone conditions; and application of research findings overtime. The desired social mix can be most effectively and efficiently provided by an integrated approach to coastal zone management. The analysis required for ICM performs an overall resource management auditing role; it forces decision makers to ask relevant questions relating to coastal ecosystems and processes, coastal zone pressure trends, trade offs, environmental impacts and various aspects of response strategies, including sources of finance and human/ institutional capital resource potential. In macro-policy terms, ICM can be seen as a component of sustainable resource management within a regional/national economic development strategy' (Bower and Turner, 1998, p.45).

It is apparent that the fundamental objective of ICM is to optimise/maximise the value of the coastal product. However, when there are multiple resource uses and conflicting claims or pressures for resource allocation, there is obviously the need for harmonising the different interests and having an integrated approach to coastal zone management. As Bower and Turner put it again, 'because the resources of a coastal zone can generate a range of different products and services, not all of which are naturally compatible, conflicts are likely and trade offs are necessary. This situation is exacerbated by the variety of different stake-holders that are usually present in any given coastal zone. Moreover, the coastal zone resource base is now under severe pressure from the sheer 'scale' of the resource demands that are being generated. Parts of the coastal zone have become increasingly susceptible (more vulnerable) to stress and shock and consequent environmental economic damage by climate and other natural geophysical factors, together with population, urbanisation, waste generation and disposal pressures' (ibid, p.42).

As Clark puts it, 'a major purpose of ICZM is to coordinate the initiatives of the various coastal economic sectors towards long term optimal socio-economic outcomes, including resolution of use conflicts and beneficial trade offs. This integrated multiple-sector approach is designed to coordinate and jointly guide the activities of two or more economic sectors in planning and management ... This supports a programmatic goal to optimise resource conservation, public use and economic development ... The integrated approach to ICZM is particularly essential for effective multiple use approaches. The concept of greatest yield from the best multiple-use plan takes into view that specific resource systems are always components of a larger ecological system that contains many other resources with economic and social values ... Also taken into account is the fact that component resource systems naturally tend to be highly integrated and dependent upon one another. In summary, in no other part of the earth is integrated, multi-sectoral resource planning and management more needed than at the coast' (Clark, 1996, pp.40-41).

Cicin-Sain and Knecht point out five dimensions of integration (Cicin-Sain and Knecht, 1998, p.45). They are: (1) Intersectoral integration, which involves integration among different sectors along the coast (e.g., oil and gas development, fisheries, coastal tourism, marine mammal protection, port development) and integration between coastal and marine sectors and land based sectors that affect the coastal, and ocean environment (such as agriculture, forestry, and mining). Intersectoral integration also addresses conflicts among government agencies in different sectors. (2) Inter governmental integration or integration among different levels of government (national, provincial, local). This is needed to harmonise policies which address different public needs. (3) Spatial integration or integration between land and ocean sides of the coastal zone. This is needed for the formation of consistent goals and policies for the 'wet side' and 'dry side' of the coast. (4) International integration or integration among nations. This is essential when trans-boundary issues like pollution, conservation of migratory fish stock, passage of ships, etc. are involved. (5) Science-management integration or integration among the different disciplines important in coastal and ocean management (e.g., natural sciences, social science, engineering) and management entities (institution). This is important for proper planning, implementation and monitoring of the coastal management programme.

As Clark points out, 'integration is the sine-que non of ICZM. The ICZM strategy requires 'horizontal integration' among various economic sectors and the national agencies (including their private sector clintele). As an example, integration may be needed among fisheries, tourism, oil and gas development, and public works where these sectors are all attempting to use to coastal zone simultaneously...Almost every sector has a strong stake in the coastal area. If would be virtually impossible to allocate the coast to a single one of these economic sectors for development or even to give one of these economic sectors for development or even to give one or two sectors a priority for coastal development. In fact, it is the intense conflicts over use of the coastal area. It would be virtually impossible to allocate the coast to a single one of these economic sectors for development or even to give one or two sectors a priority for coastal development. In fact, it is the intense conflicts over use of the coast that arise among the various sectors of stake-holders that make the ICZM process so necessary...Because the ICZM process operates at the interface between land and water there is often intense conflicts between private (or quasi-private) property based operations in shore land and public (common) property-based activities in the tide lands and coastal waters. Thus, the ICZM process may have an important mediating role between conflicting wetside and dryside interests. This essential role should not be played out competitively, sector against sector. Rather, the ICZM mediating/ coordinating entity must look at all sectors with legitimate interests to find the most broadly compatible solutions. The integrated approach of ICZM is particularly essential for effective multiple use approaches' (Clark, 1996, pp.40-41).

4.3.4. Economic advantage of ICM

The benefits of ICM has been highlighted by the Coastal Zone Management sub-group of the Inter-Governmental Panel on Climate Change in 1992. It noted that 'the benefits of integrated coastal zone planning and management are generally recognised and considered desirable as a management tool to address complex coastal resource use issues' (Tol, *et al.* 1996, p.40). It is also pointed out that 'taking a pro-active approach towards coastal zone management, involving investments at an early stage, is financially advantageous in the long run' (ibid, p.40).

The theoretical argument of the economic advantage of ICM is based on the following possibilities: (1) the presence of economies of scale, and (2) the presence of external effects, either positive or negative.

Tol *et. al.* observe that 'it is commonly agreed that the integration of separate but familiar categories of economic activity may give rise to economies of scale, and hence, an overall increase in productivity. The same may hold true for the integration of sectoral CZM strategies into an integrated approach. An integrated approach on a larger scale may reduce costs, i.e., the costs of an integrated approach are lower than the cumulative costs of separate sectoral approaches. First of all, these cost reductions are due to the larger scale as such, which often makes it possible to economise on capital, labour and other inputs. An example is the tourist sector. A geographical cluster of recreational activities not only attracts more tourists per activity, but also allows for sharing of infrastructural and promotional investments, lowering the cost per unit. Another example is nature conservation. The connection of two nature reserves not only leads to a whole that is greater than the sum of its parts, but also to economising on equipment and staff. Second, a larger scale of operation often provides for the critical mass to induct technological change and learning-by-doing' (ibid, p.42).

The economic underpinning of this argument is presented in fig. 4.2.

Figure 4.2
Comparative advantage of ICM

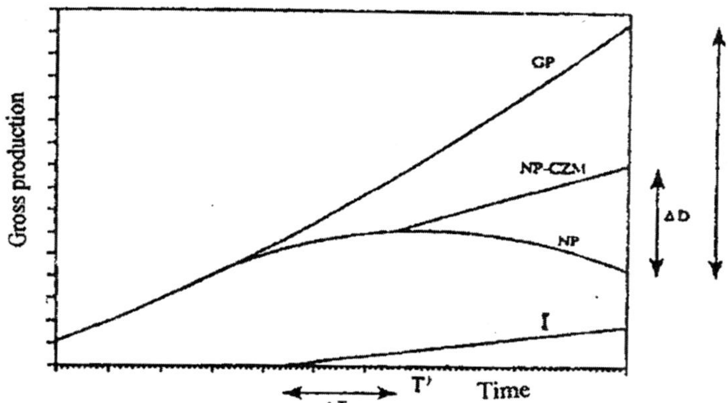

Source: Adapted from Tol. *et al.* 1996, p.41.

The upper line (GP) represents total gross production in a particular area, country or region. It increases as a result of population growth, technological progress and economic development. Damage (D), however, increases too, due to accelerated sea level rise, pollution, congestion, over exploitation of resources, etc. In case no coastal zone management measures are taken, the increase in damage will be higher than the increase in total gross production, resulting in a net production (NP) showing less and less growth, leading to a collapse. Rededuction of damage (ΔD) can be achieved by proactive investments in CZM (I). Due to the long lead times needed for the effectuation of the measures taken, it will take some time before actual reduction in damage is realised. This time lag is indicated by T.During this period there will be no benefits arising from the investments. Later, however, reduction in damage enables net production (NP - CZM) to continue to increase, which can be considered as the gain from ICM initiative (I).

It is also argued that integrated planning requires better

management and induces a longer time lag between the decision-making process and its full implementation. Moreover, if the management costs of an integrated approach are kept under control, an increase in policy scale should lead to overall cost reduction.

The second component of benefits of integration, i.e., the presence of external effect is summarised by Tol *et at.* thus: 'the presence of external effects - also known as externalities, external economies or external diseconomies - are defined as the (uncompensated) benefits or damages that an economic agent enjoys or suffers as the unintended result of the economic activities of another agent. As the term itself indicates, these effects are external to the market and no market price is obtained. This characteristic implies that the market cannot be relied upon to provide an efficient allocation of resources. This, in turn, requires government intervention. If externalities are present among separate sectors in the coastal zone, policy coordination among these sectors is justified to realise least-cost solutions. Thus, the presence of external effects requires policy coordination at a supra-sectoral level ... In general, policy coordination should be sought at that level where the externalities are manifest - the so-called optimal policy level. This is the only level at which management strategies are both effective and efficient' (ibid, pp.43-44).

The comparative advantage of ICM over a sectoral approach is shown in fig.4.3.

Fig. 4.3

Comparative advantage of ICM over sectoral approach

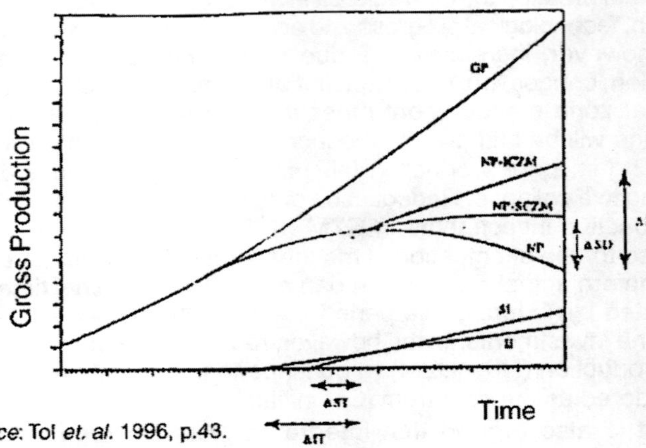

Source: Tol *et. al.* 1996, p.43.

The upper line (GP) represents gross production. The lower line (NP) representing net production results from the gross production and the damage. Reduction of damage can be achieved by proactive investments in sectoral (ΔSD) or integrated CZM (ΔID). The time lag between the start of the investments is larger for integrated (ΔIT) than for sectoral (ΔST) CZM, because the former involves more extensive planning. The investments in sectoral CZM (SI) rise faster than the investments in integrated CZM (II), because of the externalities. Also, the net production with integrated CZM (NP - ICZM) is higher than the net production with sectoral CZM (NP - SCZM), again because of the external effects.

4.4. Socio-political/cultural reasons

Coastal zone management initiatives are usually considered as responses to demands to resolve problems arising from such issues as conflicting uses of coastal resources, urbanisation, access, pollution and environmental degradation.

The socio-political reason for coastal zone management is very much embedded in the concept of sustainable development. Sustainable development demands fulfilment of the following requirements: (a) integration of conservation and development, (b) satisfaction of basic human needs, (c) opportunities to fulfil other non-material human needs, (d) progress towards equity and social justice, (e) respect and support for cultural diversity, (f) provision for social self-determination and the nurturing of self-reliance and (g) maintenance of ecological integrity (Kay and Alder, 1999, p.15). Quoting Reid, Kay and Alder also note that sustainability is 'not just about managing and allocating natural capital. It is also about deciding who has the power both to do this and to institute whatever social, economic and political reforms are considered necessary' (ibid, p.15).

Now it is generally accepted that coastal resources can only be effectively evaluated and managed in the total context of the social and cultural environment. Effective resource planning provides for decision making which allocates resources over space and time according to the needs, aspirations and desires of society, taking into account society's ability to exploit resources, its social and political institutions, and its legal and administrative arrangements.

The primacy of social concerns in coastal zone management is borne out of the adverse impact of certain coastal activities on the coastal community. Typical sources of such impacts are ports and tourism. Referring to the adverse impact of ports on the coastal society, Key and Alder state that 'the thousands of ports around the world can be multi-functional or used for a single commodity such as mineral exports or containers. Irrespective of the type, port development results in a number of environmental and social impacts. Generally, port developments involve the manipulation of coastal areas by dredging, land reclamation and clearing of coastal forests. Socially, port development can displace pre-existing coastal inhabitants, limiting areas for subsistence and recreation, and creating increased local traffic (road and rail). In worst scenarios, port development constrains dwellers from using the area for subsistence and income generation' (ibid, p.31).

Social issues related to coastal tourism development and recreational activities include the displacement of indigenous residents, restricted access to coastal resources for income generation and subsistence, loss of wilderness opportunities, conflicts between users, changes to the area's amenity and possible life style changes.

The fundamental social objective of ICM is to minimise the social costs of development and to harmonise the process of development by horizontal (sectoral/ spatial) and vertical (hierarchical) integration of management. Sustainable development of the coast demands ensuring intra-generational and inter-generational equity both of which involve paying attention to social choice and valuation of present and future development activities.

Referring to the significance of social and cultural factors in coastal zone management, Kay and Alder observe 'the cultural and social structure of a coastal nation is often the hidden determinant of its organisational approach to coastal management ... It could be argued that most, if not all, coastal programmes are influenced by cultural beliefs' (ibid, pp.81-85). These authors also note that 'cultural factors play a central, if not the central, role in the successful management of coastal areas ... The cultural norms of a coastal nation will shape the boundaries of a coastal programme, often long before notions of the exact details of programme design have been considered' (ibid, p.133). Ironically, however, these writers also admit that much of the development and implementation of coastal planning and management systems are essentially founded on the cultural norms of western developed countries (ibid, p.134).

4.5. Other arguments for ICM

A different, but very powerful argument for coastal zone management focusses on three factors which are considered to provide the 'big push' for ICM, world wide. They are (1) global change,

(2) sustainable development and (3) epistemological changes (Vallega, 1999, pp.10-12). With regaid to the first, i.e., global change, Vallega notes that 'the international research programmes on climate change and subsequent changes in biochemical cycles, on the one hand, and social change, on the other, made it clear that special attention should have been given to coastal areas. In particular, investigations of sea-level variations dependent on atmospheric warming made it possible to design scenarios of coastal erosion and its impacts on the national and subnational scales. The rapid growth in assessing these physical processes and consequences for the coastal ecosystems, man-made facilities and settlement organisation made it self-evident that ad-hoc coastal management programmes were needed' (ibid, p. 10).

With regard to the second, i.e., 'sustainable development' concept, it is stated that 'during the 1980's theoretical approaches within the UNESCO framework, mainly in the context of the Man and Biosphere (MAB) programme led to defining the concept of sustainable development. It was intended as a system of goals consisting of: (1) the integrity of the ecosystem, (2) economic efficiency, and (3) social equity including the rights of future generations. The World Commission on Environment and Development (1984-1987) moved from that speculative basis to propose sustainable development as a political paradigm able to guarantee the contextual pursuit of the environmental and development goals on any scale and to trace a new course to reduce the gap between developed and developing countries. This view of the commission was agreed by the UN General Assembly which decided ... to convene the UN Conference on Environment and Development (UNCED, Rio de Janeriro , 1992). That political process enabled integrated management ... throughout the world' (ibid, pp.10-11). It may be noted here that the role of UNCED in the development of ICM concept and practice was recognised in the last chapter.

The third factor, i.e., 'epistemological changes' is highlighted by Vallego. Vallego notes that 'during the 1980s, mainly within the UNESCO framework, intense epistemological discussion developed involving important components of the scientific community. It concerned the innovative role of the theory of complexity, also called the theory of the complex system, vis-a-vis the conventional epistemological background, more or less rooted in positivism and structuralism, and using disjunctive and deductive logical approaches

... the theory of complexity has led to global. views of reality by selecting and focussing on those elements closely referring to the objective assessment and basing investigations on them. In so doing, scientists were able to provide goal-oriented views tailored to the guidelines of Agenda-21 which as regards the coastal area, recommend working out holistic and management-oriented approaches' (ibid, p.11).

Vallega argues that 'as far as coastal systems are concerned, the three paths (global change, sustainable development and the epistemology of complexity) have converged on the same goal: ICM. Research on global change provided the awareness of the need to harmonise human action with the evolution of nature. The sustainable development principle designed the final goal to which the specific goals, pursued in the single coastal areas, should be correlated. The theory of complexity made it possible to build methodological frameworks tailored to the concept of integrated management, (ibid, p.12).

It may not be out of place to note here that the ICM process, notwithstanding its diverse origin is appearing to be a tool to promote globalisation. This seems to be the message Borgesse conveys while referring to vertical integration in his foreward to Vallega's book. Borgesse states that 'vertical integration, of course must not stop at the state level, but must continue through the regional level upto the United Nations, in a system that must be as consistent, coherent, comprehensive and participatory as its parts. At the local level this kind of horizontally and vertically integrated management/governance system is often called 'co-management' system, and this may well be one of the most fertile socio-political concepts of our time... It may bind or 'integrate' multinational companies into local communities as participants in the common task of enhancing sustainable development. It may enhance the process of democratization, domestically and internationally. One might go as far as to say; this is the emerging shape of democracy in the next century; for democracy, as everything else is bound to change. Quite conceivably, the political party based democratic system, the 'Westminister model', which, emanating from the UK and France, has conquered the world, may not be there to stay for long. Widely corrupted and 'commercialised' in the 'north' it may not have been the most suitable system for the south to begin with. A community based democracy may accord better with the historical evolution and the indigenous cultures of developing countries than a political party based system' (ibid, p. xiii), Borges, also argues that 'the socio-political map is going through a process of basic reshuffling through two, simultaneous and complementary processes: states are breaking up and/or devolving powers to smaller units, yielding to cultural, linguistic, religious or similar pressures. States are yielding sovereign powers to larger, regional organizations ('economic integration organisation') due to economic, environmental and ecological imperatives. The emergence of local co-management systems for integrated coastal area management may well be a part of this process' (ibid, p. xiii).

It would appear that the ICM is not an accident in economic history, but part of a well planned and designed strategy for globalisation. Every component of this strategy, particularly vertical and horizontal integration, capacity building, indigenous participation, etc. are crucial for realizing the goal of ICM and globalisation.

4.6. The holistic view

A holistic approach to ICM was recognized by the World Commission on Environment and Development in 1987. It stated that '...looking into the next century, the Commission is convinced that sustainable development, if not survival itself, depends on significant advances in the management of the oceans' (WCED, 1989). It also noted that this management must consider five areas: inland areas (river catchments), coastal lands, coastal waters, offshore waters and high seas (Ductotoy and Pullen, 1999, p. 5).

A holistic approach to coastal zone management should have the ecological, economic, social, cultural and even political process and issues in mind. It should address and resolve the conflicts emanating and prevailing in the coast in these fields. It may be noted that the problems prevailing in these areas are not isolated and mutually exclusive issues but manifestations of a 'cumulative process' of coastal interaction.

The ICM concept as it exists today is truly holistic. It recognises the ecological, economic, social, cultural and administrative nexus and rightly demands the incorporation and integration of these variables in the ICM process. The concept has matured over the last three decades and significantly after the UNCED (1992) declaration of Agenda 21. This is partly indicated by El-Sabh, *et. al.* when they noted that 'between 1972 (Stockholm) and 1996 (Rimouski), global awareness has moved from a sectoral to a comprehensive and integrated approach, from the projection of the marine environment and coastal resources to sustainable development. Significant progress has been made at the international level during the last two decades, as demonstrated by many events that indicates a growth in capacity for integrated coastal management. These include the Law of the Sea Convention, the Climate and Biodiversity Conventions; Agenda 21, the Barbados Action Plan for Small Island Developing States, the Noorwijk, Lisbon, Halifax, and Rimouski recommendations on integrated coastal management, the Agreement on Straddling Stock and Highly Migratory Stocks, the Global Plan of Action on Protection of the Marine Environment from Land-based Activities and the International Coral Reef Initiative', (El-Sabh, *et. al.* 1998, p.18).

Agenda 21 of the UNCED commits the coastal states to fulfil the following requirements (Ducrotoy and Pullen, 1999, pp.5-6).

1. The need to provide for an integrated policy and decision-making process, including all involved sectors, to promote compatibility and a balance of uses; this includes cooperation and coordination between the multitude of government departments, ministries and agencies, both federal and regional that have responsibilities in the coastal zone.
2. The need to apply preventive and precautionary approaches in project planning and implementation, including prior assessment and systematic observation of the impacts of major projects.
3. The need to promote the development and application of methods, such as natural resource and environmental accounting, that reflects changes in value resulting from uses of coastal and marine areas, including pollution, erosion, loss of resources and habitat destruction.
4. The need to provide access for concerned individuals, groups and organisations to relevant information and opportunities for consultation and participation in planning and decision making.

The holistic or integrated approach to ICM is further evident from the current global focus on certain themes which are common or central to the advancement of the concept of 'integrated coastal zone management and sustainable development'. These themes include (a) integration and cooperation (regional, national and international), (b) enhancing conservation and protection of coastal ecosystems, (c) education, training and capacity building for coastal zone management, (d) science and technology in support of coastal zone management, (e) data and information management and exchange, (f) integrating traditional knowledge with conventional science, (g) ameliorating the impact of natural disasters and climate change, (h) empowering local communities through community-based management, (i) legislation, regulations and socio-economic instruments and (j) enhancing political will and sustained commitment to the coastal zone.

Some scholars think that there are still significant efforts to be anticipated in the coming years relative to the implementation of many international agreements. El-Sabh, *et. al.*, for example, observe that 'the change from the past narrow boundaries of thinking and action for conservation and protection of the marine environment has a number of institutional implications which the parties overseeing the ICZM programme now have to face. Management actions should involve strengthening of institutional arrangements and empowerment of local authorities, a reiteration of customary rights and strengthening of community organisation, developing sustainable livelihoods as alternative employment, enforcing regulatory measures to control new entrants to coastal zone fisheries, curtailing destructive fishing practices, and promoting awareness of the concepts and practice of sustainable development at all levels of government and in the affected communities. Public education and community revitalisation will also be required to reduce resistance from some of the potentially affected interest groups' (El-Sabh, *et. al.* p. 18).

A point further highlighted by these writers is the fact that 'whereas in the past, coastal zone conservation and protection objectives often conflicted with economic development goals, new avenues of socio-economic development that are sustainable and equitable are now being sought. Sustainable socio-economic development of coastal regions cannot be achieved without the close cooperation of scientists, government officials and the general public. New partnerships between the public and the private sector and universities can support efforts to bring about sustainable development and economic diversification of coastal zones. Integrated management of coastal zone resources must rest on new models and instruments that consider both natural ecosystems and the needs of the human communities involved in efforts to develop and protect them. A better understanding of coastal zone development processes and the establishment of new indicators can help communities assess the costs, benefits and the environmental, economic and social risks associated with development' (ibid, p.19).

A holistic view of ICM deeply rooted in sustainable development principles should ensure that all coastal activities should be ecologically, economically, socially, politically and culturally viable and sustainable.

It might appear that the holistic approach to ICM is too complex and idealistic with multiple layers of integration and functions.

4.7. Summary

The rationale for coastal zone management has been broadly highlighted in this chapter. As a starting point, this chapter has presented the notion of the coastal zone and the natural resource base. It has discussed the background and need for ICM under four sections; ecological, economic, socio-political/ cultural and other.

The major ecological issues noted are pollution, threats to biological diversity and adverse natural processes.

The economic argument has focused on the multiple use conflicts and the need to integrate and harmonise the various uses of the coastal zones. The economic advantages of integration has been briefly explained. The major economic uses noted are human settlements (housing), agriculture, aquaculture, fishing, forestry, mining, petroleum industry, other manufacturing industries, infrastructure, ports and marinas, coastal tourism, waste disposal, water supply projects, shore protection works, national security and marine excavation.

The socio-political-cultural arguments are fundamentally based on the principles of social choice and sustainability.

Other arguments favouring ICM find their basis in 'globalisation', strategically planned through the instruments of the UN.

The holistic approach to ICM noted in this chapter recognises the need to integrate the ecological, economic, social, cultural and political issues of the coastal zones and the sustainability of ICM with respect to these parameters.

5

Coastal Zone Management in Kerala—The Resource Base

5.1. Introduction

The general arguments for coastal zone management have been put forward in the last chapter. The objective of this chapter is to give a picture of the coastal resource base of Keral as a prelude to a study of coastal activities and coastal issues attempted in the next two chapters, respectively.

5.2. Coastal resources

The coastal resources of Kerala may be broadly classified into natural, human, physical and other resources. These resources constitute the basis of all economic and non-economic activities of the coast. They provide inputs for the production of valuable goods and for the provision of valuable services in the coast. Sustainable use of these resources is the crux of coastal zone management. An outline of these resources is given in the following sub-sections.

5.2.1. Natural resources

The natural resources of the coast of Kerala are vast. They include the living and non-living resources of the coast, found in the 'dry' side and the 'wet' side and in the different layers of soil, water and air. They constitute the ecological basis of coastal economic and social life. They also form the coastal physical and natural environment.

5.2.1.1. The coast line

An aggregate measure of the natural resource base of the coast is the coastal length. Kerala has a coastal length of 590 km spread over nine coastal districts. The district-wise distribution of the coast line of Kerala is given in table 5.1.

Table 5.1
District-wise distribution of coast line of Kerala

S. No.	*District*	*Length of coast line*	
		Length (Km)	*Percentage to total*
1.	Thiruvanathapuram	78	13.2
2.	Kollam	37	6.3
3.	Alappuzha	82	13.9
4.	Ernakulam	46	7.8
5.	Thrissur	54	9.2
6.	Malappuram	70	11.8
7.	Kozhikode	71	12.0
8.	Kannur	82	14.0
9.	Kasargode	70	11.8
	Total	590	100.00

Source: Department of Fisheries, 1998, p.l.

Table 5.1 makes it clear that the maximum (14 per cent) length of coast line is present in Alappuzha and Kannur districts and the minimum (6.3 per cent) in Kollam district.

Some of the notable features of these coasts have been pointed out in the Kerala state Gazetteer. It notes that 'the shore lines of Kerala with a generally straight configuration has a number of offsets towards east and the major ones are at Kotekunnu, north of Azhikkal and ,Kadalur, South of Badagara. These are due to faults. Between Kotekunnu and Alleppey, the coast line moves inward into the land. The concavity of the coast line may be related to the structural feature and also to the resistance of rocks exposed to the high wave action during the South West monsoon in this region. The curved coast line of Kerala is exactly in North-East direction of ninth degree and eighth degree channels between Laccadive and Maldive islands' (Nair, 1986, p.71).

It is also noted that 'out of the ... total coast line, about 360 km in different reaches is subject to active erosion' (ibid, p. 71).The Gazetteer further notes that 'the chain of Kayals admixed with the estuaries formed at the mouth of the rivers retain a perennial water body almost parallel to the shore line. Heavy tidal inflow during monsoon and other tidal peaks result in the breaking of the narrow sandy ridge between these water columns and the sea. Likewise during dry seasons, the existing openings may be barred by accumulated sediments. Tidal action may thus result in breaking and building up of sand bars which in turn may cause considerable changes in the total configuration of the coast line' (ibid , p.71).

Apart from these phenomena, the Gazetteer reports that 'the coast line might have been subjected to serious alterations through river channel changes, Geomorphological observations have revealed shifting of river mouths by long distances in considerably short periods. The coastal stretch, generally occupied by sand bars and spits, intertwined in many a place by overhanging cliffs and sub-parallel rock ridges manifest a compound aspect of submergence and emergence. The rock exposures and cliffs along the coast line are of 3 to 29 metres in elevation. The cliffs are invariably capped by laterites and are made up of incoherent sedimentary formations downwards. Because of this they are subject to heavy under cutting, resulting in profile recession. Close scrutiny of satellite imageries covering the area suggest that these cliffs as well as sub-parallel rock ridges might have evolved as the result of NW-SE and N.N.W.S.S.E. fractures' (ibid, p. 72).

It also noted that the rock-ridges close to the shoreline may be considered as remnants of erstwhile sea-cliffs. Hardly above waiter level, these ridges are seen to extend into the shelf area sloping westward to limits not yet determined. On the shore front where they appear to be protruding rock-ridges, metamorphosed sedimentaries are in prominence but, the subaqueous parts constitute laterites which are characteristically reddish brown' (ibid, p.72).

5.2.1.2. Continental shelf area

Kerala has a continental shelf area of 39139 km^2, stretching up to 200 m dept. The depth-wise and district wise distribution of this area is given in table 5.2.

Table 5.2 reveals that Kannur and Kozhikode districts have the maximum of continental shelf area, i.e., 16.0 per cent and 15.50 per cent respectively. Ernakulam, Kollam and Thrissur districts have only comparatively small percentage of the continental shelf area.

5.2.1.3. Fishing grounds and potential

The seas off Kerala has the unique feature of receiving discharge from an incredible 41 small and medium rivers and harbouring an even larger number of estuaries and backwaters. This coupled with the monsoons and other natural process make Kerala coast the home for an unlimited number of fin fishes and shell fishes.

The major fishing grounds of Kerala coast are (a) Wadge Bank, (b) Quilon Bank and (c) Chettuva Bank. Table 5.3 gives details of these fishing grounds.

Table 5.2
Distribution of continental shelf area of Kerala

S. No.	District	Depth range							
		0-20 m		20-80 m		80-200 m		0-200 m	
		Area (Km^2)	Per cent	Area (Km^2)	Per cent	Area (Km^2)	Per cent	Area (Km^2)	Per cent
1.	Thiruvananthapuram	154	3.4	2930	12.0	1091	10.7	4175	10.7
2.	Kollam	349	7.8	1821	7.5	719	7.0	2882	7.4
3.	Allappuzha	742	16.6	2900	11.9	1139	11.1	4781	12.2
4.	Ernakulam	614	13.7	977	4.0	592	5.8	2183	5.6
5.	Thrissur	461	10.3	1792	7.3	714	7.0	2967	7.6
6.	Malappuram	512	11.5	3713	15.2	871	8.5	5096	13.0
7.	Kozhikode	717	16.0	3772	15.4	1591	15.6	6080	15.5
8.	Kannur	527	11.8	3726	15.20	1999	19.55	6247	16.0
9.	Kasargode	397	8.9	2811	11.50	1508	14.75	4713	12.0
	Total	4473	100.00	24442	100.00	10224	100.00	39139	100.00

Source : Department of Fisheries, 1992, p. 47.

Table 5.3.
Major fishing ground of Kerala coast

S. No.	Name of fishing ground	Location	Area (Km^2)	Potential (tonnes)
1.	Wadge Bank	Latitude 7°N and 80°N Longitude 36° and 78°E	12000	73,000- 88,000 (large stocks of perches nemipterids, rays, cuttle fish, carangids, lizard fish, cat fish, etc.)
2.	Quilon Bank	Latitude 08°30' N and 09°10' N Longitude 75°25' E and 76°15' N	3300	5,300 (rich resources of deep sea lobsters, deep sea prawns and deep sea fishes)
3.	Chettuva Bank	Latitude 10°31' N and 10°33' N Longitude 75°09' E 75°15' E	28	(deep sea lobsters, prawns and fishes)

Source : Department of Fisheries, 1992, p. 63

The FAO/UNDP Pelagic Fisheries Project (Report No.2) has confirmed the presence of a large number ot species, particularly oil-saardine, mackerel, anchovies, ribbon fishes, cat fishes, silver bellies and lesser sardines in the neritic waters between 19 and 40 fathoms (Silas, *et. al.* 1976, p.19).

The potential yield of commercially important species within the 200 m depth range of the south-west coast of India which covers the Kerala coast is given in table 5.4.

Table 5.4

Potential yield of commercially important species of fishes within 200 m depth range in south-west coast of India.

(Tonnes)

S. No.	Fishes	Depth range 0-50 m	50-200 m	Total 0-200 m
1.	Elasmobranchs	15,000	30,000	45,000
2.	Cat fishes	40,000	80,000	120,000
3.	Perches	20,000	100,000	120,000
4.	Sciaenids	20,000	—	20,000
5.	Leiognathus	15,000	—	15,000
6.	Oil sardines	180,000	—	180,000
7.	Other sardines	40,000	—	40,000
8.	Anchoviella	40,000	120,000	160,000
9.	Other clupeids	10,000	—	10,000
10.	Ribbon fishes	30,000	80,000	110,000
11.	Carangids	30,000	80,000	110,000
12.	Mackerel	80,000	—	80,000
13.	Seer fish	10,000	—	10,000
14.	Tuna and allied fishes	10,000	50,000	60,000
15.	Penaeid prawns	80,000	15,000	95,000
16.	Other crustaceans	5,000	5,000	10,000
17.	Cephalopods	5,000	30,000	35,000
18.	Other fishes	70,000	130,000	200,000

Source: Department of Fisheries, 1992 pp.64-65.

The estimated potential of the south-west coast of India is 1.42 million tonnes. of these, aoout 70-80 per cent, i.e., a little more than one million tonnes is assumed to be the share of Kerala.

5.2.1.4. Mineral sand and oil

The state's coast is known for its rich deposits of mineral sands. The Kerala State Gazetteer notes that 'the coastal tract in Quilon and Alleppey districts along Chavara-Neendakara area and upto Kayamkulam is endowed with large deposits of mineral sands, occurring as beach placers containing ilmenite, rutile, monozite, zircon, silimanite, leucoxene, garnet, etc. (Kerala Gazetteer Department, 1989, p. 375).

The potential for mining petroleum off Cochin has been reported on several occasions in the past. It is, however, understood that the Kerala coast is classified under category-III for oil mining potential and investments priority.

5.2.1.5. Backwaters and canals

Another major feature of the coastal zones of Kerala is the presence of a large number of backwaters and canals. These are estuaries and lagoons which are mostly inter-connected by natural or man-made canals. These water bodies are locally known as 'Kayals'. Referring to these water bodies, the Kerala State Gazetteer notes:

'The string of backwaters (Kayals) generally running parallel, to the coast and having arms extending between the offshore bars occupy extensive area. The Kayals are considered to be of three major categories on the basis of their geomorphological and geological setting of the coastal plain. They are (1) those contained within the beach ridge complex area such as Vembanad and Kayamkulam Kayals, (2) those occuring in the Warkalli terrain but have undergone some modification of morphology along the coasts by growth of spits and (3) those occuring within the Warkalli terrain extending to the eastern margin of the coastal plain such as the Ashtamudi Kayal. Of these, the first category have their long axis running parallel to the shoreline and are very narrow when compared to the length. Set well within the strand plain, these Kayals are separated from the sea by large barrier spits interrupted by tidal passes. On the contrary, the Ashtamudi Kayal of the third category has its longest axis perpendicular to the shore. The margins of Ashtamudi Kayal are fringed with dipping laterite hills of tertiary age which are steadily wearing back due to human interference.

There is considerable freshwater inflow into the Kayals from upland, particularly during the rainy season. When the rivers are in spate, the Kayals over flow and discharge sizeable quantities of sediment into the sea. During the dry season, the sea water may tide up into the Kayals for considerable distances. This result in seasonal fluctuations in salinity, rate of sedimentation and organic transport.

The important backwaters in the coastal tract contained within Kasargode and Cannanore districts are Kumbla, Kalnad, Bekal, Chittari and Kavvai. Among these, the first four are the estuaries formed at the mouths of the respective rivers. The Kavvai Kayal extends parallel to the coast for a distance of 21 km, with outlets at the mouths of Karingote and Ezhimala rivers. Three other rivers, viz. Peruvamba, Kavvai and Ramapuram rivers also drain into this lake. There are a few islets (thuruths) in this Kayal, the major ones being Madakkal, Edalakkad, and Vadakkekad. To the south, this kayal is connected to Payangadi-Valapattanam rivers by Sultan's canal. The project for converting the northern outlet of this Kayal into a minor fishing port is half-way on. Extensive made-lands is a peculiar feature around this Kayal. Study of old maps reveal considerable narrowing of Kavvai Kayal. The wide mouth of Valapattanam-Payangadi rivers has been converted into a minor fishing port.

The Sultan's canal, about 3.2 km in length is an artificial canal dug by Ali Raja (1766) when managing the Kolattiri domains for Hyder Ali. It connects Ezhimala river with the estuary of Payangadi-Valapattanam rivers and can provide uninterrupted water communication at all seasons.

The Agalapuzha, literally meaning 'broad river' in Calicut district also may be considered as a Kayal. The backwater extends to a north-south distance of 25.6 km parallel to the sea upto its merger with the Elathur river close to its mouth. No significant rivers drain into it at present and nearly all the drainage form the Ghats at this point is intercepted by the main stream and tributaries of the Kotta river. It would seem as if the Kotta river had at one time found its way to the sea by this outlet instead of by the channel now in use and indeed even now the water level in the Kotta river sometimes rise so high as to threaten to breach through the narrow isthmus separating it from the Agalapuzha, the water level of which rises of course much less rapidly in floods. This difference in the level of floods necessitates the maintenance of a water-lock at the entrance of the Payoli canal from the Kotta river. The man-made Payoli canal of about 1.6 km in length connects Agalapuzha to Kotta river.

Another important artificial water course in Calicut district is the Conolly canal, inter-connecting the three rivers, Elathur, Kallai and Beypur. It was imperfectly completed in 1948 as part of a scheme to extend inland navigation facilities available in Travancore area towards Malabar. The canal cuts through several small ridges and hence is of irregular width. The Kallai estuary is wide enough to be treated as a small backwater.

There are two canals branching off from Bharathapuzha from near its mouth towards right and left. The canal on the right runs north upto Tirur. The leftward canal known as Ponnani canal runs south for a distance of 3.2 km and connects itself with Velliankode kayal and runs further on upto Chettuvai river. This backwater system consists of a group of lagoons the drainage of which is completely controlled by tidal action. Velliankode Kayal is connected to Chavakkad Kayal through narrow creeks. No stream of importance drains itself into either Velliankode system of Chavakkad Kayal. Running about 24 km, the systems get connected to the sea in the south through Chetwai river.

The freshwater lakes Enamakkal and Manakkodi in Trichur taluk are interconnected and may be treated as a single system. Fed by the Karuvannoor, Viyoor and Wadakkancheri rivers, the system extends over an area of 25 km^2 . This system drains out into the backwaters through two narrow outlets at Enamakkal and Karanchira. Bunding at these points facilitates cultivation of paddy in the marginal beds of these lakes. Large scale reclamation has been effected following modern devices to check saltwater incursion from the backwaters. The Muriyad lake in Mukundapuram taluk, which is much smaller in extent than the above is fed by several small streams and its surplus waters flow into the Karuvannur river during rainy seasons. It is brought under cultivation during the dry season. The irregular shaped marshy body, partly extending to Palghat district can hardly be considered a lake; and has been considerably narrowed down through reclamation and alteration into paddy fields.

Apart from Ponnani canal, there are three more navigation canals in Trichur district, viz. the Conolly canal lying between Chavakked and Mukundapuram taluks, the Shanmugham canal in Mukundapuram taluk and the Puthenthodu in Trichur taluk. The Conolly canal, 12.8 km long connects Karanchira puzha with the backwaters at Vallivattom. The Shanmughom canal branches off from Conolly canal and runs 7 km long upto Irinjalakuda. Puthenthodu, the other canal, connects Trichur to Karuvannur puzha.

There are two small backwaters in the Parur taluk of Ernakulam district; the northern one is the Kodungallur kayal and the southern one is the Varapuzha Kayal. The Periyar falls in the Varapuzha Kayal. A north to south canal of length 11.2 km connects the villages of Cheranellur and Edappally in Kanayannur taluk. Another canal, 8 km long, flows along the boundaries of Elamkulam and Ernakulam.

Although the Vembanad estuary has its mouth in Cochin, much of its extent lies within Alleppey district. Vembanad, the largest Kayal in Kerala, extends from Cochin to Alleppey for a distance of 83 km at widths ranging from about 15 km to a few hundred metres. The area of this lake is approximately 205 km^2. Five important rivers, viz. the Muvattupuzha, the Minachil, the Manimala, the Pampa and the Achankoil discharge their waters into this Kayal. Draining a total catchment area of about 6630 km^2, these rivers discharge about 5,61,000 MC ft. of water annually. The Vembanad Kayal is bordered by the taluks of Ambalapuzha and Shertallai of Alleppey district and Vaikom, Kottayam and Changanacherry of Kottayam district.

The low lands around the southern margins of Vembanad Kayal have been extensively rnade into paddy fields through constructing bunds and pumping out waters within. Since the tidal effect reached upto the southern margin of the lake, the waters remain highly saline except in rainy season, rendering 'puncha' cultivation unproductive. In order to prevent saline intrusion into the lake and the connected water bodies further south, a bed-regulator across the neck of the lake connecting Thannirmukkom on the west to Vechur on the east has been constructed. This regulator is the longest of its kind in India.

There are many islands and 'thuruths' inside the Kodungallur-Vembanad Kayals. The promfnent among them are Willington island, Vypin and Ramanthuruth. Cheria Kadamakudi, Ponjikara (Bolgatty),

Vallarpadom, Valia Kadamakudi, Kumbalam, Panangad, Cheppanam, Nettur, Pizhala, Kankattuthuruth, Korampadom, Cheranellur, Chathannur, Pathiramanal, Pallippuram and Perumpalam are the other inlets of significance.

South of Vembanad is the 30.4 km long Kayamkulam Kayal, with an area extent of 59.6 km^2 from Karthikapally to Panmana. The shallow parts of this Kayal have been altered into agricultural fields and the waterbody is considerably narrowed down. The Chavara-Panmana thodu connects it to Ashtamudi Kayal. It has a narrow outlet to sea at Kayamkulam.

The Ashtamudi Kayal in Quilon district is unique in its configuration and extent. The name itself is derived from the fact that this backwater branches off into eight creeks, known by different local names. Running north from Quilon, Ashtamudi Kayal is 16 km long while the total width is about 15 km. Average width of individual creeks is around 3 km. The Kallada river empties through this Kayal. The outlet to the sea is at Neendakara which now has been protected as a fishing port. A bridge, 408.6 m (1338 feet) long spans the backwater to the east of Neendakara.

South of Ashtamudi, there is a small but deep backwater known as Paravur Kayal. Its outlet to sea is often hindered by sand bars. The Ithikara river empties into this Kayal. The Kollam thodu connects Paravur Kayal to Ashtamudi. Another one, the Paravur thodu, likewise connects it to the Edava and Nadayara Kayals to the south. These two small kayals lying partly in Trivandrum district are also separated from the sea by sand bars which are cut only in rainy season. A chain of Kayals interconnected by man-made canals run down to Trivandrum facilitating inland navigation along the coastal zone. This water way, if properly repaired and maintained would provide a straight route from Trivandrum to Tirur. The Kayals in Trivandrum district from north to south are Anjuthengu, Kadinamkulam and Veli. These are comparatively small and shallow. To provide an uninterrupted water way two tunnels have been constructed across the Warkalli cliffs, of lengths 283 m and 721 m respectively' (Nair, 1986, pp.66-70).

The district-wise distribution of backwaters of Kerala is shown in table 5.5.

Table 5.5 makes it clear that nearly half of the backwater area of the state is located in the districts of Alappuzha and Ernakulam. These districts together accounted for about 48 per cent of the backwater area. A sizeable part (15.69 per cent) of the backwaters

Table 5.5
District-wise distribution of backwaters of Kerala

Sl. No.	*District*	*Sl. No.*	*Name of backwater*	*Area (ha.)*	*%*
1.	Thiruvananthapuram	1.	Poovar Kayal	30.93	
		2.	Poonthura Kayal	97.59	
		3.	Veli Kayal	22.48	
		4.	Kadinamkulam Kayal	346.88	
		5.	Anchuthengu Kayal	521.75	
		6.	Edava-Nadayara Kayal	157.65	
			Total	1177.28	2.55
2.	Kollam	7.	Paravoor Kayal	662.46	
		8.	Ashtamudi Kayal	6424.15	
		9.	Kayamkulam Kayal	140.58	
			Total	7227.19	15.67
3.	Alappuzha	10.	Kayamkulam Kayal	1511.75	
		11.	Poomeen Kayal	3.39	
		12.	Vadakkel Kayal	1.46	
		13.	Chethi Kayal	4.11	
		14.	Arthingal Kayal	5.96	
		15.	Pozhikal Kayal	20.41	
		16.	Vettakkalchal Kayal	27.10	
		17.	Vembanad Kayal	10661.23	
			Total	12235.39	26.52
4.	Kottayam	18.	Vembanad Kayal	2926.77	6.34
			Total	2926.77	6.34
5.	Ernakulam	19.	Vembanad Kayal	2257.89	
		20.	Kochi Kayal	7503.80	
			Total	9761.69	21.16
6.	Thrissur	21.	Azhikode Kayal	82.02	
		22.	Kodungalloor Kayal	613.81	
		23.	Chettuva Kayal	713.87	
		24.	Pattikara Kayal	—	
		25.	Menakkady Kayal	—	
			Total	1409.70	3.06
7.	Malappuram	26.	Puthuponnani	150.83	
		27.	Ponnani Kayal	757.19	
		28.	Poorapuzha	62.98	
		29.	Kadalundi Kayal	323.56	
			Total	1294.56	2.81
8.	Kozhikode	30.	Kadalundi Kayal	83.85	
		31.	Beypore Kayal	783.74	
		32.	Kallai puzha	160.13	
		33.	Korapuzha	1038.08	
		34.	Payyoli puzha	26.70	
		35.	Kottapuzha	584.12	
		36.	New Mahe puzha	88.28	
			Total	2764.90	5.99

(Contd. Table. 5.5)

(Table. 5.5 Contd.)

Sl. No.	District	Sl. No.	Name of backwater	Area (ha.)	%
9.	Kannur	37.	Mahe	91.89	
		38.	Dharmadam Kayal	359.06	
		39.	Valapattanam	3077.64	
		40.	Palakkode	598.25	
		41.	Cheruvathur	30.58	
			Total	4157.42	9.01
10.	Kasargode	42.	Cheruvathur	1123.12	
		43.	Nileswaram	824.69	
		44.	Chittari Kayal	89.33	
		45.	Bekal Kayal	43.37	
		46.	Kappil Pozhi	2.22	
		47.	Neembil Kayal	22.47	
		48.	Chandragiri	575.81	
		49.	Mogral puthur	89.74	
		50.	Kumbala	221.54	
		51.	Suvarnagiri	6.22	
		52.	Manjeswaram	158.41	
		53.	Thalappady	17.12	
			Total	3174.04	6.88
			Grand Total	46128.94	100.00

Source: Department of Fisheries, 2002, pp.126-129.

is also found in Kollam district. Thiruvananthapuram, Thrissur and Malappuram districts have only comparatively limited stretches of backwater. The block/panchayat-wise distribution of backwaters of Kerala is given in Appendix 5.1.

The district-wise distribution of brackishwater area in Kerala is shown in table 5.6.

Table 5.6
District-wise distribution of brackishwater area in Kerala*

Sl.No.	District	Area (ha.)	%
1.	Thiruvananthapuram	1424	2.18
2.	Kollam	8604	13.19
3.	Alappuzha	15223	23.34
4.	Kottayam	4327	6.63
5.	Ernakulam	16213	24.86
6.	Thrissur	4272	6.55
7.	Malappuram	1796	2.75
8.	Kozhikode	4162	6.38
9.	Kannur	5944	9.11
10	Kasargode	3248	4.98
	Total	65213	100.00

* Brackishwater area includes backwaters and canals, but excludes prawn filtration fields.

Source: Department of Fisheries, 2002, p.123.

It is apparent from table 5.6 that approximately half of the brackishwater areas of the state is in the districts of Ernakulara and Alleppey. Kollam and Kannur districts are also found to have notable extent of area under brackishwater. The taluk-wise distribution of brackishwater area in the state is given in appendix 5.2.

The district-wise distribution of estuaries (locally called 'azhi'/ 'pozhi') in Kerala is presented in table 5.7.

Table 5.7 indicates that out of a total of 84 estuaries listed in the table, Munambam estuary in Ernakulam district, with 3000 m length of the barmouth is the largest. The next in extent is the Mahe estuary with 2000 m length of the barmouth. The Dharmadam and Mattool-Azhikal estuaries in Kannur district and the Puthuponnani pozhi and Poorapuzha pozhi in Malappuram district are also of notable size.

Table 5.7
District-wise distribution of estuaries (Azhi/Pozhi) in Kerala

S. No.	*District*	*S. No.*	*Name of the estuary*	*Length of the barmouth (m) (approximate)*	*Azhi/Pozhi*
1	Thiruvananthapuram	1.	Pozhiyoor		Pozhi
		2.	Karichal Pozhy		Pozhi
		3.	Poovar		Pozhi
		4.	Poonthura (Panathura)		Pozhi
		5.	Veli		Pozhi
		6.	Kadinamkulam		Pozhi
		7.	Anchuthengu		Pozhi
		8.	Muthalapozhy		Pozhi
		9.	Edava-Nadayara		Pozhi
2.	Kollam	10.	Paravoor Pozhi	100	Pozhi
		11.	Neendakara Azhi	450	Azhi
		12.	Azheekal Pozhi	150	Pozhi
		13.	Kayamkulam		Pozhi
		14.	Thottappally		Pozhi
		15.	Andhakaran Azhi		Pozhi
		16.	Poomeen Pozhi		Pozhi
3.	Alappuzha	17.	Vadakkal		Pozhi
		18.	Chetti Pozhi		Pozhi
		19.	Arthungal Pozhi		Pozhi
		20.	Pozhichal		Pozhi
		21.	Vattakkalchal		Pozhi
4.	Ernakulam	22.	Azheecode		Azhi
		23.	Munambam	3000	Azhi
		24.	Cheepuchira		Pozhi
		25.	Arappathodu Arappu		Pozhi

(Contd. Table. 5.7)

(Table. 5.7 Contd.)

S. No.	*District*	*S. No.*	*Name of the estuary*	*Length of the barmouth (m) (approximate)*	*Azhi/Pozhi*
		26.	Cheradi Arappu		Pozhi
		27.	Kuniyaru Arappu		Pozhi
		28.	Pokkali Arappu		Pozhi
		29.	Koolimuttom Arappu		Pozhi
		30.	Arathukadavu Arappu		Pozhi
		31.	Mepparath Arappu		Pozhi
5.	Thrissur	32.	Korrikuzhi Arappu		
		33.	Kozhimbram Arppu		
		34.	Karayamattom Arappu		Azhi
		35.	Chettuva Azhi		Azhi
		36.	Munakkakaavu Azhi		Azhi
		37.	Kodungalloor		
		38.	Veliamkode	8	Azhi
		39.	Puthupponnani Pozhi	500	Pozhi
		40.	Ponnani Azhi	350	Azhi
6.	Malappuram	41.	Poorapuzha pozhi	500	Pozhi
		42.	Kadalundikadavu Azhi	100	Azhi
		43.	Ottumpuramettungal		Azhi
		44.	Kadalundi		Azhi
		45.	Beypore	150	Azhi
		46.	Kallai	80	Azhi
		47.	Korappuzha		Azhi
		48.	Kottackal Azhi		Azhi
		49.	Thikkodi Pozhi		Pozhi
		50.	Madakkarathodu Pozhi		Pozhi
7.	Kozhikode	51.	Naduthode Pozhi		Azhi
		52.	Kallintavidethodu Pozhi		Pozhi
		53.	Chombal Ayikkara Pozhi		Pozhi
		54.	Kulluzhothi Azhi	75	Azhi
		55.	Payyoli		Azhi
		56.	Azhithala	75	Azhi
		57.	Mahe	2000	Azhi
		58.	Korattapuzha		Azhi
8.	Kannur	59.	New Mahe	75	Azhi
		60.	Dharmadam	800	Azhi
		61.	Muzhzppilangad	75	Azhi
		62.	Valapattanam		Azhi
		63.	Palakkode	50	Azhi
		64.	Ayikkara Kanal Azhi		Azhi
		65.	Cheruvathur		Pozhi
		66.	Kadalayi		Pozhi
		67.	Mattool Azhikkal	800	Azhi
		68.	Edakkadu Kavinagom		Pozhi
		69.	Edakkadu Munambu		Azhi

(Contd. Table. 5.7)

(Table. 5.7 Contd.)

S. No.	*District*	*S. No.*	*Name of the estuary*	*Length of the barmouth (m) (approximate)*	*Azhi/Pozhi*
		70.	Kavvayi		Pozhi
9.	Kasargode	71.	Cheruvathur		Azhi
		72.	Nileswaram (Thykadappuram)		Azhi
		73.	Chittari Pozhi		Pozhi
		74.	Bekal Pozhi		Pozhi
		75.	Kappil Pozhi		Pozhi
		76.	Neembil Pozhi		Pozhi
		77.	Chandragiri		Azhi
		78.	Mogral Puthur		Azhi
		79.	Kumbala		Azhi
		80.	Suvarnagiri		Pozhi
		81.	Manjeswaram		Azhi
		82.	Talappady	14	Azhi
		83.	Azhithalapadne		Azhi
		84.	Kannuvatheertha		Pozhi

Source: Department of Fisheries, 2002, pp.132-135.

5.2.1.6. Mangrove areas

The mangrove resources of the Kerala coast are fast depleting. Their total area now comprise a mere 1924 ha. The district-wise distribution of area under mangroves is given in table 5.8.

Table 5.8

Districtwise distribution of area under mangroves in Kerala

S. No.	*Districts*	*Area (ha.)*	*Percent*
1.	Thiruvanathapuram	195	10.13
2.	Kollam	376	19.54
3.	Alappuzha	79	4.10
4.	Kottayam	340	17.67
5.	Ernakulam	453	23.54
6.	Thrissur	26	1.35
7.	Malappuram	—	—
8.	Kozhikode	24	1.25
9.	Kannur	375	19.49
10.	Kasargode	56	2.91
	Total	1924	100.00

Source: Department of Fisheries, 2002, pp. 136-142.

It is apparent from table 5.8 that the bulk of the mangrove areas of Kerala are located in the districts of Ernakulam, Kollam, Kottayam and Kannur. The block/panchayat-vdse distribution of mangroves in Kerala is given in appendix 5.3.

5.2.1.7. Prawn filtration fields

The state has a total number of 23 traditional prawn filtration fields with a total area of 2727.13 ha. There are also about 10146.12 ha. of modified/improved traditional prawn filtration fields in the state. Altogether, the state has 12873.25 ha. of prawn filtration fields. These fields are distributed in the districts of Alappuzha, Ernakulam, Thrissur, Kozhikode, Kannur and Kasargode. The district-wise distribution of the traditional and modified/improved traditional prawn filtration fields and their area are given in table 5.9.

Table 5.9 makes it clear that the majority of the fields and the bulk of the area are located in the districts of Ernakulaim, Thrissur, Alappuzha and Kannur. Details of areas suitable for aquaculture are given in appendix 5.4. Details of brackish water fish/prawn farms owned by Department of Fisheries are given in appendix 5.5.

Table 5.9
District-wise distribution of traditional and modified/improved traditional prawn filtration fields in Kerala

S.No.	*District*	*No. of traditional prawn filtration fields*	*Area of traditional fields (ha.)*	*Area of modified/improved traditional prawn filtration fields (ha.)*	*Total area of filtration fields (ha.)*	*Per-cent of total area*
1.	Thiruvananthapuram	—	—	2.22	2.22	0.01
2.	Kollam	—	—	98.56	98.56	0.76
3.	Alappuzha	46	229.53	255.06	484.59	3.75
4.	Kottayam	—	—	63.99	63.99	0.49
5.	Ernakulam	152	2116.63	8611.84	10728.47	83.33
6.	Thrissur	11	303.69	653.18	956.87	7.43
7.	Malappuram	—	—	—	—	—
8.	Kozhikode	3	7.57	—	7.57	0.05
9.	Kannur	20	69.69	452.38	522.07	4.05
10.	Kasargode	2	0.02	8.89	8.91	0.07
	Total	234	2727.13	10146.12	12873.25	100.00

Source: Department of Fisheries, 2002, p.130.

5.2.1.8. Areas of outstanding natural beauty

The state has a number of areas of outstanding natural beauty on the coast. Table 5.10 gives details of areas of outstanding natural beauty along the coast of Kerala.

It may be noted that there are several other beaches in all the coastal districts of the state, especially in Trichur, Malappuram, Kozhikode, Kannur and Kasargod, many of which did not occur in table 5.10. The beaches in Kodungalloor, Ponnani, Kozhikode, Tellicherry, Dharmadom, Muzhappilangad, Payyannur (Ezhimala) and Kasargode may be particularly noteworthy.

5.2.1.9. Herritage sites and historical areas

The state has an abundance of heritage sites and historical areas along the coast line. In fact, every locality must be having its tale of treachery and defeat and its history sleeping in the tomb of the dead. It appears however, that most of these heritage/historical sites are neglected or abandoned. Very few of them are now protected and promoted to attract tourists. Table 5.11 gives details of some of the heritage sites along the coast of Kerala.

Table 5.10

Areas of outstanding natural beauty along the coasts of Kerala

S.No.	*Name of place*	*District*	*Notable features*
1.	Poovar South	Thiruvananthapuram	Wide beach, backwater
2.	Pulinkudi-Kovalam	do	Rocky cliff, extensive stable beach
3.	Sankumugham	do	Beach, archeological sites, palace, park
4.	Veli	do	Tourist village, backwater, beach tourism, park
5.	Papanasam-Varkala	do	Cliff, beach, artician springs, temple
6.	Edava	Kollam	Barrier beach and backwater at close proximity, coconut groves
7.	Kappil	do	Barrier beach, extensive backwater, coastal road
8.	Pozhikkara	do	Pozhi (permanently connected to sea with canal, temple, coconut groves
9.	Mundakkal (Jonnapuram)	do	Park, extensive stable beach
10.	Thirumullavaram	do	Bay, beaches, coconut groves, temple, pond
11.	Palliyamthuruth	do	Uninhabited island (inlet) with beautiful backwater surroundings
12.	Alappuzha	Alappuzha	Extensive stable beach, park, pier suitable for recreational fishing
13.	Fort Kochi	Ernakulam	Wide beach with backwater
14.	Cherai	do	Extensive beach with sea and backwater frontage, park
15.	Beкal	Kasargode	Fort on high cliff, wide beaches around, backwater at the vicinity,
16.	Kottikulam	do	Promontory and pocket beaches around

Source: Baba, *et. al.*, 1995, p.40.

Table 5.11

Details of some of the heritage sites of Kerala coast

S.No.	Name of the site	Artefacts	District
1.	Sankumugham	Temple	Thiruvananthapuram
2.	Vettukad	Church	do
3.	Papanasam	—	do
4.	Pozhikkara-Paravur	Church	Kollam
5.	Neendakara	do	do
6.	Arthungal	do	Alappuzha

Source : Baba, *et. al.* 1995, p.41.

It may be noted that several of the heritage sites are not properly listed and the attempt made by the Department of Fisheries in the 'Pan Fish Book' series needs to be perfected.

Table 5.12 gives details of some of the historical areas along the coasts of Kerala.

It may be noted that the historical areas noted in table 5.12 is not at all exhaustive and it in fact does not include the numerous fortresses, churches and cemeteries built by the Dutch, the Portuguese, the French and the English during the previous era of colonisation of the country. Taking stock of these cultural acquisitions may be of some value for promoting the sustainable development of the coastal zones of Kerala. Its economic and non-economic value will be highlighted in the later chapters.

5.2.2. Human resources

About 75.43 per cent of the total population of the state is residing in coastal districts (State Planning Board, 2000, p.178). Table 5.13 gives the district-wise distribution of population of Kerala during 1991.

Table 5.13 shows that coastal districts like Thiruvananthapuram, Thrissur, Ernakulam, Malappurarn and Kozhikode accounted for the bulk of the coastal population.

A close view of the human resources of the coastal zone can be obtained by looking at the population of the coastal panchayats, municipalities and corporations of the state. Table 5.14 gives details of population of coastal panchayats, municipalities and corporations of the state.

Table 5.12

Details of some of the historical areas of Kerala coast

S.No.	*Name of the area*	*District*	*Artefacts*
1.	Kottukal	Thiruvananthapuram	Vizhinjam Bhagavathy temple
2.	Shanmugham	do	Palace, mandapam
3.	Anjengo fort	do	Fort
4.	Thangassery	Kollam	Fort and light house
5.	Karunagapally	do	Buddha image
6.	Ambalapuzha	Alappuzha	Buddha image Karumadi
7.	Vaikom	Kottayam	Temple with fine ponds of mural paintings
8.	Mattancherry	Ernakulam	St. Francis church
9.	Chennamangalam	do	Granite stone, Hebrew inscriptions
10.	Chennamangalam	do	Pallipuram fort
11.	Chennamangalam	do	Manjipra temple
12.	Chennamangalam	do	Kottayi kovilakom palace—site of Raja of Villarvattath
13.	Chennamangalam	do	Vaipikkotta seminary built by Portuguese in 18" century
14.	Parur	do	Stone inscriptions
15.	Chemencherry Quilandy	Kozhikode	Kappad pillar monument of the arrival of Vasco de Gama
16.	Bekal	Kasargode	Bekal Fort

Source : Baba, *et. al.* 1995, p.42.

Table 5.13

District-wise distribution of population in Kerala in 1991

S.No.	*District*	*Population*	*Percent*
1.	Thiruvananthapuram	29,46,650	10.12
2.	Kollam	24,07,566	8.27
3.	Pathanamthitta	11,88.332	4.08
4.	Alappuzha	20,01,217	6.88
5.	Kottayam	18,28,217	6.28
6.	Idukki	10,78,066	3.70
7.	Ernakulam	28,17,236	9.68
8.	Thrissur	27,37,311	9.40
9.	Palakkad	23.82,235	8.18
10.	Malappuram	30,96,330	10.64
11.	Kozhikode	26,19,941	9.00
12.	Wayanad	6,72,128	2.31
13.	Kannur	22,51,727	7.73
14.	Kasargode	10,71,508	3.68
	Total	2,90,98.518	100.00

Source: State Planning Board, 2001, p. 178.

Table 5.14
Details of population of coastal panchayats, municipalities and corporations in Kerala*

S. No.	District	Number of coastal Pancha-yats	Municipalities	Corpo-rations	Total coastal population	Percent of total
1.	Thiruvanantha-puram	26	2	1	12,94,618	14.22
2.	Kollam	24	2	0	9,95,233	10.94
3.	Alappuzha	26	3	0	9,76,992	10.74
4.	Kottayam	5	1	0	1,19,010	1.31
5.	Ernakulam	22	2	1	12,29,899	13.52
6.	Thrissur	33	2	0	8,83,696	9.71
7.	Malappuram	16	2	0	7,07,853	7.78
8.	Kozihikode	28	2	1	14,10,914	15.51
9.	Kannur	29	4	0	9,74,789	10.71
10.	Kasargode	13	2	0	5,06,399	5.57
	Total	222	22	3	90,99,403	100.00

* includes non-coastal areas which are not strictly subject to control under Coastal Regulation Zone (CRZ) notification.

Source: Compiled from Baba *et al.* 1998, pp. 103-107.

The total population of the coastal panchayats, municipalities and corporations subject to CRZ regulations was found to be around 91 lakhs. Of these, the highest percentage was in Kozhikode district (15.51) followed by Thiruvananthapuram (14.22), Ernakulam (13.52), Kollam (10.94), Alappuzha (10.74), Kannur (10.71), Thrissur (9.71), Malappuram (7.78), Kasargode (5.57) and Kottayam (1.31) in that order.

It is significant to note here that the predominant human resource component of the coast is the fishermen population. The total marine fishermen population of the state in 1999-2000 was estimated to be 8,08,638 of which 2,50,680 were males, 2,42,801 females and 3,15,157 children. The number of active marine fishermen was found to be 1,84,849. The district-wise details of marine fishermen population and active fishermen are given in table 5.15.

Table 5.15
District-wise details of marine fishermen population and active marine fishermen in Kerala in 1999-2000.

S. No.	District	Fishermen population	Percent	Active fishermen	Percent
1.	Thiruvanathapuram	170135	21.04	51488	27.85
2.	Kollam	95752	11.84	20531	11.11
3.	Alappuzha	113647	14.05	30435	16.46
4.	Kottayam	—	—	—	—
5.	Ernakulam	73981	9.15	15157	8.20

S. No.	*District*	*Fishermen population*	*Percent*	*Active fishermen*	*Percent*
6.	Thrissur	71183	8.80	9694	5.24
7.	Malappuram	81641	10.10	23131	12.51
8.	Kozhikode	100754	12.46	18312	9.91
9.	Kannur	56909	7.04	5404	2.92
10.	Kasargode	44636	5.52	10697	5.79
	Total	808638	100.00	184849	100.00

* *Inland district*

Source: Department of Fisheries, 2000 b, p. 7.

Table 5.15, makes it clear that about 47 per cent of the marine fishermen population is in the three southern districts of Thiruvananthapuram, Kollam and Alappuzha. Ernakulam and Kozhikode districts together accounted for about 22 per cent of the marine fishermen population of the state.

As far as the percentage of working (active) marine fishermen are concerned, the three southern districts (Thiruvananthapuram, Kollam and Alapnuzha) again dominated with 55.42 per cent. Among the northern districts, Malappuram and Kozhikode showed higher percentages of working fishermen. The district-wise and village-wise distribution of marine fishermen population of Kerala is given in appendix 5.6.

It is significant to note here that the bulk of the inland fishermen population of the state are also found in the coastal districts of the

Table 5.16

District-wise details of inland fishermen population and active inland fishermen in Kerala in 1998-99

Sl. No	*District*	*Fisherman population*	*%*	*Active Fishermen*	*%*
1.	Thiruvananthapuram	1351	0.59	350	0.66
2.	Kollam	34323	14.92	8080	15.33
3.	Pathanamthitta	1450	0.63	466	0.88
4.	Alappuzha	62388	27.12	10140	19.25
5.	Kottayam	24985	10.86	6664	12.65
6.	Idukki	52	0.02	30	0.06
7.	Ernakulam	64482	28.03	16118	30.60
8.	Thrissur	19947	8.67	4832	9.17
9.	Palakkad	1041	0.45	495	0.94
10.	Malappuram	4387	1.91	1227	2.33
11.	Kozhikode	12124	5.27	2814	5.34
12.	Wayanad	1039	0.45	254	0.48
13.	Kannur	1548	0.67	920	1.74
14.	Kasargode	953	0.41	285	0.54
	Total	230070	100.00	52675	100.00

Source: Department of Fisheries, 2000 b, p. 6.

state. Out of a total inland fishermen population of 2,30,070 in 1998-99, about 2,01,503 (88 per cent) are found in the coastal districts of Thiruvananthapuram, Kollam, Alappuzha, Ernakulam, Thrissur, Malappuram, Kozhikode, Kannur and Kasargode. Among the interior districts, Kottayam is found to have a significant component of inland fishermen population.

About 22.89 per cent of the inland fishermen population of the state, i.e., 52,675 are active (working) fishermen. Table 5.16 gives the district-wise details of inland fishermen population and working fishermen in Kerala in 1998-99.

It is apparent from Table 5.16 that the majority of the inland fishermen population of the state are found in the districts of Ernakulam (28.03 per cent), Alappuzha (27.12 per cent), Kollam (14.92 per cent), Kottayam (10.86 per cent), Thrissur (8.67 per cent) and Kozhikode (5.27 per cent). The percentages of active fishermen area also high in the districts of Ernakulam (30.60 per cent). Alappuzha (19.25 per cent), Kollam (15.33 per cent), Kottayam (12.65 per cent) Thrissur (9.17 per cent) and Kozhikode (5.34 per cent). The district-wise and village-wise distribution of inland fishermen population of Kerala is given in appendix 5.7.

The considerable presence of inland fishermen in these districts has import for coastal zone management in Kerala. The CZM issues of Kerala are discussed in later sections.

5.2.3. Physical capital

The physical capital available in the coastal zones consists of primarily the instruments of production used by the fishing industry and the infrastructure existing in the coasts. These are the 'produced' means of production used for the production of further goods and services in the coast. Considering the predominance of the fisheries sector and the complexity of including the capital investments in other sectors, the attempt in this section is to present only the capital components in the fisheries sector and the related infrastructure existing in the coast.

5.2.3.1. Fishing crafts and gears

The most important physical capital and instrument of production used by the coastal community in the state is the fishing vessels. The state had a combination of 44,836 fishing crafts in 1998, consisting of 4259 mechanised boats, 22,723 motorised crafts and 17,854 non-motorised crafts (Department of Fisheries, 2000 a, p. 26). The district-wise distribution of these crafts is given in table 5.17.

It is evident from Table 5.17 that the majority of mechanised crafts are distributed in the districts of Ernakulam, Kollam, Kozhikode

Table 5.17
District-wise distribution of fishing crafts in Kerala during 1998

Sl. No.	District	Mechanised	%	Motorised	%	Non-motorised	%	Total	%
1.	Thiruvananthapuram	31	0.73	3556	15.65	2765	15.49	6352	14.17
2.	Kollam	1127	26.46	2924	12.87	2596	14.54	6647	14.83
3.	Alappuzha	248	5.82	5017	26.48	2246	12.58	8511	18.98
4.	Krnakulam	1325	31.11	1015	4.47	2008	11.25	4348	9.70
5.	Thrissur	131	3.08	2391	10.52	1351	7.51	3873	8.64
6.	Malappuram	219	5.14	242	1.06	5	0.02	466	1.04
7.	Kozikode	616	14.46	3738	16.45	5389	30.18	9743	21.72
8.	Kannur	440	10.33	1733	7.63	1151	6.45	3324	7.41
9.	Kasargode	122	2.86	1107	4.87	343	1.92	1572	3.51
	Total	4259	100.00	22723	100.00	17854	100.00	44836	100.00

Source: Department of Fisheries, 2000 a, p. 26.

Table 5.18
District-wise distribution of fishing gears in Kerala during 1990

Sl. No.	District	Gear Type											
		Ring seine	*Boat seine*	*Shore seine*	*Purse seine*	*Gill net*	*Drift net*	*Encircling net*	*Trawl net*	*Cast net*	*Hook and line*	*Others*	*Total*
1.	Thiruvananthapuram	3	403	408	-	4955	161	254	31	129	6477	517	13338
2.	Kollam	118	54	359	-	3365	496	1098	1385	2024	5025	152	14076
3.	Alappuzha	519	4	493	-	3312	302	2634	362	3607	1035	2314	14582
4.	Ernakulam	280	41	193	40	2698	179	438	1432	2074	121	1074	8570
5.	Thrissur	133	159	1	-	3285	97	273	194	170	396	254	4962
6.	Malappuram	36	1	-	-	735	6	118	277	106	100	109	1488
7.	Kozhikode	72	343	43	-	3268	81	169	1228	415	402	1047	7068
8.	Kannur	1	41	10	-	889	218	52	422	662	914	2338	5547
9.	Kasargode	62	10	-	-	1074	51	1	475	103	54	350	2180
	Total	1224	1056	1507	40	23581	1591	5037	5806	9290	14524	8155	71811

Source: Department of Fisheries, 1993, p. 62.

and Kannur. As far as motorised crafts are concerned, the major concentration is in the districts of Alappuzha, Thiruvananthapuram, Kozhikode, Kollam and Thrissur. A sizeable part of the non-motorised crafts is also found in the districts of Kozhikode, Thiruvananthapuram, Kollam and Alappuzha.

A major component of the physical capital constituting a major productive investment in the industry is the fishing gears. The state has got a variety of gears ranging from hook and line to ring seine, boat seine, shore seine, purse seine, gillnet, driftnet, trawl net, castnet, encircling net, etc. Table 5.18 gives details of the distribution of different types of fishing gears in the coastal districts of Kerala during 1990.

It appears from table 5.18 that the most prevalent gears in all the districts are gillnet, trawlnet, castnet, hook and line and 'other' gears. Ring seine is predominant in Alappuzha, Ernakulam, Thrissur and Kollam districts, while boat seine is more popular in Thiruvananthapuram, Thrissur and Kozhikode. Shore seine is more frequent in the districts of Thiruvananthapuram, Kollam, Alappuzha and Ernakulam. Trawlnet is predominant in Ernakulam, Kollam and Kozhikode. Purse seine is found only in Ernakulam district. Hook and line is predominant in Thiruvananthapuram and Kollam and to some extent in Alappuzha and Kannur.

Details of stake nets and Chinese nets licensed in the backwater fishery by the Department of Fisheries in 1980-81 is given in table 5.19.

Table 5.19

Details of stake net and chinese net licensed by the Department of Fisheries in 1990-91

S. No.	*District*	*Stake net*	*Chinese net*
1.	Thiruvananthapuram	-	
2.	Kollam	-	-
3.	Alappuzha	2073	417
4.	Kottayam	722	117
5.	Ernakulam	3626	977
6.	Thrissur	472	42
7.	Malappuram	32	-
8.	Kozhikode	156	-
9.	Kannur	687	-
10.	Kasargode	267	-
	Total	8035	1553

Source : Department of Fisheries, 1993, p. 31.

Table 5.19 makes it clear that the majority of stakenets are in the districts of Ernakulam, Alappuzha and Kottayam. A sizeable number is found in Kannur district as well. Chinese nets are found licensed only in the districts of Alleppey, Ernakulam, Trichur and Kottayam.

5.2.3.2. Boat building yards

The state had 30 boat building yards operating in the coastal zone in 1992. Two of these units were in the public sector and 23 in the private sector (Department of Fisheries, 1993, p.3). The public sector units were the Government Boat Building Yard operating from Sakthikulangara in Quilon district and the Government Boat Building Yard working at Beypore in Kozhikode district.

Among the private sector boat builders in 1990, 10 each were operating from Kollam and Ernakulam districts and four from Alappuzha district (Department of Fisheries, 1991, p.127).

5.2.3.3. Net making units

During 1992, the state had four net making units. Two of these

Table 5.20

Details of minor fishing harbours and landing centres constructed and under construction in Kerala

	1. Minor Fishing Harbours		
A.	***Constructed***	***B.***	***Under Construction***
1.	Vizhinjam, Stage I	1.	Vizhinjam, Stage II.
2.	Vizhinjam, Stage II	2.	Thangassery
3.	Neendakra	3.	Kayamkulam
4.	Munambam	4.	Munambam
5.	Puthiappa	5.	Chombal
	2. Fish Landing Centres		
A.	***Constructed***	***B.***	***Under construction***
1.	Vizhinjam South	1.	Poovar
2.	Vizinjam North	2.	Kadapra
3.	South Paravur	3.	Kattoor Pallathai
4.	Thottapally	4.	Thikkodi
5.	Arthungal	5.	Moylali Kadappuram
6.	Punnapra	6.	Kanhangad
7.	Chettuvai		
8.	Munnakadavu		
9.	Ponnani		
10.	Beypore		
11.	Vellayil Beach		
12.	Vallikunnu		
13.	Quilandy		
14.	Palakode		
15.	New Mahe		
16.	Chalilogopalapetta		
17.	Dharmadom		
18.	Cannanore		
19.	Baliapattam		
20.	Neeleswaram		
21.	Cheruvathoor		
22.	Kasargod		

Source : Department of Animal Husbandry and Dairying, 2001, pp. 94-97.

units were in the public sector and two in the private sector (Department of Fisheries, 1992, p. 3).

5.2.3.4. Fishing harbours

A major investment in the coastal zone made exclusively for the benefit of the fishing industry is in the fishing harbours and fish landing centres. The state has at present one major fishing harbour, 10 minor fishing harbours (five under construction) and 28 fish landing centres (six under construction). The major harbour is at Cochin. Table 5.20 gives details of minor fishing harbours and landing centres constructed and under construction.

Table 5.21 gives the district-wise distribution of fishing harbours in Kerala.

Table 5.21
District-wise distribution of fishing harbours in Kerala

S.No	*Name of harbour*	*Location (District)*
Major Fishihg harbour		
	Cochin	Ernakulam
Medium fishing harbour		
1.	Neendakara	Kollam
2.	Vizhinjam	Thiruvanathapuram
Minor fishing harbour		
1.	Thangassery	Kollam
2.	Munambam	Ernakulam
3.	Ponnani	Malappuram
4.	Puthiyappa	Kozhikode
5.	Beypore	Kozhikode
6.	Chombal	Kozhikode
7.	Mopla Bay	Kannur
8.	Azhikal	Kannur

Source: Department of Fisheries (1993), p.58.

Table 5.22 gives details of fish landing centres catering for the mechanised boats in Kerala.

Table 5.22
Fish landing centres for mechanised boats

S.No.	*Name of landing centre*	*Location (district)*
1.	South Paravur	Kollam
2.	Thottappally	Alappuzha
3.	Munnakkadavu	Thrissur
4	Chettuvai	Thrissur
5	Palakode	Kannur
6	Dharmadom	Kannur
7	New Mahe	Kannur
8	Neeleswaram	Kasargode
9	Cheruvathoor	Kasargode
10.	Kasargode	Kasargode

Source: Department of Fisheries, 1993, p. 57.

Table 5.23 gives details fish landing centres proposed for traditional fishermen in Kerala.

Table 5.23
Details of fish landing centres proposed for traditional fishermen in Kerala

S.No.	Name of landing centre	S.No.	Name of landing centre
Thruvanathapuram district			
1.	Paruthiyoor	5.	Puthukurichi (Mariandu)
2.	Poovar	6.	Mampally
3.	Pulluvila	7.	Chilakkoor
4.	Poonthura	8.	Adimalathura
Quilon district			
9.	Paravoor	12.	Puthanthura
10.	Pallithottam	13.	Cheriazhikal
11.	Sakthikulangara	14.	Azhikkal
Alappuzha district			
15.	Thurayilkadavu	19.	Kattoor
16.	Kallikadu	20.	Vadakkal (South and North)
17.	Pathiankara	21.	Andhakaranazhi
18.	Punnapra (South and North)		
Ernakulam district			
22.	Chellanam	25.	Cherayi
23.	Kannamali	26.	Munambam
24.	Nayarambalam		
Thrissur district			
27.	Azhikode	30.	Engandiyoor
28.	Kaipamangalam	31.	Edakazhiyoor
29.	Nattika	32.	Blangad
Malappuram district			
33.	Palapetty	37.	Paravanna
34.	Puthuponnani	38.	Thevarkadappuram
35.	Mukkadi	39.	Koraman Kadappuram
36..	Koottayi		
Kozhikode district			
40.	Puthiyakadavu	43.	Thikkody
41.	Elathoor	44.	Kuriyadi
42.	Quilandy		
Kannur district			
45.	Kurichiyil	47.	Thayyil
46.	Edakkad	48.	Mattul
Kasargode district			
49.	Padanna	53.	Koyipady
50.	Hosdurg	54.	Manjeswaram
51.	Kottikulam	55.	Chittarikadapuram
52.	Kasaba		

Source: Department of Fisheries, 1993, pp. 55-56.

5.2.3.5. Fishermen training centres

Another major investment made in the coastal zones of Kerala was in the facilities for fishermen training and education. Table 5.24

gives the details of fishermen training centres working in the coastal districts of Kerala.

Table 5.24
Fishermen training centres working in Kerala

S.No.	Name of centre	Year of establishment
1.	Fishermen training centre, Vizhinjgam	1961
2.	Fishermen training centre, Neendakara	1963
3.	Fishermen training centre, Ernakulam	1956
4.	Fishermen training centre, Beypore	1956
5.	Fishermen training centre, Kannur	1963

Source: Department of Fisheries, 1993, p. 84.

Table 5.25 gives details of fisheries technical high schools working in the coastal districts of Kerala.

Table 5.25
Details of fisheries technical high schools working in Kerala

S.No.	Name of school	Year of establishment
1.	Regional Fisheries Technical High School, Thiruvananthapuram	1968
2.	Regional Fisheries Technical High School, Kollam	1984
3.	Regional Fisheries Technical High School, Alappuzha	1984
4.	Regional Fisheries Technical High School, Ernakulam	1968
5.	Regional Fisheries Technical High School, Chavakkad	1981
6.	Regional Fisheries Technical High School, Tanur	1981
7.	Regional Fisheries Technical High School, Beypore	1981
8.	Regional Fisheries Technical High School, Kannur	1968

Source: Department of Fisheries, 1993, pp.85-86.

Table 5.26 gives details of schools with vocational higher secondary course in fisheries in Kerala during 1990.

Table 5.26
Details of schools with vocational higher secondary course in fisheries in Kerala in 1990

S.No.	Name of school	S.No.	Courses
Thiruvananthapuram district			
1.	Government High School, Poovar	1.	Fish processing technology
		2.	Fishing craft and gear technology
2.	Government Regional Fisheries Technical High School, Valiathura	1.	Fish processing technology
		2.	Fishing craft and gear technology

(Contd. Table 5.27)

(Table. 5.27 Contd.)

S.No.	*Name of school*	*S.No.*	*Courses*
Kollam district			
3.	Government Regional Fisheries Technical High School, Alappad	1.	Fish processing technology
		2.	Aquaculture
4.	Government High School, Cheriazheekal	1.	Fish processing technology
		2.	Aquaculture
Alapuzha district			
5.	Government Regional Fisheries Technical High School, Arthinkal	1.	Aquaculture
		2.	Maintencance and operation of marine engines
Ernakulam district			
6.	Government Regional Fisheries Technical High School, Thevara	1.	Aquaculture
		2.	Maintenance and operation of marine engines
7.	Government High School, Njarakkal	1.	Auaculture
		2.	Fish processing technology
8.	Government High School, Kaitharam	1.	Fishing craft and gear technology
		2.	Maintenance and operation of marine engines
		3.	Fish processing technology
9.	Government High School, Kadamakudy	1.	Aquaculture
		2.	Fish processing technology
Malappuram district			
10.	Government Regional Fisheries Technical High School, Tanur	1.	Fish processing technology
		2.	Maintenance and operation of marine engines
Kozhikode district			
11.	Government Regional Fisheries Technical High School, Beypore	1.	Fish processing technology
		2.	Fishing craft and gear technology
12.	Government High School, Madapally	1.	Fish processing technology
		2.	Fishing craft and gear technology
Kannur district			
13.	Government Regional Fisheries Technical High School, Azheekal	1.	Aquaculture
		2.	Maintenance and operation of marine engines

Source: Department of Fisheries, 1993, pp.87-88.

Table 5.27 gives details of nodal institutions which impart training and technical know-how to the fishing industry in Kerala.

Table 5.27
Nodal institutions which impart training and technical know-how to fishing industry in Kerala

S.No.	*Name of Institution*	*Year of establishment*
1.	Central Marine Fisheries Research Institute, Cochin, with research centres at Calicut and Vizhinjam	1947
2.	Central Institute of Fisheries Technology, Cochin with research centre at Calicut.	1957
3.	Central Institute of Fisheries Nautrical and Engineering Training, Cochin	1963
4.	Marine Products Export Development Authority, Cochin	1972
5.	Integrated Fisheries Project, Cochin	1952
6.	Fishery Survey of India, Cochin	1946
7.	National Institute of Oceanography (Cochin Centre)	1966
8.	School of Industrial Fisheries, CUSAT, Cochin*	1976
9.	College of Fisheries, Panangad, Cochin	1978

* In addition to those noted in the source
Source: Department of Fisheries, 1993, p. 89.

5.2.3.6. Infrastructure for processing and marketing

During 1989, the state had 410 units engaged in processing and preservation of fish. Of these, 18 units were in the public/ cooperative sector and 392 in the private sector. Among the private sector units, 90 were freezing plants, 21 canning plants and 281 ice-plants and cold storages (Department of Fisheries, 1993, pp.4-5).

Table 5.28 gives details of processing units operating in the coastal zones of Kerala during 1989.

Table 5.28
Details of processing units operating in the coastal zones of Kerala during 1989

S. No.	*District*	*No. of units*	*Ice production caspacity (tonnes/ day)*	*Ice storage capacity (tonnes)*	*Freash fish storage capacity (tonnes)*	*Freezing capacity (tonnes/ day)*	*Frozen fish storage capacity (tonnes)*
1.	Thiruvananthapuram	22	171	35	–	–	–
2.	Kollam	65	709	952	178	168	1913
3.	Alappuzha	80	877	640	33	273	38
4.	Kottayam	56	6	1	20	–	–
5.	Ernakulam	71	410	415	469	521	–
6.	Thrissur	19	113	186	28	–	–
7.	Malappuram	22	177	105	50	–	–
8.	Kozhikode	43	414	190	45	35	1065
9.	Kannur	26	285	375	90	11	120
10.	Kasargode	6	103	150	–	–	–
	Total	**410**	**3265**	**3049**	**913**	**1108**	**3136**

Source: Department of Fisheries, 1991, pp. 131-145.

It is apparent from table 5.28 that the bulk of the processing facilities are concentrated in the districts of Ernakulam, Kollam, Alappuzha and Kozhikode. Freezing capacity is found only in the districts of Kollam, Alappuzha, Ernakulam, Kozhikode and Kannur.

The coastal zones of Kerala has an extensive infrastructure for marketing of fish. Table 5.29 provides details of major fish markets of Kerala.

Table 5.29
Details of major fish markets of Kerala

S.No.	*Name of market*	*Location*	
		Taluk	*District*
Fresh fish market			
1.	Nedumanged	Nedumangdd	Trivandrum
2.	Palayam	Trivandrum	do
3.	Quilon	Quilon	Quilon
4.	Kundara	Kottarakara	do
5.	Kottarakara	do	do
6.	Punaloor	Pathanapuram	do
7.	Kayamkulam	Karthikapally	Alleppey
8.	Purakkad	Ambalapuzha	do
9.	Alleppey	do	do
10.	Sherthalai	Sherthalai	do
11.	Kottayam	Kottayam	Kottayam
12.	Palai	Meenachil	do
13.	Kanjirappally	Kanjirappally	do
14.	Mundakayam	do	do
15.	Peerumede	Peerumede	Idukki
16.	Talappara	do	do
17.	Munnar	Devikulam	do
18.	Muvattapuzha	Muvattupuzha	Ernakulam
19.	Alwaye	Alwaye	do
20.	Mattancherry	Cochin	do
21.	Ernakulam	Kanayannur	Ernakulam
22.	Chalakkudy	Mukundapuram	Trichur
23.	Trichur	Trichur	do
24.	Kunnamkulam	do	do
25.	Kadappuram	Chowghat	do
26.	Chowghat	do	do
27.	Ponnani	Ponnani	Malappuram
28.	Angadippuram	Perinthalmanna	do
29.	Paravanna	Tirur	do
30.	Kuttayi	do	do
31.	Tirur	do	do
32.	Tanur	do	do
33.	Vallikunnu	do	do
34.	Parappanangadi	do	do
35.	Kadalundi	do	do
36.	Feroke	do	do

(Contd. Table. 5.29)

(Table. 5.29 Contd.)

S.No.	*Name of market*	*Location*	
		Taluk	*District*
37.	Nilambur	Ernad	Malappura
38.	Ernad	do	do
39.	Olavakode	Palghat	Palghat
40.	Palghat	do	do
41.	Ottapalam	Ottaplam	do
42.	Shornur	do	do
43.	Chittur	Chittur	do
44.	Sholayar	do	do
45.	Beypore	Kozhikode	Kozhikode
46.	Calicut	do	do
47.	Quilandy	Quilandy	do
48.	Kuttiyadi	do	do
49.	Badagara	Badagara	do
50.	Vythiri	South Wynad	Wynad
51.	Mananthody	North Wynad	do
52.	Tellicherry	Tellicherry	Cannanore
53.	Mattannur	do	do
54.	Cannanore	Cannanore	do
55.	Madai	do	do
56.	Hosdurg	Hosdurg	Kasargode
57.	Kasargode	Kasargode	do
58.	Manjeswaram	do	do
Cured fish market			
1.	Parakode	Kunnathur	Quilon
2.	Changanacherry	Changanacherry	Kottayam
3.	Athirampuzha	Kottayam	do
4.	Alwaye	Alwaye	Ernakulam
5.	Vaniamkulam	Ottappalam	Palghat

Source: Department of Fisheries, 1991, pp. 246-247.

Table 5.29 makes it clear that the majority of the leading markets for fish are operating in the coastal zones of the state.

It is significant to note here that the coastal zone is also the base for operation of a large number of marine product export units. Table 5.30 gives details of the number of registered exporters of marine products from Kerala during 1990.

Table 5.30

Details of the number of registered exporters of marine products from Kerala During 1990

S.No.	*District*	*Exporters (No).*
1.	Thiruvananthapuram	1
2.	Kollam	14
3.	Alappuzha	21
4.	Kottayam	3

(Contd. Table. 5.30)

(Table. 5.30 Contd.)

S.No.	*District*	*Exporters (No).*
5.	Ernakulam	86
6.	Thrissur	—
7.	Malappuram	—
8.	Kozhikode	8
9.	Kannur	1
10.	Kasargode	—
	Total	**134**

Source: Department of Fisheries, 1991, pp. 148-153.

The majority of the exporters are having their bases in Ernakulam, Alappuzha and Kollam districts.

5.2.3.7. Coastal health facilities

The state has a net-work of health centres established in the coast for the benefit of coastal community. Table 5.31 gives details of fisheries dispensaries operating along the coastal stretch of Kerala.

Table 5.31

Details of fisheries dispensaries operating along the coasts of Kerala

S.No.	*Location*	*S.No.*	*Location*
Thiruvananthapuram		**Kollam district**	
1.	Edava	4.	Alappad
2.	Puthukurichi	5.	Paravoor
3.	Thiruvallam	6.	Azhikal
Alappuzha District		**Ernakulam district**	
7.	Arattupuzha	11.	Chellanam
8.	Pallithode	12.	Nayarambalam
9.	Panoor Pallana	13.	Puthuvaippu
10.	Thottappally		
Thrissur district		**Malappuram district**	
14.	Andathode	20.	Koottayikadappuram
15.	Edavilangu	21.	Parappanagadi
16.	Karimpuram	22.	Thevarkadappuram
17.	Koolimuttom	23.	Vallikunnu
18.	Nattika	24.	Velliyangodekadappuram
19.	Punnayoor		
Kozhikode district		**Kannur district**	
25.	Ayanikkad beach	31.	Arikkady
26.	Badagara	32.	Ettikulam
27.	Ezhukudikkal beach	33.	Mavila kadappuram
28.	Kottakkal	34.	Muzhappilangadu
29.	Madappally		
30.	Puthiyappa		
Kasargode district			
35.	Kumbala	38.	Padna kadappuram
36.	Ajanoor	39.	Valiaparamba
37.	Thaikadapuram		

Source: Department of Fisheries, 1993, p. 92.

It appears that the health facilities are more evenly distributed along the coasts of the state.

5.2.4. Other Infrastructure

The other infrastructural resources available to the coast consist of the net-work of roads, railways, waterways, ports, light houses, etc.

5.2.4.1. Roads

There is a good network of roads along the coastal zones of Kerala. Baba, *et. al.* noted that 'many stretches of the National Highways, NH 47 and NH 17 passes through or are very close to the coastal zone while NH 49 terminates at Cochin. Besides the National Highways, there are state highways, PWD roads and village/ panchayat roads in this zone. The coastal zone, especially of the south and central Kerala are well connected by a good network of roads' (Baba, *et. al.,* 1995, p.20).

Construction of link roads connecting the coastal villages with the national highways and other roads was a major component of the coastal (fisheries) development strategy followed by the Government of Kerala. This has been noted by this writer earlier when he wrote that 'the role of transportation to connect the fish landing centres with the nearby markets, railway stations and bus terminals was recognised by the government and a programme for the construction of coastal roads and link roads was chalked out by the government in the middle sixties. Between 1966 and 1980, about 59 link roads were constructed by the government to facilitate the quick transportation of fish from landing centres to the hinterland markets and for despatch to the processing centres for export' (Korakandy, 1994, pp. 213-214).

Table 5.32 gives details of link roads constructed by the Department of Fisheries from 1981-82 to 1989-90.

Table 5.32

Details of link-road constructed by the Department of Fisheries from 1981-82 to 1989-90

Year	*Link road constructed (length in km.)*
1981-82	26
1982-83	23
1983-84	11
1984-85	19
1985-86	15
1986-87	13
1987-88	10
1988-89	5
1989-90	1

Source: Department of Fisheries, 1991, p. 231.

It is significant to note here that many of the roads constructed by other departments and agencies prior to the implementation of CRZ notification in Kerala are not included in table 5.32. It is also likely that the implementation of CRZ notification has dampened the efforts to construct new roads in the coastal zones.

5.2.4.2. Railways

The coastal zones of Kerala is very well connected by railways. Baba *et. al.* note that 'many sections of Kanyakumari-Mangalore railway lino passes through or lie close to the coastal zone' (Baba, *et. al.* 1995, p. 20).

Table 5.33 gives details of railway stations located in or near the coastal zones of Kerala.

Table 5.33
Details of railway stations located in or near the coastal zones of Kerala

S.No.	*Name of station*	*S.No.*	*Name of stations*
1.	Nemom	31.	Alleppey
2.	Trivandrum Central	32.	Thumboli
3.	Trivandrum Pettah	33.	Kalavur
4.	Kochuveli	34.	Mararikulam
5.	Veli	35.	Thiruvizha
6.	Kazhakuttam	36.	Shertalai
7.	Kaniapuram	37.	Vayalar
8.	Murukkumpuzha	38.	Thuravur
9.	Perunguzhi	39.	Ezthupunna
10.	Chirayinkil	40.	Arur
11.	Kadakavur	41.	Kumbalam
12.	Akathumuri	42.	Thirunettur
13.	Varkala	43.	Ernakulam Jn.
14.	Edava	44.	Mattancheri Halt
15.	Kappil	45.	Cochin Harbour Terminus
16.	Paravur	46.	Tanur
17.	Iravipuram	47.	Parappanagadi
18.	Quilon Jn.	48.	Vallikunnu
19.	Perinad	49.	Kadalundi
20.	Munrothuruthu	50.	Feroke
21.	Sasthamkotta	51.	Kallayi
22.	Karunagapally	52.	Calicut
23.	Ochira	53.	Vellayil
24.	Kayamkulam Jn.	54.	West Hill
25.	Cheppad	55.	Elathur
26.	Harippad	56.	Chemencheri
27.	Karuvatta	57.	Quilandi
28.	Thakazhi	58.	Vellerekkad
29.	Ambalapuzha	59.	Tikkoti
30.	Punnapra	60.	Payyoli

(Contd. Table. 5.33)

(Table. 5.33 Contd.)

S.No.	*Name of station*	*S.No.*	*Name of stations*
61.	Iringal	76.	Payangadi
62.	Badagara	77.	Elimala
63.	Nadapuram	78.	Payyannur
64.	Mukkali	79.	Trikkaripur
65.	Mahe	80.	Chandera
66.	Jagannath Temple Gate	81.	Cheruvathur
67.	Tellicherry	82.	Nileswaram
68.	Dharmadom	83.	Kanjangad
69.	Edakkot	84.	Pallikara
70.	Cannanore South	85.	Kottikulam
71.	Cannanore	86.	Kalanad
72.	Chirakkal	87.	Kasargod
73.	Valapattanam	88.	Kumbla
74.	Pappinisseri	89.	Uppla
75.	Kannapuram	90.	Manjeswaram

Source: Southern Railway, 1998, pp. 64-70.

It is evident from table 5.33 that the railway line connects the entire stretch of the coastal zone of Kerala, except for some portions lying between Ernakulam and Malappuram districts and predominantly occurring in the Thrissur district.

5.2.4.3. Waterways

The coastal zone of Kerala has one of the longest waterways in the country, connecting former Travancore, Cochin and Malabar regions from one end to the other. This water route is known as the West Coast canal. The Kerala State Gazetteer noted in 1989 that 'the West Coast canal system which starts from Hosdurg in the north and ends at Trivandrum in the south, the capital of the state, is 558.4 km in length, including the uncut portion of 47.5 km from Azhikal to Badagara. During its course, it is parallel to the west coast flanked by the Arabian Sea at a distance varying from 0.4 to 11.3 kms. It joins up a series of natural lagoons and backwaters which are fed by several streams and rivers originating on the Western Ghats, the gaps in between being connected by artificial canals. It connects practically every district in the state from north to south. In its course at certain points it lies between several taluks of different districts, such as the Vembanad lake. This main canal is split up into various reaches, and is known as such, probably because it was existing or commissioned as such previously' (Kerala Gazetteers Department, 1989, pp.649-650).

Table 5.34. presents details of different stretches of the west coast canal.

Table 5.34
Details of different stretches of the west coast canal

S.No.	Name of stretch	Length (km.)
1.	Hosdurg to Azhikkal	54.5
2.	Azhikkal to Badagara (including the uncut portion)	47.5
3.	Badagara to Kadalundi	72.4
4.	Kadalundi to Ponnani	61.2
5.	Ponnani to Ala	79.8
6.	Ala to Cochin	35.4
7.	Cochin to Alleppey	70.8
8.	Alleppey to Quilon	74.8
9.	Quilon to Trivandrum	62.0
	Total	**558.4**

Source: Kerala Gazetters Department, 1989, p. 650.

It is significant to note here that the west coast canal system almost entirely connects the coastal stretches of Kerala. Proper management of this infrastructure is, however, an issue for coastal zone management in Kerala. This issue is discussed at some length in chapters six and seven.

5.2.4.4. Ports

Ports constitute another major component of the infrastructure of the coast. There are seventeen ports in Kerala, comprising one major port, three intermediate ports and thirteen minor ports. Table 5.35 gives details of major, intermediate and minor ports of Kerala.

Table 5.35
Details of major, intermediate and minor ports of Kerala

Sl. No.	Name (location of Ports)
Major ports	
1.	Cochin
Intermediate ports	
2.	Neendakara
3.	Alappuzha
4.	Beypore
Minor ports	
5.	Kovalam-Vizhinjam
6.	Valiathura
7.	Thankasseri
8.	Kayamkulam
9.	Munabam-Kodungalloor
10.	Ponnani
11.	Vadakara
12.	Thalasseri
13.	Kannur
14.	Azhikkal
15.	Neeleswaram
16.	Kasargod
17.	Manjeswaram

Source: State Planning Board, 2001, p.138.

The major port is administered by the central government and other ports by the state government. Recently the Government of Kerala has notified the establishment of a new port at Manakkodam near Shertalai (The New Indian Express, 27.6.2002). Proper management of these ports is integral for the sustainable development of the coast.

5.2.4.5. Light houses

Light houses constitute a major amenity for the coastal people. In the course of fisheries development planning in the state, the Government of Kerala had established a number of light houses (guide lights) along the coasts of Kerala. There were a few guide lights existing even prior to that. Table 5.36 gives details of light houses (guidelights) existing in the coastal zone of Kerala in 2001.

Table 5.36

Details of light houses (guide lights) existing in the coastal zones of Kerala in 2001

S.No.	*Name of light house*	*Location*	*District*	*Condition*
1.	Vizhinjam light house	Kovalam	Thiruvananthapuram	Working
2.	Anjuthengu light house	Anjuthengu Fort	do	do
3.	Thankasseri light house	Thankasseri	Kollam	do
4.	Kovilthottam light house	Kovilthottam, near KMML	do	do
5.	Andhakaranazhi light house	Andhakaranazhi	Alappuzha	do
6.	Mararikulam-Chettipozhi light house	Mararikulam-Chettiponzhi bar	do	do
7.	Alappuzha beach light house	Alappuzha beach (near Rest House)	do	do
8.	Muhamma light house	Near Muhamma jetty	do	do
9.	Kumarakom guide light	Near Kumarakom jetty	Kottayam	do
10.	Monekkor light house	Kumbalangi Panchayat	Ernakulam	do
11.	Fort Cochin light house	Fort Cochin, (Bar mouth)	do	do
12.	Vypeen light house	Vypeen	do	do
13.	Nattika beach light house	Nattika beach	Thrissur	do
14.	Chettuva light house	Kadapuram beach	do	do

(Contd. Table. 5.36)

(Table. 5.36 Contd.)

S.No.	*Name of light house*	*Location*	*District*	*Condition*
15.	Akalad light house	Akalad	Thrissur	Not working
16.	Blangad light house	Blangad beach	do	working
17.	Parvanna light house	Parvanna beach	Malappuram	do
18.	Vakkad light house	Vakkad Central beach	do	do
19.	Koottayi light house	Koottayi south	do	do
20.	Thanur light house	Thanur	do	Not working
21.	Cheppapadi light house	Cheppapadi	do	do
22.	Thikkodi light house	Thikkodi	Kozhikode	Working
23.	Thalasseri light house	Thalasseri	Kannur	do
24.	Payyambalam light house	Payyambalam	do	do
25.	Azheekal light house	Azheekal	do	do
26.	Ezhimala lilght house	Ezimala	do	do
27.	Kasargode beach light house	Kasargode beach	Kasargode	do

Source: Department of Fisheries, 2001, series - 1,2,4,5,7,8,10,11,12 and 14.

It is worth noting here that these light houses, apart from providing a public utility, serve as landmarks in the economic history of the coastal zone.

5.3. Summary

This chapter gave a general outline of the coastal resource base. The resources considered included the natural, human and physical capital and the infrastructure available to the coast. The natural resources noted included the coastline, the continental shelf, fishing grounds, mineral sand and oil, backwaters and canals, mangrove areas and prawn filtration fields, areas of outstanding natural beauty and heritage sites and historical areas.

The human resources of the coastal zone were discussed in terms of the total population, total fishermen population, marine fishermen, inland fishermen, active fishermen, etc.

The physical capital available to the coast was discussed primarily in terms of the capital assets of the fishing industry in the form of fishing crafts and gears, boat building yards, net making units, fishing harbours, fishermen training centres, infrastructure for processing and marketing and coastal health facilities.

Among the other infrastructure considered are roads, railways, waterways, ports and light houses.

The chapter, by and large, recognised the resource base of the coast and their relevance in the sustainable development of the coastal zone.

6

Coastal Zone Management in Kerala—Coastal Activities

6.1. Introduction

The attempt in the last chapter was to give an account of the resource base of the coastal zones of Kerala. This chapter seeks to examine the various coastal activities of Kerala as a prelude to an understanding of the coastal issues which are delineated in the next chapter. The major coastal activities considered are: (l) fisheries, (2) aquaculture, (3) agriculture. (4) mining, (5) manufacturing (coir, cashew processing, fish processing, fertilizers and chemicals), (6) tourism, (7) ports and harbour, (8) inland water transport, (9) urban development and (10) other uses. The first nine activities fall generally in the category of economic uses and the last in the group of non-economic (socio-cultural) uses. The above activities encompass the 'land side' and 'water side' uses of the coast. An approximate picture of the 'land side' activities of the coast may he got from the 'land-use' pattern of the coast. The attempt in the next section is to look at the land-use pattern along the demarcated coastal zones of Kerala. In the ensuing section the various coastal activities are discussed at some length.

6.1.1. Land-use pattern

The land-use pattern on the 'land side' of the coastal zone of the state has been worked out by the Centre for Earth Science Studies (Baba, *et. al.*, 1998, p.108-147). The landuse categories noted by the Centre (CESS) in its land-use map consisted of the following; (l) Forest, (2) Agricultural land, (3) Waterbody, (4) Wetland, (5) Built-up land, (6) Transportation, (7) Coastal structures, (8) Other features. The above land uses have been further divided into a number of specific uses. Table 6.1 gives details of land use classification followed by the Centre for Earth Science Studies.

Table 6.1
Details of land-use classification followed by the centre for Earth Science Studies

S. No.	*Land Use*
1.0	**Forest**
1.1	Reserve forest
1.2	Social forest
2.0	**Agricultural land**
2.1	Paddy
2.2	Coconut
2.3	Mixed vegetation
2.4	Waste land
2.5	Others
3.0	**Water Body**
3.1	Estuary/kayal
3.2	River/stream
3.3	Freshwater body
3.4	Pond/tank
3.5	Irrigation canal
4.0	**Wetland**
4.1	Beach
4.2	Tidal flat with mangrove
4.3	Tidal flat without mangrove
4.4	Filtration pond
4.5	Marsh/swamp/non-tidal
5.0	**Built-up land**
5.1	Clustered settlement
5.2	Settlement with vegetation
5.3	Industrial area
5.4	Other major establishment
6.0	**Transportation**
6.1	Road (highway)
6.2	Other road
6.3	Railway
7.0	**Coastal structures**
7.1	Harbour/port
7.2	Fish landing centre
7.3	Seawall/ groyne
8.0	**Other features**
8.1	Rocky cliff
8.2	Laterite cliff
8.3	Sand dune/ sandy area with vegetation
8.4	Sand dune/ sandy area without vegetation
8.5	Reclaimed
8.6	Mining area
8.7	Waste dumping/drains/effluent discharge site
8.8	Vacant/open land
8.9	Area of outstanding natural beauty
8.10	Historical area
8.11	Heritage area

Source : Baba, *et. al.*, 1998, Vol. III.

It may be noted here that the land-use data given by the Centre do not show specific details of area under different categories of water bodies, transportation, coastal structures, and other features like rocky cliffs, laterite cliffs, area of outstanding natural beauty, historical areas, heritage areas, etc. mentioned elsewhere in the report. A general description of the land use parameters followed by the CESS is given in appendix 6.1. Table 6.2 shows the land-use pattern in CRZ areas of Kerala as worked out by the CESS.

Table 6.2
Land-use pattern in CRZ areas of Kerala

S. No.	*Land use*	*Area (ha)*	*Per cent*
1.0	**Forest**		
1.1	Reserve forest	—	—
1.2	Social forest	1.045	0.21
2.0	**Agricultural land**		
2.1	Paddy	29.748	6.06
2.2	Coconut	129.583	26.51
2.3	Mixed crop	185.114	37.87
2.4	Waste land	3.515	0.73
2.5	Others	0.723	0.15
3.0	**Water body**	19.179	3.92
4.0	**Wet land**		
4.1	Beach	24.193	4.95
4.2	Tidal flat with mangroves	2.347	0.48
4.3	Tidal flat without mangrove	0.806	0.16
4.4	Filtration pond	17.740	3.63
4.5	Marsh/swamp (non-tidal)	4.747	0.97
5.0	**Built-up area**		
5.1	Clustered settlement	9.195	1.88
5.2	Settlement with vegetation	32.454	6.64
5.3	Industrial area	0.927	0.19
5.4	Other (major)	4.116	0.84
6.0	**Transportation**	—	—
7.0	**Coastal Structure**	—	—
8.0	**Other features**	—	—
8.1	Rocky cliff	—	—
8.2	Laterite cliff	—	—
8.3	Sand dune with vegetation	4.835	0.99
8.4	Sand dune without vegetation	5.538	1.13
8.5	Reclaimed area	3.110	0.64
8.6	Mining area	0.627	0.14
8.7	Waste / effluent/ dumping site	0.041	0.00
8.8	Vacant/open land	6.511	1.33
	Total CRZ area	488.830	100.00

Source : Baba, *et. al.*, 1998, Vol.I and II, pp.146-147.

It appears from table 6.2 that out of a total area of about 488.83 hectares falling within the CRZ limits as worked out by the Centre, about 75.24 per cent constituted agricultural land, four per cent water bodies, 10 per cent wetland, 10 per cent built up area and the remaining by other features like sand dunes with and without vegetation, reclaimed areas, mining areas, social forests, waste dumping sites and open lands.

The most important single landuse noted was area under mixed crop (37.87). Area under coconut formed the next most important use (26.551). Area under paddy cultivation accounted for 6.06 per cent of the land use. Beaches constituted 4.95 per cent of the CRZ area. Similarly, the filtration ponds constituted 3.63 per cent. Tidal flats with mangroves formed only 0.48 per cent of the CRZ. Settlements with vegetation occupied about 6.64 per cent of the CRZ area while clustered settlements accounted for only 1.88 per cent. Areas under industries were a mere 0.19 per cent. Mining areas constituted 0.14 per cent. Sensitive areas of sand dunes with vegetation formed one per cent of the CRZ, while sand dunes without vegetation covered 1.13 per cent of CRZ. About 0.64 per cent of the CRZ was reclaimed area. The land-use pattern of the CRZ at the district level is presented in appendix 6.2.

It may be noted here that the land-use pattern of the very narrow strip of CRZ (upto 500 m from the high tide line) is only indicative of the multiple uses to which the coastal zone is put to and the complex interactions this land use pattern may cause to the coastal economy, environment and culture. Considering the limitations of the land-use data of the microcosm of the CRZ and the diverse impacts and interactions the various activities of the 'land side' and the 'water side' of the coast may cause to the coastal zone, the attempt in the next section is to give an account of the various coastal activities noted earlier.

6.1.2. Fisheries

Fisheries constitute the most predominant activity of the coast undertaken both on the 'land side' and the 'water side'. On the land side, the inland fisheries of the state as carried out in all the coastal districts and the interior districts make one component of fisheries. Taking a holistic view of ICM and the effects of upland activities on the coast, especially on fisheries, the inland fisheries of the state as a whole (including all the districts) may be considered as relevant for analysing the economic and non-economic values. The counterpart of inland fisheries, on the 'land side', is marine fisheries on the 'water side', which is exclusively a coastal zone activity. A closer look at the fisheries sector of the state is made in the following sections.

6.1.2.1. Trend in production

Fish production in the state since 1997 has shown an increasing trend, with total production increasing from 5.69 lakh tonnes in 1997-98 to 6.68 lakh tonnes in 1999-2000. However, taking a long term view of the trend in output since 1990-91, it is seen that the total output of the industry has shown some up and down movements. Table 6.3 gives the trend in fish production in Kerala between 1990-91 and 1999-2000.

Table 6.3
Trend in fish production in Kerala between 1990-91 and 1999-2000

(in lakh tonnes)

Year	*Marine*	*Inland*	*Total*	*Inland as per cent of total*
1990-91	6.78	0.36	7.14	5.04
1991-92	5.40	0.40	5.80	6.89
1992-93	5.53	0.42	5.95	7.06
1993-94	5.59	0.45	6.04	7.45
1994-95	5.49	0.48	5.97	8.04
1995-96	5.53	0.50	5.83	8.57
1996-97	6.61	0.52	7.13	7.29
1997-98	5.11	0.58	5.69	10.19
1998-99	5.82	0.66	6.48	10.18
1999-00	5.94	0.74	6.58	11.25

Source : State Planning Board, 2001, p.65.

It appears from table 6.3 that total fish production in the state was at its peak in 1990-91 when it stood at 7.14 lakh tonnes and then slumped to 5.80 lakh tonnes during the next year but agin rose to reach 7.13 lakh tonnes during 1996-97 after slight falls in 1994-95 and 1995-96. The table, also shows that inland fish production in the state was showing a steady increase from 0.36 lakh tonnes in 1990-91 to 0.74 lakh tonnes in 1999-00. The share of inland fisheries in total fish production has increased from 5.04 per cent in 1990-91 to 11.25 per cent in 1999-00. This is partly indicative of the growing importance of inland fisheries (aquaculture) in the fisheries sector of the state and having implications for ICM in Kerala. The relative fall in the share of output of marine fisheries also has similar portends for ICM and sustainable development of the coast. These issues will be discussed in the next chapter.

6.1.2.1.1. Species-wise trend in production

A closer look at the trend in fish production in Kerala in terms of the species composition is indicated to reveal the possible implications for fisheries management and coastal zone management in the state. Table 6.4 shows the trend in (species-wise) inland fish production in Kerala between 1994-95 and 1999-00.

It is apparent from table 6.4 that prawn constituted the single most important species in total inland fish production in the state contributing to about 21.79 per cent to 25.45 per cent of the output during the period. The actual output of this species increased from 12,265 tonnes in 1994-95 to 16,459 tonnes in 1999-00. The relative share of this species has, however, come down from 25.45 per cent in 1994-95 to 22.20 per cent in 1999-00. This declining share in the output of this species, which is a high priced item meant for export, is likely to have its impact on the working of the processing sector, which is also a major coastal zone activity in the state.

Another major species, which is showing a comparatively high level of output is tilapia, the share of which also showed some decrease from about 15 per cent during 1996-98 to about 11 per cent during 1998-00. Etroplus, a high priced variety, which is predominantly sold in the domestic market also showed a decreasing trend in its relative share which decreased from about nine per cent in the early years to about seven per cent in the last two years. The actual output of this species has remained more or less static during the entire period. The relative share of species like murrels, catfish and jewfish also showed a declining trend. It is interesting to note that the relative share of all 'other' species of fishes as a group has shown an increasing trend from around 23 per cent in the early years to around 42 per cent in the last two years. This outcome seems to be the result of intensive aquaculture in the state which has implications for coastal zone management in the future. This issue will be further probed in the section on aquaculture and in the next chapter. Trend in the production of major and minor varieties of inland fishes in Kerala is given in appendix 6.3.

The trend in the production of major varieties of marine fish in Kerala in recent years may also be noted. Table 6.5 presents the trend (species-wise) in marine fish production in Kerala between 1994 and 1999.

Table 6.4
Trend (species-wise) in inland fish production in Kerala between 1994-95 and 1999-00 (in tonnes)

S. No.	Species	1994-95	Per cent of total	1995-96	Per cent of total	1996-97	Per cent of total	1997-98	Per cent of total	1998-99	Per cent of total	1999-00	Per cent of total
1.	Prawns	12265	25.45	11984	24.15	12531	24.05	13010	22.35	14346	21.79	16459	22.20
2.	Etroplus	4468	9.27	4660	9.39	4883	9.37	4964	8.53	4756	7.22	4860	6.56
3.	Murrels	4179	8.67	4386	8.84	4618	8.86	4568	7.85	4369	6.64	4596	6.20
4.	Tilapia	6836	14.18	7347	14.81	7732	14.84	8532	14.65	7219	10.96	8510	11.48
5.	Catfish	4546	9.43	4882	9.84	4928	9.46	5239	9.00	4420	6.71	4816	6.50
6.	Jewfish	2566	5.32	2652	5.34	2791	5.36	3181	5.46	3012	4.57	3054	4.12
7.	Others	13332	27.66	13695	27.60	14622	28.06	18721	32.16	27733	42.11	31835	42.94
	Total	**48192**	**100.00**	**49606**	**100.00**	**52105**	**100.00**	**58215**	**100.00**	**65855**	**100.00**	**74130**	100.00

Source: State Planning Board, 2001, p.56

Table 6.5

Trend (species-wise) in marine fish production in Kerala between 1994 and 1999 (in tonnes)

S. No.	*Species*	*1994*	*1995*	*1996*	*1997*	*1998*	*1999*	*Average of 1994-99 Quantity*	*Average of 1994-99 Per cent*
1.	Elasmobranches	5887	4109	4422	3915	4110	3677	4368	0.80
2.	Catfish	499	308	390	192	213	248	308	0.06
3.	Chirocentrus	1450	983	1379	1380	1340	380	1152	0.21
4.	a) Oil Sardine	1554	13328	30607	93636	77795	143152	60013	11.01
	b) Other Sardine	16482	46131	6737	15573	19889	29090	22317	4.10
5.	Anchoviella	31710	36683	29744	26315	31629	26047	30355	5.57
6.	Thrissocles and other Clupeids	20196	14509	26604	15430	19041	10835	17769	3.26
7.	Perches	60180	47620	71157	46763	42370	40989	51513	9.45
8.	Red mullets	382	174	33	111	358	122	197	0.04
9.	Seiaenids	16734	9979	17720	9952	13431	7607	12571	2.31
10.	Ribbon fishes	15435	4641	21884	18976	16579	16542	15676	2.87
11	Carrangids	15836	13075	15193	22401	16091	—	16519	3.03
12.	Leiognathide	4238	4005	4536	4732	5118	6154	4798	0.88
13	Lactarius	1135	561	2208	1791	3016	1645	1726	0.32
14.	Pomfrets	3391	1675	3644	2644	2858	1964	2697	0.49
15.	Mackerel	111879	78515	128411	82429	61499	82469	90867	16.68
16.	Seerfish	5837	5910	4828	4216	5669	2945	4901	0.90
17.	Tunnies	14395	10977	17923	16018	11561	17708	14764	2.71
18.	Solas	20999	12385	15768	20375	16747	25433	18618	3.42
19.	a) Prawns	71974	43406	46279	56562	58575	44706	53584	9.80
	b) Lebsters and other Crustaceans	25252	13700	12808	10703	16164	513	13190	2.42
20.	Cephalopods	38275	43942	34557	37058	33267	31881	36497	6.70
21	Miscellaneous	57093	125030	75173	83597	85376	13180	73242	13.41
	Total	**540813**	**531646**	**572005**	**574774**	**542696**	**507287**	**544870**	**100.00**

Source: State Planning Board, 2001, p.S.57.

Table 6.5 shows that some of the predominant varieties of marine fishes caught in the state during this period are oil sardine, mackerel, prawn, perches, etc. The average catch of these species was more than 50,000 tonnes in all cases. The average output of mackerel was the highest at 90,867 tonnes. Oil sardine came next with 60,013 tonnes and prawns in the third position with 53,584 tonnes of output. Perches contributed 51,513 tonnes. These four species individually contributed to about 16.68 per cent, 11.01 per cent, 9.50 per cent and 9.45 per cent respectively of the total marine fish production of the state during this period. The output of prawns was primarily meant for export, as a high priced variety. The output of cephalopods which constituted 6.7 per cent of the total output should also be considered in this category.

It is also apparent from table 6.5 that the output of pomfret and seerfish, two of the traditional table fishes of the state, was remarkably low and showing a more or less declining trend.

A major characteristic of marine fish production discernible in table 6.5 is the high degree of fluctuation in the output of most varieties of fish and typically in the output of oil sardine, mackerel, prawn and perches which constitute the bulk species. It may be noted here that the large scale fluctuation in the landings (production) of these and other species of marine fish in Kerala will have its implication for the management of fisheries and the coastal zones of Kerala as far as they affect the economy, culture and environment of the coast. These Issues are considered in the next chapter. Yet, in retrospective, it is pointed out here that it is such fluctuations and collapses in the output of the marine fishing industry that called for drastic control measures on the working of the industry, in the past. The impact of those controls and the emergence of new conflicts, all, now call for greater measures of regulations and jurisdictions, which pave the way for ICM initiatives in Kerala.

6.1.2.1.2. District-wise trend in production

The regional variation in the output of the fishing industry and its implication for coastal zone management in Kerala can be understood from the district-wise trend in the output of the industry. Table 6.6 shows the trend in inland fish production in the coastal and non-coastal districts of Kerala during 1997-98 and 1998-99.

Table 6.6
Trend in inland fish production in Kerala during 1997-98 and 1998-99.

(in tonnes)

S. No.	District	1997-98	Per cent of total	1998-99	Per cent of total
1.	Thiruvananthapuram	732	1.25	1174	1.78
2.	Kollam	6547	11.25	7502	11.39
3.	Pathanamthitta	833	1.43	1120	1.70
4.	Alappuzha	11326	19.45	11670	17.72
5.	Kottayam	3509	6.03	3881	5.89
6.	Idukki	610	1.05	581	0.88
7.	Ernakulam	21904	37.63	21474	32.60
8.	Thrissur	5092	8.75	7168	10.88
9.	Palakkad	3237	5.56	6561	9.96
10.	Malappuran	839	1.44	1031	1.56
11.	Kozhikode	1735	2.98	1807	2.74
12.	Wayanad	113	0.19	206	0.31
13.	Kannur	1675	2.88	1614	2.45
14	Kasargode	63	0.11	66	0.10
	Total	**58215**	**100.00**	**65855**	**100.00**

Source : Department of Fisheries, 2000 (b), pp.8-9 and 2000 (c), pp.8-9.

It appears from table 6.6 that the districts of Ernakulam, Alappuzha, Kollam, Thrissur and Palakkad contributed to the bulk of inland fish production in the state. The share of interior districts like, Idukki, Pathanamthitta and Wayanad and coastal districts of Thiruvananthapuram, Malappuram, Kozhikode, Kannur and Kasargode is found to be meagre. The table also shows slight improvement in the shares of districts like Thiruvananthapuram, Kollam, Pathanamthitta, Thrissur, Palakkad, Malappuram and Wayanad during 1998-99 compared to the previous year. In the case of all other districts, their relative share showed some decrease. The decrease was maximum in Ernakulam district. Here, the actual production also has shown some decrease. Such decreases were noticed only in Kannur and Idukki districts during this period. Any further fall in production in these districts or decrease in the relative share of any district can have adverse consequence on the fishery sector of the district and that should call for ICM efforts to contain the problem.

The trend in the output of marine fisheries, at the district level may also be looked at. Table 6.7 gives the trend in marine fish production in the coastal districts of Kerala during 1997-98 and 1998-99.

Table 6.7
Trend in marine fish production in the coastal districts of Kerala during 1997-98 and 1998-99

(in tonnes)

S. No.	*District*	*1997-98*	*per cent of total*	*1998-99*	*per cent of total*
1.	Thiruvananthapuram	40837	7.99	47881	8.22
2.	Kollam	93935	18.38	111780	19.19
3.	Alappuzha	83868	16.41	91626	15.73
4.	Ernakulam	57313	11.21	73977	12.70
5.	Thrissur	60773	11.89	53182	9.13
6.	Malappuram	25630	5.01	30869	5.30
7.	Kozhikode	103184	20.19	125527	21.55
8.	Kannur	29371	5.74	27666	4.75
9.	Kasargode	16176	3.16	19981	3.43
	Total	**511087**	**100.00**	**582489**	**100.00**

Source : Department of Fisheries, 2000 a, pp.13-25.

Table 6.7 shows that nearly 70 per cent of the marine fish production in Kerala during 1998-99 was concentrated in the districts of Kollam, Alappuzha, Ernakulam and Kozhikode. Among these districts Kozhikode contributed the highest share of 21.55 per cent of the total output, followed by Kollam (19.19 per cent), Alappuzha (15.73 per cent) and Ernakulam (12.70 per cent). Among the other districts, Thiruvananthapuram and Thrissur contributed moderately, their relative shares being 8.22 per cent and 9.13 per cent, respectively. The relative shares of Malappuram, Kannur and Kasargode are found to be quite low. This might appear quite unwarranted especially if one looks at the length of the coastline of these districts and the relatively high level of output of these districts during the early decades of fisheries development planning in the state. As already noted in chapter five (table 5.1), these districts have a significant stretch of the coastal length of Kerala. The comparatively high level of output and the high productivity prevailing in these districts have been noted by this author earlier (Korakandy, 1994, pp.232-237). The downward drift in the output of these districts was attributed to the meagre technological changes initiated in these districts and the overall by-passing of development efforts in these districts. It appears now that the number of fishing crafts and the number of fishermen population and active fishermen are all low in these districts (see tables 5.15, 5.17 and 5.18). This observed situation may perhaps be the consequence of many cumulative factors which ultimately led to the historic fall in the output of these districts. Any further deterioration in the output of these districts will have greater implication for coastal zone management in these districts, especially in allocating resources for alternative employment and uses. Simultaneously, notable transformation in the coastal zone activities in these districts can also be considered as indicative of the economic compulsions and trade offs taking place in the area. These issues will be further probed in the ensuing chapters.

6.1.2.2. Trend in employment

Fisheries provide employment to a large section of the population in the state in both marine fisheries and inland fisheries. The major fields of employment include actual fishing, fish culture, fish processing, fish marketing, boat building, making and repairing of nets, etc. In this section the employment generated in the actual operation of fishing alone is considered. Table 6.8 gives details of fishermen employed in the inland fishing sector of Kerala during 1990-91 and 1998-99.

Table 6.8
Details of fishermen employed in inland fishing in kerala during 1990-91 and 1998-99

S. No.	District	1990-91	1998-99	% increase over 1990-91	% of total in 1998-99
1.	Thiruvananthapuram	316	350	10.75	0.66
2.	Kollam	7820	8080	3.32	15.33
3.	Alappuzha	13401	10140	-24.33	19.25
4.	Pathanamthitta	180	466	159.00	0.88
5.	Kottayam	5183	6664	28.57	12.65
6.	Idukki	-	30	100.00	0.05
7.	Ernakulam	13818	16118	16.64	30.59
8.	Thrissur	5106	4832	-5.36	9.17
9.	Palakkad	101	495	390.00	0.93
10.	Malappuram	931	1227	31.79	2.33
11	Wayanad	215	254	18.13	0.48
12	Kozhikode	2670	2814	5.39	5.34
13	Kannur	234	920	293.16	1.74
14.	Kasargode	196	285	45.40	0.54
	Total	**50173**	**52675**	**4.98**	**100.00**

Source : 1. Department of Fisheries, 1993, p.7.
2. Department of Fisheries, 2000 b, p.6.

Table 6.8 makes it clear that the number of inland fishermen increased from 50173 during 1990-91 to 52675 during 1998-99. It constituted an increase of nearly five per cent. Among all districts, the maximum number of active inland fishermen was found in Ernakulam district where they constituted 30.59 per cent of the active inland fishermen of the state during 1998-99. Here, the number of fishermen increased by 16.64 per cent from 13818 in 1990-91 to 16118 in 1998-99.

In Alappuzha, where the next highest number of fishermen were found, the number decreased by 24.33 per cent from 13401 in 1990-91 to 10140 in 1998-99. In Thrissur also the number of inland fishermen showed some decrease over this period. In all other districts the number of fishermen showed some increase, with the maximum, percentage increase being noted in Palakkad, Kannur and Pathanamthitta districts.

The absolute and relative changes in employment in inland fisheries, particularly in the coastal districts of the state have significance for fisheries and coastal zone management in Kerala. The issue of unemployment is discussed in chapter seven.

Table 6.9 gives details of fishermen employed in marine fishing in Kerala during 1990-91 and 1999-00.

Table 6.9
Details of fishermen employed in marine fishing in Kerala during 1990-91 and 1999-00.

S. No.	*District*	*1990-91*	*1999-00*	*Per cent increase over 1990-91*	*Per cent of total in 1999-00*
1.	Thiruvananthapuram	29841	51488	72.54	27.85
2.	Kollam	17234	20531	19.13	11.10
3.	Alappuzha	23013	30435	32.25	16.46
4.	Ernakulam	14027	15157	8.05	8.20
5.	Thrissur	12210	9694	-20.60	5.24
6.	Malappuram	15598	23131	48.29	12.51
7.	Kozhikode	19425	18312	-5.73	9.91
8.	Kannur	12345	5404	-56.22	2.92
9.	Kasargode	9879	10697	8.28	5.78
	Total	**153570**	**184849**	**20.36**	**100.00**

Source : 1. Department of Fisheries, 1993, p.49.
2. Department of Fisheries, 2000 a, p.7,

Table 6.9 shows that the number of marine fishermen employed in the state increased from 153570 in 1990-91 to 184849 in 1999-00, registering an increase of 20.36 per cent. The majority of these fishermen were found in the districts of Thiruvananthapuram, Kollam, Alappuzha and Malappuram. Here, they accounted for 68 per cent of the active fishermen of the state. Among these districts, Thiruvananthapuram alone accounted for 27.85 per cent and

Alappuzha for 16.46 per cent. Malappuram and Kollam accounted for 12.51 per cent and 11.10 per cent respectively.

Among all coastal districts, Thiruvananthapuram registered maximum increase in the number of active marine fishermen where the number increased from 29841 in 1990-91 to 51488 in 1999-00. It amounted to a 72.54 per cent increase. The other districts where the member of active fishermen increased significantly are Malappuram, Alappuzha and Kollam. Here, the number increased by 48.29 per cent, 32.25 per cent and 19.13 per cent respectively. Curiously, the number of active marine fishermen in Thrissur, Kozhikode and Kannur districts showed a decrease, the decrease being absolutely high in Kannur district. Kasargode district showed slight increase in the number of working marine fishermen.

The fact that marine fishermen in Thiruvananthapuram, Alappuzha, Malappuram and Kollam are heavily dependent on coastal marine fishing as are inland fishermen in Ernakulam, Alappuzha and Kollam, drives home the ecological, economic and socio-cultural values of fisheries in these districts and the role of ICM in maintaining these values.

6.1.2.3. Trend in earnings

Earnings from the fisheries sector have increased considerably over the years. Table 6.10 shows the contribution of fisheries to the gross domestic product (GDP) of Kerala from 1994-95 to 1999-00.

Table 6.10

Contribution of fisheries to the gross domestic product of Kerala at factor cost from 1994-95 to 1999-00

(Rs Lakhs at current prices)

S. No.	*Year*	*Fisheries*	*GDP*	*Fisheries as per cent of GDP*
1.	1994-95	74805	3187663	2.34
2.	1995-96	93449	3876232	2.41
3.	1996-97	113754	4445990	2.56
4.	1997-98	130817	5187234	2.52
5.	1998-99	150440	6044063	2.49
6.	1999-00	173007	7095262	2.44

Source: State Planning Board, 2001, p.S.5.

It appears from table 6.10 that the contribution of fisheries to the state's domestic product is not significant. In spite of this, it would be interesting to look at the contribution of fisheries to the value added by the primary sector of the economy.

Table 6.11 gives details of value added by the primary sector and fisheries in Kerala from 1994-95 to 1999-00.

Table 6.11
Details of value added by the primary sector and fisheries in Kerala from 1994-95 to 1999-00

(Rs lakhs at current prices)

Year	*Primary sector*	*Fisheries*	*Fisheries as per cent of primary sector*
1994-95	980385	74805	7.63
1995-96	1188088	93449	7.86
1996-97	1329636	113754	8.55
1997-98	1528731	130817	8.55
1998-99*	1725736	150440	8.71
1999-00*	1948687	173007	8.87

* Provisional estimates

Source: State Planning Board, 2001, p.S.5.

Table 6.11 takes it clear that the share of the fisheries sector in the value added by the primary sector is comparatively more, but still less than 10 per cent during the entire period. It would be interesting to look at the contribution of fisheries to the net domestic product at the district level. Table 6.12 gives details of the contribution of fisheries to the net domestic product of the districts of Kerala during 1999-00.

Table 6.12
Contribution of fisheries to the net domestic product of the districts of Kerala during 1999-00

(Rs lakhs at current prices)

S. No.	*District*	*Fisheries*	*GDP*	*Fisheries as per cent of GDP*
1.	Thiruvananthapuram	6889	658370	1.04
2.	Kollam	35660	473226	6.90
3.	Pathanamthitta	182	231226	0.07
4.	Alappuzha	13735	493121	2.78
5.	Kottayam	1123	421896	0.26
6.	Idukki	76	273876	0.02
7.	Ernakulam	29746	740098	4.01
8.	Thrissur	9576	617776	1.55
9.	Palakkad	577	463761	0.12
10.	Malappuram	13947	487201	2.86
11.	Kozhikode	30277	523776	5.78
12.	Wayanad	0	219409	0
13.	Kannur	5904	443928	1.33
14.	Kasargode	7072	207311	3.41
	Total	**151764**	**6255675**	**2.42**

Source: State Planning Board, 2001, p.S.13.

It is apparent from table 6.12 that the contribution of fisheries to the net domestic product of the districts was generally very low in all the districts. The coastal districts, however, showed a slightly better position,particularly in the districts of Kollam, Ernakulam, Alappuzha, Kozhikode, Kasargode and Malappuram.

Once again, the contribution of fisheries to the value added by the primary sector of the districts may be looked at. Table 6.13 presents details of value added by the primary sector and fisheries in the districts of Kerala during 1999-00.

Table 6.13
Details of value added by the primary sector and fisheries in the districts of Kerala during 1999-00

(Rs lakhs at current prices)*

S. No.	*District*	*Primary sector*	*Fisheries*	*Fisheries as per cent of primary sector*
1.	Thiruvananthapuram	156191	6889	4.41
2.	Kollam	123387	32660	26.46
3.	Pathanamthitta	79945	182	0.22
4.	Alappuzha	152023	13735	9.03
5.	Kottayam	125757	1123	0.89
6.	Idukki	170295	76	0.04
7.	Ernakulam	144144	29746	20.63
8.	Thrissur	132996	9576	7.20
9.	Palakkad	147881	577	0.39
10.	Malappuram	153344	13947	9.09
11.	Kozhikode	108140	30277	27.99
12.	Wayanad	153928	0	0
13.	Kannur	100780	5904	5.85
14.	Kasargode	47804	7072	14.79
	Total	**1796615**	**151764**	**8.44**

* provisional estimates

Source: State Planning Board, 2001, p.S.13.

What is strikingly apparent from table 6.13 is the fact that the share of fisheries in the value added by the primary sector is significantly high in the districts of Kozhikode, Kollam and Ernakulam. It was as high as 28 per cent in Kozhikode district. This share was noticeable and greater than the state average in Kasargode, Malappuram, and Alappuzha districts. Among the other coastal districts, the contribution of fisheries to the value added by the primary sector was the lowest in Thiruvananthapuram district.

It appears from the above tables that the contribution of fisheries to the state's domestic product is not quite significant at

Table 6.14
Percentage of fishermen households with different levels of income in the districts of Kerala (1998)

S No.	*District*	*Annual Income (Rs.)*						
		<1000	*1000-3000*	*3000-5000*	*5000-7000*	*7000-10000*	*10000-20000*	*>20,0000*
1.	Thiruvananthapuram	4.00	52.65	30.15	8.60	3.00	1.00	0.60
2.	Kollam	0.20	30.65	36.00	18.40	9.90	4.40	0.60
3.	Pathanamthitta	—	12.73	56.90	21.55	8.50	0.32	—
4.	Alappuzha	3.50	43.50	34.17	12.60	5.10	1.15	0.14
5.	Kottayam	1.30	42.50	34.50	15.40	6.20	0.45	0.10
6.	Idukki	15.00	48.00	25.46	11.54	—	—	—
7.	Ernakulam	0.20	35.10	40.10	15.85	6.25	1.00	0.70
8.	Thrissur	6.50	42.20	27.28	9.90	10.55	3.25	0.22
9.	Palakkad	0.50	18.00	16.46	8.93	37.00	16.46	0.65
10	Malappuram	0.30	12.15	38.60	20.30	16.40	12.00	0.21
11.	Kozhikode	4.20	48.30	27.20	11.20	5.91	2.65	0.54
12.	Wayanad	12.00	17.70	14.10	10.65	31.60	13.95	—
13.	Kannur	3.50	32.45	30.60	17.40	9.56	6.35	0.14
14.	Kasargode	1.55	64.20	26.40	5.50	1.35	0.60	0.40
	Total	**4.01**	**35.54**	**30.46**	**13.32**	**11.54**	**4.79**	**0.34**

Source: Department of Fisheries, 2000 c, p.8.

the macro-level. But at the district level, this contribution is significant in districts like Kollam, Ernakulam, Kozhikode and Kasargode. More importantly its role among primary sector activities is predominant in the districts of Kozhikode, Kollam, Ernakulam and Kasargode. It may be noted here that the above findings have significance in the planning for ICM in the coastal districts of Kerala. This conclusion can be further buttressed by looking at the degree of dependence of fishermen households on fishing in the different districts of the state as reflected in the percentage of fishermen households with different levels of income. Table 6.14 gives the percentage of fishermen households with different levels of income in the districts of Kerala.

Table 6.14 illustrates the point that the nodal income bracket was Rs 1000-3000 for a large percentage of fishermen households in the districts of Thiruvananthapuram (52.65 per cent), Alappuzha (43.50 per cent), Kottayam (42.50 per cent), Idukki (48.00 per cent), Thrissur (42.20 per cent), Kozhikode (48.30 per cent)and Kasargod (64.20 per cent).The nodal income bracket was however, Rs 3000-5000 for the corresponding percentage of fishermen households in Kollam (36.00 per cent), Pathanamthitta (56.90 per cent), Ernakulam (40.10 per cent) and Malappuram (38.60 per cent) districts. About 66 per cent of the fishermen households in the state belonged to these two income brackets. Another 13 per cent of the fishermen households in the state was seen in the income range of Rs 5000-7000. A further 12 per cent had incomes ranging from Rs 7000 to Rs 10000.There were very few households (4.79 per cent) in the income range of Rs 10,000-20,000. Families with income above Rs 20,000 was just 0.34 per cent. At the bottom end of the economic scale, there were about 4.01 per cent of fishermen families with annual income less than Rs 1000. It may be noted that the per capita income of the state at current prices in 1998-99 (provisional estimate) was Rs 16,811 (State Planning Board, 2001, p.S.11). Comparing the nodal income of the large majority of fishermen households in the state (as revealed above) with the per capita income of the state in 1998-99 (Rs 16,811), it would appear that the contribution of fisheries to the personal (per capita) income of the fishermen is quite meagre. But this contribution being the main stay of the fishermen households and a sizeable part of the value added by the primary sector in many districts, the proper management of this sector will be of crucial importance in any ICM programme for Kerala.

Table 6.15
Trend in the quantity and value of marine products exported from Kerala and india from 1990-91 to 1999-00

Year	Kerala		India		Share of Kerala (Per cent)	
	Quantity	Value	Quantity	Value	Quantity	Value
1990-91	50997	313.79	139419	893.37	36.58	35.12
1991-92	58743	444.47	171820	1375.89	34.19	32.30
1992-93	49094	414.25	209025	1768.56	23.49	23.42
1993-94	63848	622.12	243960	2503.62	26.17	24.85
1994-95	74653	817.09	307337	3573.27	24.29	22.85
1995-96	78895	856.90	296277	3501.11	26.63	24.48
1996-97	92288	936.22	378199	4121.36	24.40	22.72
1997-98	89366	948.02	385818	4697.48	23.16	20.18
1998-99	70641	816.55	302934	4626.87	23.32	17.65
1999-00	92148	1146.96	343131	5116.67	26.826	22.42

Source: State Planning Board, 2001, p.S.171.

6.1.2.4. Trend in foreign exchange earnings

One of the major contributions of fisheries to the Kerala economy is as a foreign exchange earner. The foreign exchange earned by the state by exporting marine products has increased steadily over the years. Table 6.15 shows the trend in the quantity and value of marine products exported from Kerala and India from 1990-91 to 1999-00.

It is quite evident from table 6.15 that the contribution of the state to the foreign exchange earned by the country from the export of marine products is quite significant. The table, however, also reveals that the share of the state in the total quantity and value of marine products exported from the country is declining over the years. This down swing in the relative quantity and value of marine products exported from the state seems to have started since 1992-93 and this apparently should be the result of a higher rate of growth in export by other states. This is reflected in the declining share of marine products exports from Cochin and Thiruvananthapuram ports. Table 6.16 shows the trend in the export of marine products from Cochin and Thiruvananthapuram ports and all India from 1995-96 to 2001-02.

Table 6.16

Trend in the export of marine products from Cochin and Thiruvananthapuram ports and all India from 1995-96 to 2001-02

(Quantity in tonnes: value in Rs crores)

Year		*Cochin*	*Thiruvananthapuram*	*Total*	*All India*	*Share of Cochin and Thiruvananthapuram as per cent of All India*
1995-96	Q.	78682	214	78896	296277	26.62
	V.	854	3	857	3501	24.47
1996-97	Q.	91616	672	92288	378199	24.40
	V.	926	11	937	4121	22.73
1997-98	Q.	88708	658	89366	385818	23.16
	V.	938	10	948	4697	20.18
1998-99	Q.	69991	651	70642	302994	23.31
	V.	808	9	817	4627	17.65
1999-00	Q.	91543	605	92148	343031	26.86
	V.	1137	10	1147	5117	22.41
2000-01	Q.	88355	497	88852	440473	20.17
	V.	1034	13	1047	6444	16.24
2001-02	Q.	72035	721	72756	424470	17.14
	V.	931	20	951	5957	15.96

Source: MPEDA, Annual Reports, 1995-96 to 2001-02 and other records.

Table 6.16 makes it clear that the relative share of Cochin and Thiruvananthapuram in the quantity and value of marine products exported from the country has come down from 26.62 per cent and 24.47 per cent respectively in 1995-96 to 17.14 per cent and 15.96 per cent respectively in 2001-02. This is notwithstanding a better position in 1999-00. The crucial question arising from the above trends in the export of marine products from Kerala is the un-sustainability of the marine products processing industry and its impacts on the fisheries sector of Kerala, both on the capture side and the culture side. With the prevailing ecological, economic, social and cultural interactions in the coast, management of the fisheries sector in the ICM mode is quite essential. These issues are further highlighted in the ensuing sections and in chapter seven.

6.1.3. Aquaculture

Aquaculture is one of the 'land-side' activities of the coast, which has the potential to become a major coastal zone activity in Kerala. The natural resources available in the coast in the form of backwaters, brackish water areas, mangrove swamps, prawn filtration fields, areas suitable for aquaculture, etc. have been pointed out in chapter five.

Aquaculture is reported to be a traditional activity in the backwater areas of Kerala, particularly in the districts of Ernakulam, Alappuzha, Thrissur and Kannur. Seasonal culture of prawns in the agricultural (*pokkali*) fields was a lucrative occupation in the past. The 'Master Plan for Fisheries Development' in Kerala notes that 'prawn filtration in paddy fields. in Kerala is a unique feature in Indian fisheries. Extensive paddy fields known as *Pokkali* fields adjacent to the backwaters in the Cochin, Kanayannoor, Parur, Mukundapuram, Crangannoore, Vaikom and Shertalai taluks, afford excellent prawn fisheries. Cultivation in these fields is restricted to a single crop from July to September and then prawn culture by automatic stocking is resorted to. The extent of area under prawn filtration is about 4,200 hectares. Production varies from 3000 to 5000 tonnes annually of which 80 per cent is covered by prawns and the rest by mullets, pearl spots, etc. The major portion used to be cured and exported to various places in India, Burma and Ceylon but with the loss of these markets, large quantities are taken for freezing and canning' (Directorate of Fisheries, 1969, p.10).

Referring to this practice of traditional aquaculture, the National Commission on Agriculture notes that 'brackish water fish culture is practised by traditional methods, and is an old industry in India. It is mainly undertaken in the bheris in the Sunderbans area of West Bengal and in the paddy fields along the margins of backwaters in Kerala. The practice in both these regions, although differing in details, follow the same basic principle, namely, trapping-cum-holding. Fish and crustaceans in their young stages which enter the fields with the on-coming tide are trapped and grown for some months, until they attain a marketable size or are harvested wholesale before the next monsoon'. (Ministry of Agriculture and Irrigation, 1976, p.74).

Siva and Karir observe that 'traditional shrimp and aquaculture has been practised in Kerala's low-lying backwaters for centuries. There are two systems of aquaculture practised: (1) seasonal fields, where paddy is cultivated during the monsoon months (July-October) and prawn/fish cultivated during the rest of the year when fields become inundated with saline waters and (2) perennial fields where prawns are cultivated throughout the year' (Siva and Karir, 1997, p.75).

Parallel to this shrimp/fish culture in the *pokkali* fields in the central regions of Kerala, there is also the practice of rearing and harvesting prawns from *Kaypads* in the northern parts of Kannur district.

Reporting on the *Kaypad* system, Siva and Karir note that the '*Kaypods* are small plots of land where saline water intrudes Into the cultivated area. The Kaypods are often formed in small rectangular shapes, with a one feet bed on four sides ... Kaypods unlike *Pokkali*, are situated close to rivers and marshes - areas where prawn and fish breed. In a fashion similar to Pokkali, sluice gates are installed and water level are monitored; once the prawns and fish reach maturity, they are harvested ... on an average, there are two prawn crops; one from January/February to April and the second from August to December, with one paddy crop from April to July' (ibid, p.77).

Development of aquaculture was made a major priority in the government's programme for the development of inland fisheries since the Fifth Five Year Plan. Speaking on the related programmes, the Fifth Five Year Plan document notes that "the state has five brackish water fish farms set up to serve, as model demonstration farms. However, culture fisheries are yet to be developed on any significant scale. Therefore in order to generate popular enthusiasm in this direction, the existing brackish water fish farms will be reconstructed and culture of mullets, chanoes, etroplus, prawns, etc. will be taken up in a systematic manner' (State Planning Board, 1973, p.160).

The programmes for the development of aquaculture have been continued in the succeeding five year plans as well. In 1981, the Government of Kerala established the Kerala Inland Fisheries Development Corporation for the development of brackish and freshwater prawn and fish farming with seed money support facilities by availing institutional finance (Kerala Gazetteers Department, 1989, p.152). However, with the establishment of the Kerala State Co-operative Federation for Fisheries Development (MATSYAFED) this work was transferred to the MATSYAFED. The MATSYAFED had prepared plans for the development of aquaculture in 15,000 hectares with an anticipated investment of Rs 134 crores under World Bank Assistance (ibid, p.155). The project to be Implemented in seven years expected to cover 5000 hectares of public waters and 10,000 hectares of private waters. Some of the highlights of the project are given in Table 6.17.

Table 6.17

Highlights of World Bank project for prawn culture in Kerala

S.No.	*Particulars*	*Quantity*	*Value (Rs.)*
1.	Additional production of prawns	50,000 tonnes	80 Crores
2.	Additional production of fish	1,500 tonnes	1.8 Crores
3.	Additional production of coconuts	48 million nuts	9.6 Crores
4.	Additional foreign exchange earnings	—	94 Crores
5.	Employment to be generated	180 lakh man days	—
6.	Regular employment of private firms	30,000 man years	—
7.	Processing	2,250 man years	—

Source: Kerala Gazetteers Department, 1989, p.155.

The project was expected to produce huge net benefits and earn foreign exchange for the country.

The work of promotion of aquaculture in the state is now being carried out by the Agency for Development of Aquaculture in Kerala (ADAK), Fish Farmers Development Agencies (FFDA), Brackish Water Fish/Prawn Farmers' Development Agencies, etc. The major programmes implemented by these agencies include (l) integrated fish farming and inland aquaculture, (2) janakeeya matsyakrishi (people's programme for development of aquaculture), (3) integrated project for the development of prawn culture in Pokkali lands in Ernakulam district, and (4) Kuwait Fund assisted prawn culture development project.

The Kuwait Fund assisted prawn culture development project is an externally aided project, funded by the Kuwait Fund for Arab Economic Development. This scheme, though started in 1989-90 had suffered setback in 1990-91 due to the Gulf war. The project after its revival in 1991-92, has again come to a standstill with the implementation of coastal zone regulations in the state (State Planning Board, 1997, p.40).

The Janakeeya matsyakrishi programme is an integrated programme, consisting of freshwater and brackishwater farming, seed rearing, setting up of hatcheries, etc. This programme envisages optimal utilisation of the inland water resources with people's participation.

As already noted, with the introduction of coastal zone regulations in the country, the coastal aquaculture activity in the state has suffered some jolt. This seems to be reflected in the staggering output of the sector. Table 6.13 shows the details of brackishwater shrimp/scampi farming in Kerala.

Table 6.18

Details of brackish water shrimp/scampi farming in Kerala from 1999-00 to 2001-02

Year	*Estimated brackish water area (ha)*	*Area under shrimp culture (ha)*	*Estimated production (tonnes)*	*Area under scampi culture (ha)*	*Estimated production (tonnes)*	*Total area under culture (ha)*	*Total production (tonnes)*
1999-00	65000	13760	6700	—	—	13760	6700
2000-01	65000	14743	7327	—	—	14743	7327
2001-02	65000	14700	5540	770	200	15470	5740

Source: MPEDA Records, 2002.

The limited data contained in table 6.18 indicates a fall in the area under culture in the final year and an even greater or disproportionate fall in the output of shrimp in that year. The slight increase in total production made with the addition of scampi output does not alter the basic situation.

It might be interesting to note at this point that both area under shrimp culture and shrimp production from brackish water shrimp culture in the country have shown an increasing trend during this period. The area under shrimp culture has increased from 1,44,625 hectares in 1999-00 to 1,57,400 hectares in 2001-02. Shrimp production during this period also increased from 78,860 tonnes to 1,02,940 tonnes, notwithstanding the operation of coastal regulations in the country. Details of brackish water shrimp farming in India are given in appendix 6.4. The stagnating or decelerating trend in the output of the coastal aquaculture industry in Kerala needs to be examined further and possible solutions for it found in the ICM framework. This is needed in view of Its linkage with the fish processing industry, agriculture and capture fisheries. Its impact on the coastal ecology, economy, society and culture also needs to be considered to make it a sustainable avocation of the coast. An attempt is made in this direction in the next chapter and in chapter nine.

6.1.4. Agriculture

Agriculture, like aquaculture, is a predominant activity along the coastal wetlands and adjoining areas of the coasts of Kerala. Referring to the landscape of Kerala and quoting from Padmanabha Menon's History of Kerala, the Kerala State Gazetteer notes, 'the low belt which borders on the sea and the backwaters has in the course of ages become rich with the works of man, and the landscape, shaded and fanned by the feathery palm presents a chequered scheme of light and shade. As we leave the sea board, an undulating country, diversified with grassy flats, naked hills and wooded terraces, intersected by numerous torrents and rapids and profusely dotted with homesteads, orchards and cultivated fields, rolls upto the foot of the Western Ghats. Here the landscape, nobler and more intensified in grandeur, merges itself in wide forests of continuous shade' (Kerala Gazetteer Department, 1989, p.l). While writing on Travancore, quoting an earlier source, Velu Pillai noted that 'broad stretches of alluvial ricefields fringe the coast-strip and run up into the interior, gradually thinning out as they approach the high lands through which the rivers force their way' (Velu Pillai, 1940; Reprint, 1996, p.3). This description of the paddy landscape is equally applicable in the case of Malabar region as well. No doubt, economic development and cultural change have altered the picturesque landscape described above. Nevertheless, the basic economic pursuit of cultivation of crops continues in the coastal plain of Kerala, although on a limited or declining scale at present.

Describing the agricultural practice of the coast, the CESS notes that cultivation of paddy, coconut and other mixed crops like mango, jackfruit, cashew and arecanut as predominant. In the present section, the effort is to describe only the trend in the cultivation of paddy and coconut in the region.

6.1.4.1. Cultivation of paddy

Referring to the paddy cultivation practice in the state, the Kerala State Gazetteer noted in 1989 that 'paddy cultivation extends over nearly 23 per cent of the total cropped area. The main rice growing tracts are: the coastal saline area including the *kaippad* or *pokkali* areas in central Kerala, the central laterite region which runs parallel to the sea between the coastal belt and the Ghats; the sandy loam tract of Onattukara; the Kuttanad submerged area (the Netherlands of Kerala) and the upland paddy area which consists of long narrow winding paddy fields in the valleys between the hills. In all these parts the crop is raised as a rainfed crop, though irrigation facilities are now being provided on an increasing scale.

The cultivation of paddy in the backwater or Kayal areas present special features ... No crop can be grown in these parts during the monsoon season when inland water flood the lakes. Cultivation is also not possible after April when the sea water enters the areas. To control the flow of water, strong bunds are constructed and a number of water channels are provided to drain the overflow.

Near Trichur, about 8,100 hectares of paddy area are under *Kole* cultivation which is a peculiar system of cultivating paddy under submerged conditions. At the end of the monsoon, water inside the large lakes is pumped out with the help of water wheels or power-driven pumps which are kept working day and night. Afterwards, field bunds are formed, the land is prepared for cultivation, and paddy seedlings are transplanted. Occasionally during the pre-monsoon showers, the area gets flooded. When this happens the excess water is removed by using water wheels. Sometimes, even harvesting has to be done in boats ...

The Kuttanad lake area extends over 750 km^2 and the bottom of the lake is several inches below the sea level. The area remains submerged for greater part of the year and is de-watered after the monsoon is over. There are special large sluice gates which can be opened and shut to let the flood water flow into the sea and to prevent seawater flooding the lake. All the habitations in the area are situated on islands of varying sizes and the only communication between them is through boats. Rice cultivation in Kuttanad is a demonstration of what human endeavour can accomplish even without elaborate equipment. The area is divided into blocks of convenient sizes (20 to 80 hectares each) with embankments all around built with the mud taken from the bottom of the lake. Immediately after the monsoon period, the water is pumped out of the blocks with the help of electric pumps till only a few inches of it are left. The soil is then puddled and levelled and sown with paddy. The water in the channels surrounding the blocks is always at a higher level and can be turned into fields whenever needed. Only varieties that take 100 to 120 days to mature are grown. The area is divided into three classes, viz. *punja*, *kayal*, and *kari*, according to the physical conditions and the varieties grown. Yields of thousand kilograms of paddy per hectare are not uncommon. Ploughing is done soon after harvest ..' (ibid, pp.33-35).

Explaining the practice of paddy cultivation in the saline soil, the Gazetteer states, 'paddy cultivation in saline soils is a unique system prevalent in Kerala. Popular in the coastal belt of the state, nearly two-thirds of this *Pokkali* cultivation is in Ernakulam district. The name is synonymous with *Kaipad* cultivation in Cannanore district and the *Kariland* cultivation in Alleppey district which are the other two major districts adopting this type of cultivation.

It is estimated that nearly 20,000 hectares of saline soils are under cultivation in Ernakulam district, 2,000 hectares in Alleppey district and 2,000 hectares in Cannanore district. All the other coastal districts put together have about 1,400 hectares of land under this type of cultivation.

The lands for *Pokkali* cultivation are low lying marshes and swamps situated near the estuaries of streams and rivers not far from the sea. They are water logged with a poor drainage system and are subject to tidal action throughout the year with a tidal amplitude of about one metre. The soil is stiff impervious clay but rich in organic matter. It is bluish black in colour and is hard and creates deep fissures when dry and sticky when wet.

More than 95 per cent of the total area are single crop lands. These lands are cultivated during the first crop season (*Viruppu*), from May-June to September-October ... After the harvest these lands can be used for fisheries which enables the farmer to make extra money ....' (ibid, pp.36-37).

Cultivation of paddy in the wetlands of Kerala had developed much earlier and it was reported to be part of a colonial strategy to extract surplus (land revenue) from the farmers. Writing on this scheme, Tharakan observes that 'expansion of cultivable land was encouraged, not only in plantations but also in non-plantation commercial crops and even in areas for cultivation of food crops on a commercial scale, as in land reclamation for paddy. Since the policy followed towards piantations was not drastically different from that followed for non-plantation agriculture, the colonial interest could be accommodated within the same policy framework' (Tharakan, 1999, p. 372). Much of this reclamation was in the former Travancore State.

Tharakan further notes that 'the reclamation of backwater areas for paddy cultivation in Thiruvitamkur was in the Kuttanad region spread across Alappuzha and Kottayam divisions. Reclamation from the 'swamps near the coast' which was to be known as *Kayal Krishi* was part of the comprehensive scheme for increasing the output of wealth in the state envisaged by Sir T.Madhava Rao who was the Dewan between 1858 and 1870 ... Various schemes of encouragement such as tax exemptions and liberal loans were offered to land reclaimers. The estimates of total land reclaimed was around 20,000 acres in the first stage and around 50,000 acres in the second stage'. (ibid, pp. 372-373).

Referring to the land reclamation scheme, the Kerala State Gazetteer notes that 'the reclamation of paddy lands from water in Kuttanad was the child of necessity as the region was densely populated and suffered from a chronic deficit in food supply from early times. Records show that from 1009 M.E. (1833 BP) if not from an earlier period, reclamation has been going on. The general consensus of opinion is that the entire area now known as Kuttanad in the erstwhile North Travancore has emerged as a result of reclamation activities by the ryots spread over several centuries. During the eighties of the last (nineteenth) century, the pressure of an increasing population on the available food supply compelled the state also to pay increasing attention to reclamation projects to extend the area under rice cultivation.

Activity was mainly directed towards changing the water courses. The proximity of the low lying rice belt to the backwater and the sea made the intrusion of salinity a source of perennial danger in many area and considerably diminished the yield from the lands. The reclamation schemes were mostly intended to bring more lands under the rice crop and improve the yield of the existing fields by putting up barriers against the entry of brackish water from the lakes and seas and channelling the flow of freshwater from the river system to these fields. A considerable area was reclaimed in this manner for rice cultivation.

Reclamation of land from water for paddy cultivation was not confined to Kuttanad; it was practised on an extensive scale in the Cochin area of Kerala also. In Cochin there are several freshwater lakes whose beds have come to be known as *Kole* lands. The most important of these lakes are the Ennomakkal and the Mangara lakes in the Trichur taluk, which are connected by a canal and are fed by the three rivers, Karavanoor, Viyyur and Vadakkancherry. Besides these there are smaller lakes like Muriyan in Mukundapuram and the Kattampal in Thalappally. All these lakes have been reclaimed and brought under the plough. The system of cultivation is called *Kole Krishi*. The low lying lands, known as the 'rice bowls' of the state are spread over three districts, viz. Alleppey, Kottayam and Trichur. The portion in Alleppey and Kottayam districts form the Kuttanad area and that in Trichur, the *Kole* lands. The low lying lands in Kerala have more or less similar characteristics. The cultivation practices-starting from bunding and dewatering to harvesting and threshing-adopted by the cultivators in those two regions are the same.

The low lying lands in Kerala are man-made in the sense that these lands are product of land reclamation work undertaken in *Kayals* (backwater) and other water logged areas. The land reclamation in Kerala has a long history in its back, though its exact period of origin has yet to be traced out. But *Kayal* reclamation, the main part of land reclamation work and of recent origin was started since 1833. The pioneering attempt of large scale *Kayal* reclamation was started in Kuttanad region. Lured by the successful reclamation work and profitable paddy cultivation in Kuttanad area, some enterprising farmers (some were farmers in the Kuttanad area) slowly turned their attention to similar water logged areas, comprising a number of *Kayals* in Trichur area, which have later come to be known as *Kole* lands.

Reclamation in small patches has been attempted by agriculturists of the state on their own accord in several regions. But the heavy financial outlay necessary, the risk involved and the inherent uncertainty of sure success have stood in the way of a large scale or planned reclamation scheme being taken up by the ryots themselves. Hence this has to be taken up at the state level.

The Kuttanad in Alleppey district, the *Kole* lands in Trichur district and Kattampally swamp in Cannanore district are vast areas that are amenable to reclamation. Paravoor Kayal reclamation, Korapuzha reclamation, Vellayani reclamation and the Mattancherry reclamation schemes are some of the smaller schemes sponsored by the state' (Kerala Gazetteer Department, 1989, pp. 5-7).

The extent of lands that could be reclaimed from the water-logged marshes of the state was roughly assessed as 1,21,000 hectares (ibid, p.13). It is interesting to note here that during the second half of the last century, the Government of Kerala had implemented several programmes to promote cultivation of paddy in the state including legislation to prevent the conversion of paddy fields to other uses. It, nevertheless, appears that in the course of the changing national economic scenario and the prevailing situation in Kerala, the cultivation of paddy as a main agricultural crop has suffered severe setback in the state. This is reflected in the declining area under paddy cultivation in the state as shown in table 6.19.

Table 6.19 makes it clear that the aggregate area under paddy cultivation in the state has come down from 5.59 lakh hectares in 1990-91 to 3.52 lakh hectares in 1998-99, showing a decrease of about 37 per cent. At the district level, the percentage decrease was more in Thiruvananthapuram, Malappuram, Pathanamthitta, Thrissur, Kottayam, Kasargod, Kozhikode, Kollam, Alappuzha, etc. in that order. The other districts also showed relative decrease in the area under paddy cultivation, ranging fron 21.16 per cent to 29.12 per cent, the lowest percentage being in Ernakulam district.

The deteriorating trend in paddy cultivation in Kerala is further illustrated by the falling output of paddy as indicated in table 6.20.

It is evident from table 6.20 that the production of paddy in Kerala decreased from 10.86 lakhs tonnes in 1990-91 to 7.26 lakh tonnes in 1998-99, marking a decrease of 33.16 per cent. At the district level, the percentage decrease was again the maximum in Thiruvananthapuram district, followed by Malappuram, Kozhikode, Kottayam, Kollam, Pathanamthitta, etc. The actual fall in the output was, however, the maximum in Palakkad district where the output fell from 3.24 lakh tonnes in 1990-91 to 2.37 lakh tonnes in 1998-99. Significant fall in the output was noted in Thrissur, Alappuzha, Malappuram, Kollam and Thiruvananthapuram districts.

What is emerging from this apparent declining trend in the cultivated area and production of paddy in Kerala is the un-

Table 6.19
Area under paddy cultivation in Kerala from 1990-91 to 1998- 99

(Area in hectares)

S.No.	District	*1990-91*	*1991-92*	*1992-93*	*1993-94*	*1994-95*	*1995-96*	*1996-97*	*1997-98*	*1998-99*	*Decrease in 1998-99 over 1990-91 (per cent)*
1.	Thiruvananthapuram	21677	19604	18361	18103	17338	16986	13961	11368	9538	55.72
2.	Kollam	30513	27619	28460	26775	25202	23252	22223	20023	17571	42.41
3.	Pathanamthitta	14234	13153	12892	12191	11045	10860	10985	8267	7497	47.33
4.	Alappuzha	60675	55872	53344	50781	54864	44132	41447	43220	35125	42.10
5.	Kottayam	26257	23855	25448	24696	25006	24878	20200	13754	14393	45.18
6.	Idukki	5078	4851	4397	3648	4696	4660	5099	4068	3846	24 26
7.	Ernakulam	63078	65001	66158	61287	60018	56533	53988	46152	49730	21.16
8.	Thrissur	74038	69065	67151	63508	62144	58703	51544	40977	39215	47.05
9.	Palakkad	145687	147066	146095	139769	140066	135630	128359	120809	107467	26.23
10.	Malappuram	51934	50361	50908	43844	42063	37919	31098	28936	23818	54.13
11.	Kozhikode	12062	11535	10755	10162	8457	8749	8316	7988	6843	43.26
12.	Wayanad	20343	19582	21135	20946	22772	20388	17078	17926	15642	23.10
13.	Kannur	19582	20333	18334	18149	17302	16801	15421	15648	13878	29.12
14.	Kasargode	14292	13430	14170	13973	12237	11659	11107	7986	8008	43.96
	Total	**559450**	**541327**	**537608**	**507832**	**503290**	**471150**	**430826**	**387122**	**352631**	**36.96**

Source: Directorate of Economics and Statistics, 2001, p.37.

Table 6.20

Trend in the production of paddy in Kerala from 1990-91 to 1998-99

(Tonnes)

S.No.	*District*	*1990-91*	*1991-92*	*1992-93*	*1993-94*	*1994-95*	*1995-96*	*1996-97*	*1997-98*	*1998-99*	*Decrease in 1998-99 over 1990-91 (per cent)*
1.	Thiruvananthapuram	38363	33553	34816	31920	30216	31831	24877	19610	17689	53.89
2.	Kellam	58385	46086	54576	50265	46829	45370	42237	36051	33311	42.94
3.	Pathanamthitta	33226	30517	33826	29852	24984	27210	23690	18534	19467	41.41
4.	Alappuzha	131663	116089	123178	110870	99240	121047	85192	95128	91681	30.36
5.	Kottayam	62719	55166	60798	59860	56102	55609	43728	29029	35658	43.14
6.	Idukki	10953	10932	9188	7651	10098	10817	10578	8468	8995	17.86
7.	Ernakulam	102689	109484	113927	101346	101048	101951	93382	74234	84529	17.68
8.	Thrissur	129287	121723	119337	109626	114060	110698	104966	82991	74190	42.61
9.	Palakkad	324907	344738	335646	316947	313768	280405	294065	262494	237788	26.81
10.	Malappuram	80830	80346	82132	71204	70825	65208	53443	48317	42341	47.61
11.	Kozhikode	14834	13781	13008	12685	10543	10593	10429	9655	7834	47.18
12.	Wayanad	41974	42803	50337	46609	50492	46654	37563	39773	34689	17.35
13.	Kannur	32308	31249	28750	29085	26066	26050	26599	25461	22540	30.23
14.	Kasargode	24440	23883	25359	26018	20794	19583	20612	14905	16031	34.40
	Total	**1086578**	**1060350**	**1084878**	**1003938**	**975065**	**953026**	**871361**	**764610**	**726743**	**33.16**

Source: Directorate of Economics and Statistics, 2001, p.67.

sustainability of the activity. This is manifest in the growing area under current fallow and the economic compulsions for converting paddy fields into non-agricultural lands or aquaculture fields. The area under current fallow has in fact increased from 44,200 hectares in 1990-91 to 68,022 hectares in 1998-99 marking an increase of 53.39 per cent (Directorate of Economics and Statistics, 2001, p.28). The socio-economic impacts of this development in the paddy sector has been amply revealed in the continuing crisis in the Kuttanad region, where it blew out a couple of years back, leading to the destruction of plantation crops and fish farms. The need for an ICM approach taking into account the larger economic and non-economic value of paddy cultivation is indicated for sustainable development of the coastal area.

6.1.4.2. Cultivation of coconut

The palm-fringed coast of Kerala is known for its crop of coconut. Referring to its cultivation in Travancore, the Travancore State Manual notes that 'the coconut palm is the second most important crop. It is the chief money crop of the state and forms one of the main sources of revenue. The palm is a perennial which takes ten years to come into commercial production and then continues to yield profitably for about fifty years. Long before the trees cease to be productive, under-planting is possible so that the area once planted with coconuts remains under the same crop ever afterwards. Coconut products constitute the bulk of our exports. The tree supplies raw materials for several industries. The taxes on this palm bring in more than a fourth of the land revenues and the export duties on coconut products about one half of the customs revenue. The crop occupies more than a fourth of the total cultivated area. Indeed the coconut has been aptly described as the wealth of Travancore.

The coconut palm grows almost everywhere. In the lowlands, coconut forms one of the main crops. The midlands and the slopes of the high lands are also best suited for its cultivation. The seaboard, the shores of the lagoons and the banks of the river are studded with coconut trees. Coconut cultivation is now extended to higher elevations about forty to fifty miles from the sea ...

According to the official estimates, the area under coconut cultivation in 1934-35 was 5,65,590 acres, which was about fifty per cent higher than what it was sixteen years previously ... The cultivation is not on a plantation scale. The palm is grown in every back garden and is in fact ubiquitous ... more than forty per cent of the Indian coconut area lies in Travancore' (Velu Pillai, 1940, Reprint, 1996, pp.350-351).

The Manual also wrote about the problems affecting the coconut farmers and the industry during the early decades of the last century (ibid, pp.617-621). The major problems noted were the rising cost of cultivation, pests and diseases and competition from abroad. It seems that all these problems are still threatening coconut cultivation in Kerala. It would be appropriate at this stage to look at the trend in the cultivation of coconut in recent years in Kerala. Table 6.21 shows the trend in the area under cultivation of coconut from 1990-91 to 1998-99.

Table 6.21 reveals that the area under coconut cultivation in the state had increased from 8.7 lakh hectare. In 1990-91 to 9.14 lakh hectare in 1995-96 and then decreased to 8.82 lakh hectares in 1998-99. The increase from 1990-91 to 1998-99 amounted to only 1.40 per cent. At the district level, there were ups and downs in the area cultivated in most districts, but looking at 1990-91 and 1998-99 positions, it appears that all the southern districts, except Thiruvananthapuram and Idukki showed a decline in the area under coconut. Ernakulam and Malappuram districts also showed a net decline in the area under coconut. All the northern districts except Malappuram showed an increase in the area. The percentage increase was the highest in Wayanad followed by Idukki. The actual quantum of increase was, however, the maximum in Kozhikode district. The fact that the southern districts and the two other districts of Malappuram and Ernakulam are showing a net decrease in the area under coconut in recent years is indicative of the un-sustainability of the activity for various reasons. This can be further probed by looking at the trend in the production of coconut in the state. Table 6.22 gives the trend in the production of coconut in Kerala from 1990-91 to 1998-99.

Table 6.22 shows a very unsteady trend in the production of coconut in the state. Total production showed some increase upto 1994-95 when the output increased to 5336 million nuts, which thereafter fluctuated to come down to 5132 million nuts in 1998-99. Taking the 1990-91 and 1998-99 positions alone, it amounted to an increase of 21.26 per cent. At the district level, as in the case of area under coconut, all the southern districts, except Thiruvananthapuram and Idukki showed a decrease in the output in 1998-99 over the 1990-91 level of output. There were some ups and

Table 6.21
Area under coconut cultivation in Kerala from 1990-91 to 1998-99

(Area in hectares)

S.No.	District	1990-91	1991-92	1992-93	1993-94	1994-95	1995-96	1996-97	1997-98	1998-99	Change in 1998-99 over 1990-91 (percent)
1.	Thiruvananthapuram	85581	82907	86601	87976	89706	91667	89028	84308	91271	6.64
2.	Kollam	77874	75454	76658	76661	81523	81034	79374	79523	75614	-2.90
3.	Pathanamthitta	27505	26850	25635	22597	25807	23712	23346	22056	219 94	-20.03
4.	Alappuzha	66664	65254	67501	64478	68495	67030	63852	61662	58621	-12.06
5.	Kottayam	47217	46012	44992	41531	40765	40333	39603	38198	42571	-9.83
6.	Idukki	14864	16356	17298	16374	16676	17510	19261	20830	21444	44.26
7.	Ernakulam	66264	64359	65201	63900	61241	62502	69525	64816	61719	-6.85
8.	Thrissur	80856	84789	85600	87118	86206	85133	83978	76656	81171	0.38
9.	Palakkad	38153	37090	39514	43703	45503	48336	46037	48929	45439	19.09
10.	Malappuram	10245	99535	98931	103057	1067 89	106696	103924	102872	99276	-2.90
11.	Kozhikode	122062	122193	122007	119611	125709	122838	124584	122379	129506	6.09
12.	Wayanad	4510	5347	5605	6680	6980	8400	8930	9479	9948	120.57
13.	Kannur	91893	90113	93304	98579	99625	98977	98630	97365	95118	3.50
14.	Kasargode	44334	46802	48165	50028	55933	60197	55632	55271	48596	9.61
	Total	**870022**	**863061**	**877012**	**882293**	**910963**	**914370**	**902104**	**834344**	**882288**	1.40

Source: Department of Economics and Statistics, 2001, p.57.

Table 6.22
Trend in the production of coconut in Kerala from 1990-91 to 1998-99

(in million nuts)

S.No.	*District*	*1990-91*	*1991-92*	*1992-93*	*1993-94*	*1994-95*	*1995-96*	*1996-97*	*1997-98*	*1998-99*	*Change in 1998-99 over 1999-91 (per cent*
1.	Thiruvananthapuram	453	521	517	587	524	481	530	516	555	22.51
2.	Kollam	364	343	398	397	430	401	368	374	350	-3.84
3.	Pathanamthitta	145	135	141	137	128	142	135	121	118	-18.62
4.	Alappuzha	295	306	307	297	347	336	302	247	288	-2.37
5.	Kottayam	195	217	203	204	176	160	178	156	171	-12.30
6.	Idukki	63	72	85	79	71	75	67	78	87	38.09
7.	Ernakulam	346	370	432	414	389	370	402	357	345	-0.28
8.	Thrissur	465	546	634	588	614	539	566	491	534	14.83
9.	Palakkad	130	137	163	182	166	183	202	237	194	49.23
10.	Malappuram	456	500	580	601	577	558	669	634	600	31.57
11.	Kozhikode	644	751	908	814	936	925	900	929	999	55.12
12.	Wayanad	6	6	8	12	14	16	26	26	25	316.66
13.	Kannur	436	499	498	588	631	578	625	642	529	21.33
14.	Kasargode	234	238	250	292	333	391	306	402	337	44.01
	Total	**4232**	**4641**	**5124**	**5192**	**5336**	**5155**	**5276**	**5210**	**5132**	**21.26**

Source: Department of Economics and Statistics, 2001, p.83.

downs in the intervening years in most of these districts. Ernakulam district also showed a net decrease in its output. All the other districts registered a general increase in the output of coconut. The percentage increase was highest in Wayanad district but in real terms the increase was maximum in Kozhikode district where the number of nuts produced increased from 644 million nuts in 1990-91 to 999 million nuts in 1998-99.

The fact that the southern districts in general, with the possible exception of Thiruvananthapuram and Idukki are lagging in the cultivation of coconut in the state indicates of a deep rooted anomaly which has implications for the sustainable development of the region. This trend, combined with the declining trend in the cultivation of paddy in all districts of the state presents an alarming situation as far as coastal agriculture is concerned. It may be noted here that this trend needs special attention in the ICM programmes for Kerala.

6.1.5. Coastal mining

Among the known minerals of the Kerala coast, the most important are the large deposits of beach sands, glass sands and china clay. Referring to these resources, the 'Fifth Five Year Plan - Draft Outline' notes that 'extensive deposits of white quartz sands occur around Sherthallai taluk and they have been estimated at 70 million tonnes. Investigations also revealed sizeable occurrence of graphite in Thodupuzha, Neyyattinkara and Nedumangad taluks. Bauxite also occurs in certain areas in the Trivandrum, Quilon and Cannanore districts. The estimate of China clay deposits has been placed at 72.4 million tonne...." (State Planning Board, 1973, p.322).

Much earlier, referring to these resources in the Travancore region before the formation of the unified state of Kerala in 1956, Velu Pillai noted that 'the mineral possibilities of Travancore are great. So far they have been only insufficiently exploited. The sands of the beach contain some of the most valuable minerals. The deposits of monozite are by far the richest in the world both in regard to the quantity available and the proportion of the thoria content therein. Big deposits of graphite have been found in the Nedumangad taluk and it is expected that unworked deposits are still available for exploitation. Travancore plumbage should be an attractive proposition to an adventurous spirit ... The mica that has been exploited in the state by different people at various times is what is known to minerologists as Phlogopite Mica, usually amber coloured ..' (Velu Pillai, 1940, reprint 1996, p. 536).

Elaborating further, this writer states that 'all these minerals pale into insignificance in comparison with some of the so-called rare minerals in which Travancore is rich; and one or two of them she is holding a practical monopoly in the mineral industry of the whole world ... of these, the best known is monozite, a phosphate and silicate of the rare earths ceria, yttria, lanthana and didymia, while thoria is invariably present in varying proportions. The associated minerals, ilmenite and zircon, are finding an increasing market in Europe and America. Monozite is found in the pegmatites running through the granites of the country in association with mica, ilmenite, magnatite, zircon and other minerals and the deposits of workable concentration should be ultimately traced to these pegmatites, small or large, occurring all over the country along the sea-shore ... The black mineral found in such large deposits near Kolithottam, Panmana, Chavara and Neendakara ... is an iron titanium oxide ... and a very prosperous industry has grown around ilmenite as the only commercial source of titanium oxide; and Travancore with her vast deposits of ilmenite sand easily worked and cheaply transported has taken the leading place for feeding the industry ... Besides the above minerals, indications are not wanting that uranium, radium and tantalum minerals do occur in Travancore ... A very minor industry seems to centre round chrysoberyl or cat's eye in the neighbourhood of Trivandrum,... Chalcedony in blocks occur near Athappallam in Kalkulam taluk' (ibid, pp. 537-540).

Reporting on the precise situation in the mineral industry in Travancore, Velu Pillai stated that 'Travancore is not rich in minerals, though it possesses some of the most valuable and rare ones. Monazite, ilmenite and zircon are finding an increased market in Europe and America. Graphite, magnetite and mica are also found in certain localities ... There are several companies in the state carrying on mineral industry. For years mineral licenses were granted by the state. Whole areas have been leased out. Of late it has been realised that there was a tremendous amount of buying and selling of lands and speculative application for mineral licenses' (ibid, p.46).

Most interestingly, this writer reported the speech of the Dewan objecting to the unscrupulous speculation by private sector in the mineral mining sector. The Dewan's speech noted thus: 'we came to the conclusion that this kind of thing must stop and that the state must derive an adequate revenue, an adequate share of the profits which the people are making ... the production and marketing of ilmenite and silliminite are in the hands of a world combine. Until the facts are ascertained and our fair share of profit ascertained, the Government do not propose to hand over any of the mineral resources to prospectors. Of course we are bound to honour the contracts that have already been entered into, we are bound to carry out in the spirit and in the letter the contracts which are existent. No new licenses will be given to anybody unless Government after investigation are able to see what are the net profits which the venting can bring and what is the proper share which Government might obtain from that amount. This policy again is in furtherance of the idea that these being natural monopolies of the state, they must be exploited to the best advantage and the state must get the best profit out of it' (ibid, p.46).

The above policy of the state seems to have practical relevance even today when natural resources of the coast are being opened for private sector investment. It is also of significance in view of the widespread public objection to privatisation of mineral sand mining in the coastal zones of Kerala (Thomas, 7.7.2002). Indiscriminate mining of uranium-rich beach sand, Karimanal, from Kayamkulam Pozhi was challenged in the Kerala High Court in June 2001 (*The New Indian Express*, Cochin, 20.7.2001). The threat posed by sand mining on the shore, to beach ecology at the coastal stretch from Arattupuzha to Thottappilly in Alappuzha district, was reported in August 2002 (*The New Indian Express*, Cochin, 6.8.2002).

It is significant to note here that the State Government have been leasing out vast stretches of the coastal areas for mining of minerals. Table 6.23 gives details of area leased out for mining of minerals during 1999-00.

Table 6.23
Details of area leased out for mining of minerals during 1999-00.

S.No.	*Minerals*	*Area (ha.)*
1.	Clay	96.42
2.	Silica sand	44.65
3.	Bauxite	1.37
4.	Graphite	0.59
5.	Limeshell	1786.39
6.	Limestone	247.50
7.	Mineral sand	286.84
8.	Quartz	6.01
	Total	**2469.87**

Source: State Planning Board, 2001, p. S.135.

The table shows that the major part of the area leased out was for lime shell mining. Next bulk area leased out was for mineral sand mining. Table 6.24 shows details of production and sale of mineral sand in Kerala during 1999-00.

Table 6.24
Details of production and sale of mineral sand in Kerala during 1999-00

S.No.	*Name of mineral*	*Production (tonnes)*	*Sales value (Rs lakhs)*
1.	Ilmenite	136908.74	3786.42
2.	Rutile	9201.00	2941.50
3.	Zircon	14037.00	1747.09
4.	Silimenite	9595.00	244.79
5.	Lencorene	745.00	165.22
6.	Zirflor	4920.00	942.09
7.	Microzir 1 and 10	106.00	1.74
	Total	**175512.74**	**9828.85**

Source: State Planning Board, 2001, p.S.135.

Apart from the above, it is reported that the Government is embarking on a policy of extracting and processing marine sand for construction purposes with private sector participation (*The New Indian Express*, Cochin). The impact of this development on beach ecology and beach stability has to be considered before venturing for such programmes. Here again, the need for an ICM approach to development is called for.

6.1.6. Manufacturing industries

The coastal zones of Kerala can also boast of a couple of traditional and modern manufacturing industries. Among the traditional industries are coir manufacturing and cashew processing. Among the modern industries are fish processing, and fertilizers and chemicals. A brief account of these industries is given in this section.

6.1.6.1. Coir manufacturing

Coir manufacturing is one of the major traditional industries in Kerala. It provides employment to about 3,83,394 workers of whom 3,22,793 (84 per cent) are women (State Planning Board, 2001, p.114). Referring to the concentration of this industry in the coastal zones of Kerala, the Kerala Gazetteer notes that, 'the lakes, the lagoons, and the backwaters fringed with coconut palms apart from imparting to Kerala its scenic beauty and providing one of the chief tourist attraction, provide the means of livelihood to a vast section

Table 6.25

Main centres of coir retting, production and varieties of coir produced in Kerala

S. No.	Variety of coir	Centres of production	Area of retting
1.	*Anjengo*	Paravoor, Nedunganda, Vakkom, Kadakkavoor, Chirayinkeezhu, Anjengo, Perumthura, Azhoor, Kaniapuram, Murukkumpuzha, Panathara	Brackish water lagoons and lakes from Mayyanad to Thiruvallam
2.	*Ashtamudi*	Kallada, Munroe island, Perumon	Ashtamudi lake and coastal areas
3.	*Mannu Mangadan*	Chavara, Kavanad, Neendakara	Backwaters of Chavara, Kavanad and Needakara
4.	*Mangadan*	Mangad, Asramom, Kandachira, Perinad, Prakulam, Chavara South, Thevalakara, Kozhivila	Backwaters
5.	*Alappadan*	Alunkadavu, Cheriazheekal, Marthoorkulangara Alappaduthura	Lake and beach sides of Karunagapally and Karthikapally taluk
6.	*Chavara Alappadan*	Thevalakkara	Lakes and backwaters
7.	*Aratory*	Arattupuzha, Mahadevikad, Mangalam, Karuvatta, Chingoli, Pallana, Muthukulam	Kayamkulam lake and the coastal areas of Karthikapally taluk
8.	*Vaikom*	Vaikom, Sherthalai, Vechoor, Thanneermukkom, Chengada, Poochakal, Chempu, Thrinayamkandam, Kumbalangi	Vembanad lake
9.	*Aroor Special*	Aroor, Edacochi, Kumbalangi	Vembanad lake
10.	*Beach Yarn*	Muhamma, Peruneermangalam, Mararikulam, Punnapra, Mannancheri	Ponds and tanks
11.	*Parur Vannam*	Vavakkadu, Chittattukara, Pattanom, Kottapuram	Backwaters and ponds
12.	*Muppiri*	Manavalakurichi, Ethamboli, Thiruvallom	Backwaters and ponds
13.	*M.K. Yarn*	Kumbalangi, Manasseri, Anthikadavu	Backwaters
14.	*Rope Yarn*	Kandasankadavu, Manallor	Backwaters and lakes
15.	*Thin Rope yarn*	Maradu, Chittoor, Elankunnapuzha	Backwaters and lakes

Source: Kerala Gazetteers Department, 1989, pp. 531-534.

of the population. Coir industry is located in the state primarily because of the natural retting facilities provided by the backwaters. The availability of these facilities is unique in the case of Kerala. In almost all other coconut growing areas of India, the coconut husks go waste because of the absence of natural retting facilities. Though the origin of the industry dates back to the 15th century, the industry owes its rise to the pioneering efforts of a few European firms, the first of which was established in 1859' (Kerala Gazetteer Department, 1989, p.329). The Gazetteer also notes that 'in the early phases. the manufacture of coir yarn was a cottage industry in which women of the lower income groups/weaker sections of society predominated as it was a source of supplementing their meagre earnings. Hand spinning alone was carried on. The spinning wheel was unknown at this stage ... The spinning wheel was probably introduced by the adventurous Portuguese, Dutch and English colonisers who came into close contact with the people of coastal areas like Fort Cochin and Anjengo. The manufacture of coir-yarns on a commercial scale and the export of the yarn and mats and mattings manufactured out of it to outside countries, might have been an aftermath of the introduction of the spinning wheel' (ibid, p.330). Perhaps it might be the result of the ingenious ways of the Europeans to tap the resources for their advantage. The main centres of coir retting, production and varieties of coir produced in Kerala are noted in table 6.25.

Table 6.25 indicates the wide distribution of the coir producing centres and their proximity and dependence on the coastal backwater system and lakes. The coir producing centres in the northern districts of the state do not find a place in this listing. In spite of this, it can be argued here that the sustainability of this industry is very much dependent on the coastal wetlands and the backwaters.

The coir industry in Kerala consists of two major sectors, namely, the spinning sector and the manufacturing sector. The former sector accounts for over 3.50 lakh workers while the latter accommodates only 30,000 workers (State Planning Board, 2001, p.114).

The main thrust of the Government's programmes for the development of the coir industry in Kerala was to modernise the operation of spinning the yarn and to strengthen the coir cooperatives to protect the interests of the workers. As part of the modernisation of coir industry, machines have been developed for spinning of yarn and for extraction of fibre from green husk without retting process. As a result of the Government's active support to the coir cooperatives, there were about 803 coir cooperatives in the state as on 31.3.2000. Of these, 500 were active, 74 newly registered, 95 dormant and 134 under liquidation. Table 6.26 gives details of coir cooperative societies working in Kerala as on 31.3.2000.

Table 6.26
Details of coir cooperative societies working in Kerala as on 31.3.2000

S. No.	*District*	*Project office*	*No. of coir societies*		
			New and active	*Dormant*	*Total*
1.	Thiruvananthapuram	Chirayinkil	60	6	66
2.	Kollam	Kollam	99	28	127
3.	Alappuzha	Alappuzha	107	18	125
		Kayamkulam	79	2	81
4.	Kottayam }	Vaikom			
5.	Idukki }		29	1	30
6.	Ernakulam	North Paravoor	24	10	34
7.	Thrissur	Thrissur	27	4	31
8.	Malappuram }	Ponnani	27	2	29
9.	Palakkad }				
10.	Kozhikode	Kozhikode	73	16	89
11.	Kannur }	Kannur	49	8	57
12.	Kasargode }				
	Total		**574**	**95**	**669**

Source: State Planning Board, 2001, p.S. 122.

Table 6.26 indicates a fair distribution of coir cooperatives in all the districts except Wayanad and Pathanamthitta. The economic importance of these societies can be better understood from the activities undertaken by these societies. Table 6.27 shows details of activities undertaken by coir cooperative societies in Kerala during 1998-99 and 1999-00.

Table 6.27

Details of activities undertaken by coir cooperative societies in Kerala during 1998-99 and 1999-00.

S. No.	Details	1998-99	1999-00
(a) Primary societies (yarn sector)			
1.	No. of working societies	424	437
2.	No. of workers ('000)	281	275
3.	Husk purchased		
	(a) Number (lakhs)	686	615
	(b) Value (Rs. lakhs)	333	327
4.	Fibre purchased		
	(a) Quantity (tonnes)	4635	6864
	(b) Value (Rs. lakhs)	596	609
5.	Yarn produced		
	(a) Quantity (tonnes)	9362	10497
	(b)Value (Rs. lakhs)	1978	2438
6.	Wages paid (Rs. lakhs)	967	1401
(b) Manufacturing sector (product sector)			
1.	No. of working societies	34	42
2.	No. of workers	7070	7357
3.	Value of production (Rs. lakhs)	2389	2666
4.	Wages paid (Rs. lakhs)	275	434

Source: State Planning Board, 2001, p.S. 121.

Table 6.27 indicates a slight decrease in the quantity and value of husk purchased by the primary societies during 1999-00. The quantity and value of fibre purchased, however, showed some improvement as also the quantity and value of yarn produced. The number of workers, wages paid and the value of output of the manufacturing societies all showed notable increase.

Table 6.28 shows the trend in productive capital, value of output and value addition in the coir industry of Kerala from 1990-91 to 1996-97.

Table 6.28 indicates a generally rising trend in capital investment, value of output and value addition by the industry, notwithstanding some down swing in certain years. The low capital intensity and high value addition are typical of this industry.

The economic value of the coir industry can be further understood from the trend in the export of coir and coir products.

Table 6.28

Trend in productive capital, value of output and value addition in coir industry in Kerala from 1990-91 to 1996-97

(Rs in lakhs)

S. No.	*Item*	*1990-91*	*1991-92*	*1992-93*	*1993-94*	*1994-95*	*1995-96*	*1996-97*
1.	Productive Capital	1719.73	596.91	1872.92	1659.64	6743.78	4162.13	8348.24
2.	Value of output	4325.68	6496.32	8670.18	3914.45	23031.46	13878.45	18216.20
3.	Value addition	915.16	1065.80	878.47	1087.81	3515.37	3756.74	4122.03

Source: Directorate of Economics and Statistics, 2001, pp.180-183.

Table 6.29 shows the trend in the export of coir and coir products from India from 1993-94 to 1999-00.

Table 6.29
Trend in the export of coir and coir products from india from 1993-94 to 1999-00

S. No.	Year	Quantity (tonnes)	Value (Rs. Crores)
1.	1993-94	37951	129.37
2.	1994-95	48086	171.64
3.	1995-96	48277	206.84
4.	1996-97	46369	212.58
5.	1997-98	49850	238.93
6.	1998-99	55490	292.19
7.	1999-00	61031	303.05

Source: State Planning Board, 2001, p.147.

Table 6.29 indicates a significant growth in the quantity and value of coir and coir products exported from the country, the bulk of which is contributed by Kerala. About 98 per cent of the coir products exported from India is from Kerala. Maintaining this trend is vital for the sustenance of large sections of the coastal population which are directly and indirectly dependent on this sector. It may be noted that this sector has strong linkages with the primary agricultural (coconut cultivation) sector and the tertiary transport and marketing sectors. Accordingly, the sustainable development of this sector is of vital importance and concern in any ICM planning for Kerala. The 'externalities' (including pollution) which this sector produce and that other sectors cause to it are also relevant issues which are being considered in the next chapter.

6.1.6.2. Cashew processing

The cashew processing industry has a coveted place in Kerala. The state enjoys a dominant position for this industry in India. Apart from processing cashew kernels, cashew shell oil is also extracted. The industry is concentrated within a radius of 40 kms of Quilon, with a sprinkling of factories in other cashew growing areas of the state and its neighbourhood.

Referring to the beginning of the cashew processing industry in Kerala, the Kerala State Gazetteer notes that 'it was an enterprising industrialist, Mr. Joseph Pereira, who conceived in 1925 the idea of making the cashew industry an organised one' (Kerala State Gazetteer Department, 1989, p.387).

The Gazetteer gives interesting details of the distribution of the factories and their employment. Table 6.30 gives details of the distribution of cashew factories and their employment.

Table 6.30
Distribution of cashew factories in Kerala and their employment as on 1.1.1983

S. No.	*District*	*No. of Factories*	*No. of workers*
1.	Trivandrum	16	9166
2.	Quilon	229	107200
3.	Alleppey	3	6637
4.	Ernakulam	2	346
5.	Trichur	5	2575
6.	Kozhikode	2	719
7.	Cannanore	3	1094
	Total	**260**	**127737**

Source: Kerala Gazetteers Department, 1989, p.338.

The table indicates a high degree of concentration of factories and workers in Quilon district. About 90 per cent of the workforce in the industry are reported to be women. The economic importance of the cashew processing sector can be partly understood from the value of productive capital, output and value added by the sector. Table 6.31 shows the trend in productive capital, value of output and value addition in the cashew processing industry in Kerala from 1990-91 to 1996-97.

Table 6.31 makes it clear that in spite of some annual down-swings, there is an over all increase in the value of productive capital, output and value addition. Here also, the low capital intensity and high value addition are notable.

A general description of the problems prevailing in the cashew processing industry is given in the Gazetteer. It notes that 'although the cashew factories employ a large number of workers, they do not provide continuous employment all through the year. The factories are often shut down owing to insufficiency of raw cashewnuts. In a year the cashew factories could work only for less than 85 days. The Kerala State Cashew Development Corporation was set up in 1969 to relieve the unemployment faced by the workers. As they work today the factories are dependent considerably on imported nuts ... The domestic production is inadequate for sustaining the industry. The internal demand for nuts is negligible. The industry's

Table 6.31

Trend in productive capital, value of output and value addition in the cashew processing industry in Kerala from 1990-91 to 1996-97.

(Rs lakhs)

S. No.	*Item*	*1990-91*	*1991-92*	*1992-93*	*1993-94*	*1994-95*	*1995-96*	*1996-97*
1.	Productive Capital	2571.28	1336.16	3464.13	3657.31	2718.90	7977.85	13229.33
2.	Value of output	36917.70	38063.04	48479.10	45100.61	74155.73	69395.22	87418.37
3.	Value addition	6391.07	8812.32	6660.40	8799.83	12367.64	10821.93	13797.50

Source: Department of Economics and Statistics, 2001, p.183.

Table 6.32

Trend in export of cashew kernels from Kerala and India from 1990-91 to 1999-00

(Quantity in tonnes; Value in Rs crores)

Year	Kerala		India		Share of Kerala (%)	
	Quantity	Value	Quantity	Value	Quantity	Value
1990-91	44060	390.67	49874	442.20	88.00	88.30
1991-92	31630	432.46	47738	669.10	66.00	64.60
1992-93	26981	385.49	53436	745.50	51.00	51.70
1993-94	30684	454.66	69884	1046.00	44.00	43 50
1994-95	34379	538.11	77000	1246.30	45.00	43.20
1995-96	33275	606.55	70334	1240.50	47.00	48.90
1996-97	38546	731.79	68663	1285.50	56.00	56.90
1997-98	39441	746.88	76593	1396.10	52.00	54.00
1998-99	43665	940.47	77076	1360.00	57.00	57.70
1999-00*	48599	1317.20	92461	2451.50	53.00	53.70

* *Provisional*

Source: State Planning Board, 2001, p.S.173.

progress is conditioned by the changing preferences of the importing countries like U.S.A., U.S.S.R. and Japan. Fluctuations in the external price level has repercussions of a harmful nature for the industry' (ibid, pp. 333-339).

Table 6.32 shows the recent trends in the export of cashew kernels from Kerala and India.

Table 6.32 indicates an overall improvement in the quantity and value of cashew kernel exported by the state, although its share in the total export of cashew from the country is showing fluctuations both ir. terms of quantity and value. This trend seems to be the result of a heavy dependence on imported nuts for maintaining the exports. Table 6.33 gives details of import of raw cashewnut to Kerala and India from 1995-96 to 1999-00.

Table 6.33

Trend in the import of raw cashewnut to Kerala and India from 1995-96 to 1999-00

(Quantity in Tonnes; Value in Rs Crores)

Year	*Kerala*		*India*		*Share of Kerala (per cent)*	
	Quantity	*Value*	*Quantity*	*Value*	*Quantity*	*Value*
1995-96	6292	19.13	222819	760.08	2.82	2.51
1996-97	49169	159.76	212866	687.60	23.09	23.23
1997-98	70527	237.46	247181	769.60	28.53	30.85
1998-99	109660	448.82	241161	958.00	45.47	46.84
1999-00	97732	485.70	226396	1054.00	43.16	46.08

Source: State Planning Board, 2001, p.146.

It is apparent from table 6.31 that the share of the state in both the quantity and value of raw cashew imported by the country from 1995-96 to 1999-00 has been rising, indicating greater and greater dependence on imported raw material for sustaining the industry. The critical situation prevailing in the industry even earlier had been noted by the Kerala State Gazetteer. It stated that 'the volume of imports which had steeply risen (till 1978) alongside the growth of the industry has now declined owing to various factors like drop in total crop available in the cashew cultivating countries of Africa, development of processing units in these countries, resulting in reduced exports and emergence of China as a potential buyer from Tanzania because of political tie up. The domestic production is inadequate for sustaining the industry...' (Kerala State Gazetteer Department, 1989, p. 339). It appears that the situation in the cashew processing industry continues to be the same in spite of the state's efforts to enhance domestic production and supply of raw cashew nuts in the state.

Notwithstanding the above position, it is significant to note here that sustaining this industry is vital for the coastal community of Kerala, in view of the 'forward' and 'backward' linkages it provides for the growth of 'ancillary industries such as tin factories, saw mills, transport, etc. (ibid, p.338).

Hence the need for integrating this activity in the ICM plan for Kerala is obvious.

6.1.6.3. Fish processing

Fish processing is one of the most important coastal activities of Kerala at present. It is also the leading manufacturing (value adding) activity in the coast having extensive linkage effects. Incidentally, this is one of the coastal activities which is reportedly affected by the coastal zone regulations introduced by the Government of India. This issue is being discussed in chapter eight.

The fish processing industry in Kerala has a chequered history of development. Prior to independence, this industry, using traditional methods of curing and preservation was catering to the needs of colonial trade, especially in dry fish and fish oil. The industry was encouraged by the British by providing duty-free salt and providing enclosures for curing fish at major fish landing centres of the state. This situation continued even after independence for some time.

Referring to the prevailing situation, the Master Plan for Fisheries Development in Kerala, in 1969 noted that 'for preserving fish in a salted and cured state, the Fisheries Department had provided 67 fish curing yards all along the coast. Salt used to be issued to fish curers at subsidised rates. About 8000 tonnes of salt were issued for curing nearly 55,000 tonnes of fish annually. The quantity cured was about 38,000 tonnes per annum. Since the supply of salt from the Government yards was not found necessary, this scheme was abolished but the curers in those yards are allowed to cure their fish. Besides the yards mentioned above, there are innumerable private fish curing sheds in the state where extensive salt curing is done' (Directorate of Fisheries, 1969, p.11).

The changes that took place in the industry after independence have been summarised in the Master Plan. It states that 'prior to the beginning of the First Five Year Plan, there were very little ice and cold storage facilities in the state. However, the period covered by the First and Second Five Year Plans witnessed the ushering in of a number of ice making and freezing plants with facilities for cold storages. The increased demand for frozen products from foreign markets coupled with the greater availability of prawns through trawlers have paved the way for establishing quite a large number of refrigeration plants both in the public and private sectors. For the public sector there are seven ice plants, eight ice-cum-freezing plants and three simple cold storages in the state. In the private sector too, quite a large number of smaller plants has been established. Altogether, the Government owned factories provide facilities for the production of 110 tons of ice per day with cold storage capacity for 303 tonnes of fish, freezing capacity for about 44 tonnes per day and frozen storage capacity of 925 tonnes of fish. The facilities in the private sector are over 370 tonnes per day for the production of ice with cold storage capacity for nearly 260 tonnes of fresh fish, freezing capacity of 62 tonnes per day and frozen fish storage capacity of 820 tonnes of fish. The improved facilities for ice making, cold storage and freezing of fish have not only bettered the quality of fish made available in the interior markets but also promoted a brisk industry in export trade of frozen and canned prawns, lobster tails and frozen frog legs, with a number of foreign countries. In the wake of this improved facilities for handling the produce, about 18 canning factories also have come up doing business in shrimps and sardines' (ibid, pp.11-12).

Ever since the Master Plan made these observations the fish processing industry of the state has undergone fundamental changes in its structure and composition, responding to global changes in the market for its products and technological changes in the developed world. Curious is the fact that the canning sector has been almost fully wiped out. The number of ice plants, cold storages, freezing plants, canning plants and fish meal plants all put together in 1989 was reported to be 410 (Department of Fisheries, 1993, p. 4). This included 18 plants in the public/ cooperative sector and 392 plants in the private sector. Within the private sector, the break-up gives 90 freezing plants, 21 canning plants and 281 ice plants/ cold storages (ibid, pp.4-5).

The details of ice plants, cold storages and freezing plants in the public and cooperative sector is given in table 6.34.

Table 6.34
Details of ice plants, cold storages and freezing plants in the public/cooperative sector in Kerala during 1989

S. No.	District	No. of units	Capacity in tonnes for: Ice production/ day	Ice storage	Fresh fish storage	Freezing/ day	Frozen fish storage
1.	Thiruvananthapuram	2	15	-	-	-	-
2.	Kollam	2	25	-	-	-	-
3.	Alappuzha	2	5	15	16	-	-
4.	Kottayam	2	-	-	2	-	-
5.	Ernakulan	-	-	-	-	-	-
6.	Thrissur	1	5	25	25	-	-
7.	Malappuram	2	15	75	50	-	-
8.	Kozhikode	2	15	75	-	-	-
9.	Kannur	4	80	90	90	6	70
10.	Kasargode	1	5	-	-	-	-
	Total	**18**	**165**	**280**	**183**	**6**	**70**

Source: Department of Fisheries, 1991, pp.146-147.

Table 6.34 shows that a large part of the infrastructure in the public/cooperative sector for processing is located in Kannur, Malappuram, Thrissur and Alappuzha districts. Some of these facilities are reportedly not operating now while the rest are managed by the Matsyafed.

The details of ice plants, cold storages and freezing plants working in the private sector are given in table 6.35.

Table 6.35
Details of ice plants, cold storages and freezing plants in the private sector in Kerala during 1989

S. No.	District	No. of units	Capacity in tonnes for: Ice production/ day	Ice storage	Fresh fish storage	Freezing/ day	Frozen fish storage
1.	Thiruvananthapuram	20	156	35	-	-	-
2.	Kollam	63	684	952	178	168	1913
3.	Alappuzha	78	872	625	17	273	38
4.	Kottayam	54	6	1	18	-	-
5.	Ernakulam	71	410	415	469	521	-
6.	Thrissur	18	108	161	3	-	-
7.	Malappuram	20	162	30	-	-	-
8.	Kozhikode	41	399	115	45	35	1065
9.	Kannur	22	205	285	-	5	50
10.	Kasargode	5	98	150	-	-	-
	Total	**392**	**3100**	**2769**	**730**	**1002**	**3066**

Source: Department of Fisheries, 1991, pp.131-145.

Table 6.35 indicates a skewed distribution of the infrastructure for processing in the private sector. The facilities are largely concentrated in the districts of Kollam, Alappuzha, Ernakulam and Kozhikode. A comparatively large number of units seen in Kottayam are mainly retail cold storages.

The data available with the Marine Products Export Development Authority, Cochin, regarding the processing plants in Kerala are presented in table 6.36.

Table 6.36

Number and capacity of processing plants in Kerala registered with MPEDA as on 31.7.2002

(capacity in tonnes)

S. No.	*Item*	*No. of units*	*Capacity/ day*
1.	Freezing plant	100	1804.80
2.	Canning plant	2	1.50
3.	Ice plant	57	815.00
4.	Fish meal plant	0	0
5.	Cold storage	159	28.23
6.	Other storage	2	25.00
7.	Peeling shed	150	2030.10
8.	A F D Plant	1	1.60

* *Accelerated Freez Drying Plant.*

Source: MPEDA, 2002 Records

Of the 100 freezing plants shown in table 6.34, 88 were found registered in the Cochin sub-region of the MPEDA and 12 with the Quilon sub-region. The two canning plants were also registered with the Cochin sub-region. Of the 57 ice plants, 46 were registered with the Cochin sub-region and 11 with the Quilon sub-region. Among the 159 cold storages, 129 were with the Cochin sub-region and 30 with the Quilon sub-region. The two other storages noted were, both,in the Cochin sub-region. Of the 150 peeling sheds noted, 125 were registered with the Cochin sub-region and 25 with Quilon sub-region. The only one AFD unit was registered with the Cochin sub-region.

Information available with the MPEDA also show that about 206 conveyances used in the transport of fish were also registered with it. Of these, 109 were registered with the Cochin sub-region and 97 with the Quilon sub-region. The number of exporters of marine; products from the state registered with the MPEDA in July 2002 was 297 consisting of 244 in the Cochin sub-region and 53 in the Quilon sub-region.

The economic value of the fish processing industry, apart from contributing to regional employment and income and other spill-over

Table 6.37

Item-wise export of marine products from Kerala from 1997-98 to 1999-00

(Quantity in tonnes; Value in Rs crores)

S. No.	Item	1997-98				1998-99				1999-00			
		Quantity	per cent	Value	per cent	Quantity	per cent	Value	per cent	Quantity	per cent	Value	per cent
1.	Frozen shrimp	29781	33.33	529.46	55.85	25549	36.17	480.66	58.87	35710	38.75	705.61	61.52
2.	Frozen fish	21596	24.20	65.67	6.93	12182	17.24	53.18	6.51	13281	14.41	52.56	4.58
3.	Frozen squid	15933	17.80	126.26	13.32	11462	16.23	97.96	12.00	16050	17.42	140.46	12.25
4.	Frozen cuttle fish	15869	17.80	149.08	15.73	17195	24.34	150.64	18.45	19438	21.10	187.72	16.37
5.	Live items	117	0.13	3.67	0.39	121	0.17	3.13	0.38	-	-	-	-
6.	Dried items	38	0.04	0.83	0.08	89	0.13	0.84	0.10	-	-	-	-
7.	Others	6032	6.70	73.05	7.70	4043	5.72	30.14	3.69	7669	8.32	60.61	5.28
	Total	**89366**	**100.00**	**948.02**	**100.00**	**70641**	**100.00**	**816.55**	**100.00**	**92148**	**100.00**	**1146.96**	**100.00**

Source: State Planning Board, 2001, p.S.172.

benefits is predominantly in the foreign exchange earned by the sector. The trend in the foreign exchange earned by the sector has been noted in table 6.14 earlier. Table 6.37 shows the item-wise export of marine products from Kerala from 1997-98 to 1999-00.

Table 6.37, apart from showing an improvement in the quantity and value of marine products exported from the state during 1999-00 shows the predominant position of frozen prawns in the total quantity and value of marine products exported from the state during the entire period. The quantity and value of frozen cuttle fish also have shown improvement over the period, although its relative share was subject to fluctuations. What is emerging from table 6.34 and table 6.14 is the significant increase in the quantity and value of marine products exported from the state, notwithstanding some occasional slip in its course. Maintaining this trend in the export of marine products from the state is vital for the sustainability of the industry in Kerala. However, taking into account the prevailing excess capacity and the precarious position in getting raw material for the industry and the crises in the capture fisheries and the culture (aquaculture) sector, sustainability of this industry is very much at stake. The role of ICM planning is crucial in this context in Kerala.

6.1.6.4. Fertilizers and chemicals

Kerala has got a number of modern manufacturing units in the fertilizers and chemicals sector established in the coastal belt or in the upstreams having their impacts on the coastal belt. The main advantages noted for setting up of chemical industries in the Kerala coast and upstreams were 'the large capacity for generating cheap hydro-electric power, the availability of good water for process and cooling purposes and the skilled and educated labour the state could provide' (Kerala State Gazetteer, 1989, p. 402).

Some of the details regarding the major and medium chemical manufacturing units working in Kerala are provided in table 6.38.

The economic value of these enterprises would be quite high in providing both final and intermediate goods, and in creating large scale employment to the local population. In fact, the industrial units have become activity centres providing powerful stimuli for local industrial and urban growth. Assessing this potential and contribution is however, not in the scope of this study. Nevertheless, the economic value of some of these enterprises may be noted. Table 6.39 shows the details of capital investment and employment in selected public

Table 6.38

Details of major and medium chemical manufacturing units working in Kerala

S. No.	Name of manufacturing unit and location	S. No.	Products	Capacity
A. Central Sector				
1.	Fertilizers and Chemicals Travancore Limited (Plants at Udyogamandal and Ambalamedu)	1.	Ammonia	310,200 MT
		2.	Sulphuric acid	580,800 MT
		3.	Ammonium sulphate	198.000 MT
		4.	Ammonium phosphate	148,500 MT
		5.	Super phosphate	44,500 MT
		6.	Ammonium chloride	24,800 MT
		7.	Urea	330,000 MT
		8.	Phosphoric acid	148,000 MT
		9.	NPK fertilizers	485,000 MT
2.	Hindustan Insecticides Limited, Udyogamandal	1.	DDT (Dichlorodiphenyltrichloroethane)	1.344 MT
		2.	BHC (Benzene hexachloride)	3,000 MT
3.	Cochin Refineries Limited, Ambalamugal, Cochin	1.	Petroleum products	3.3 million tonnes
		2.	Asphalt	14.6 lakh drums
4.	Hindustan Organic Chemicals Limited, Ambalamugal, Cochin	1.	Phenol	40,000 MT
		2.	Acetone	20,600 MT
B. State Sector				
1.	The Travancore Sugars and Chemicals Limited, Valanjavattom, Thiruvalla	1.	Sugar	324,000 MT
		2.	Spirit	3.6 lakh gallons
2.	Travancore Titanium Products Limited, Kochuveli, Trivandrum	1.	Titanium dioxide	24,500 MT
		2.	Sulphuric acid	90,000 MT
3.	Travancore-Cochin Chemicals Limited, Udyogamandal	1.	Caustic soda	57,750 MT
		2.	Hydrochloric acid	34,650 MT
		3.	Liquid chlorine	29,700 MT
		4.	Sodium sulphide	2,100 MT

(Contd.)

(Table 6.38 contd.)

S. No.	Name of manufacturing unit and location	S. No.	Products	Capacity
4.	Kerala Minerals and Metals Limited, Kovilthottam, Chavara, Quilon	1.	Ilmenite, Rutile, Zircon, Silimenite, Leucoxene and Monozite	25,000 MT of ilmenite and corresponding quantities of allied minerals
		2.	Titanium dioxide	22,000 MT
5.	Kerala Soaps and Oils Limited, West Hill, Calicut	1.	Soaps	9,000 MT
		2.	Shark liver oil	300 MT
		3.	Glycerine	260 MT
6.	Kerala State Drugs and Pharmaceuticals Limited, Kalavoor, Alleppey	1.	Tablets	2,514 lakhs
		2.	Granules	20 MT
		3.	Capsules	–
		4.	Injectibles : a) bottles	4.50 lakhs
			b) vials	15 lakhs
			c) ampoules	60 lakhs
7.	Kerala State Detergents and Chemicals Limited, Kuttipuram, Malappuram	1.	Detergents	5,040 MT
C. Joint Sector				
1.	Kerala Chemicals and Proteins Limited, Kathikoodom, Koratty, Trichur	1.	Ossein	2,760 MT
		2.	Dicalcium phosphate	5,310 MT
2.	Kerala Chlorates and Chemicals Limited, Erazha North, Mavelikara	1.	Potassium chlorate	1,000 MT
3.	Premier-Morarji Chemical Company Limited, Kalavoor, Alleppey	1.	Sulphate of Alumina (Ferric alum)	16,500 MT
4.	Formalin Products Limited, Kalavoor, Alleppey	1.	Formaldehyde	7,500 MT
		2.	Hexamine	500 MT
		3.	Urea formaldehyde	2,000 MT
		4.	Para formaldehyde	150 MT

(Contd.)

(Table 6.38 contd.)

S. No.	Name of manufacturing unit and location	S. No.	Products	Capacity
5.	Venad Pharmaceuticals and Chemicals, Thazhakara, Mavelikara	1.	Transfusion fluids	3,000 bottles per day
6.	Carbon and Chemicals India Limited, Ambalamedu, Cochin	1.	Carbon black	17,500 MT
7.	Castols (India) Limited, Kuttipuram, Malappuram	1.	Polyols	1,200 MT
8.	Malabar Phyto Chemicals Limited, Nilamboor, Malappuram	1.	Alkaloids	13.75 MT
		2.	Papain	15 MT
		3.	Essential oils	45 MT
9.	Sri Sai Maharaj Pulp and Paper Mills Limited, Chittoor, Palghat	1.	Straw boards	3,000 MT
10.	Pigments India Limited, Thazhakad, Mukundapuram, Trichur	1.	Sodium sulphate	840 MT
		2.	Sodium and Potassium dichlorate	450 MT
		3.	Synthetic red oxide of iron	150 MT
		4.	Synthetic yellow oxide of iron	150 MT
		5.	Chromium pigments	450 MT
11.	Pragati Paints Ltd., Baliapatam, Cannanore	1.	Synthetic enamels, varnishes and paints	3,000 MT
D. Private Sector				
1.	The Tata Oil Mills Company Limited, Units at Tatapuram, Cochin and Trikoil Lane, Big Bazar, Calicut	1.	Soaps	55,300 MT
		2.	Synthetic detergents	18,400 MT
		3.	Glycerine	1.600 MT
		4.	Toilet preparations	2,100 MT
		5.	Vanaspathy	24,300 MT
		6.	Cattle and poultry feed	110.300 MT
		7.	Marine products	2,000 MT
2.	Punalur Paper Mills Limited, Punalur,	1.	Paper	50,000 MT

(Contd.)

(Table 6.38 Contd.)

S. No.	Name of manufacturing unit and location	S. No.	Products	Capacity
3.	Travancore Chemicals and Manufacturing Company Limited, Kalamassery and Kundara	1.	Copper sulphate	3,000 MT
		2.	Potiassium chlorate	3,250 MT
		3.	Sulphate of alumina, Sodium aluminate	1,020 MT
4.	The Travancore Electro-Chemical Industries Ltd. Chingavanam, Kottayam	1.	Calcium carbide	45,000 MT
		2.	Acetylene black	2,000 MT
5.	The Travancore Rayons Limited, Perumbavoor	1.	Rayon yarn	3,300 MT
		2.	Cellulose	4,000 MT
		3.	Cotton linter pulp	7,200 MT
		4.	Sulphuric acid	18,288 MT
		5	Carbon di-sulphide	3,210 MT
6.	Laxmi Starch Limited, Kundara, Quilon	1.	Starch and allied products	63,000 MT
		2.	Glucose	12,000 MT
		3.	Cattle and poultry feeds	14,000 MT
7.	The Gwalior Rayon Silk Manufacturing (Weaving) Company Limited, Birlakootam, Mavoor	1.	Rayon grade wood pulp	72,000 MT
		2.	Staple fibre	78,000 MT
8.	Cominco Binani Zinc Limited, Binanipuram	1.	Zinc	17.000 MT
		2.	Sulphuric acid	36,000 Mt
		3.	Cadmium	36 MT
9.	The Southern Gas Limited (units at Udyogamandal and Feroke, Calicut)	1.	Oxygen	15 lakhs M^3
		2.	Acetylene	1,80,000 M^3

(Contd.)

(Table 6.38 contd.)

S. No.	Name of manufacturing unit and location	S. No.	Products	Capacity
11.	Periyar Chemicals Limited, Edayar, Binanipuram	1.	Formic acid	1,500 Mt
		2.	Sodium sulphate	12,250 MT
12.	United Catalysts India limited, Edayar, Binanipuram	1.	Catalysts	2,450 MT
13.	West Coast Industrial Gases Limited, Perumanoor, Ernakulam	1.	Oxygen	11.88 lakh M
		2.	Acetylene	2.4 lakh M
14.	T. K. Chemicals, Kochuveli, Trivandrum	1.	Electrolytic managnese dioxide	900 MT
		2.	Manganous sulphate monohydrate	900 MT
15.	Kerala Acids and Chemicals Limited, Edayar	1.	Formic acid	1,200 MT
		2.	Sodium sulphate	1,870 MT
16.	The Canara Paper Mills Private Limited, Chettipuzha, Kurisumoodu, Changanacherry	1.	Craft paper	2,000 MT

Source: Kerala Gazetteers Department, 1989, pp.403-407.

sector enterprises in the fertilizers and chemicals industry in Kerala during 1998-99 and 1999-00.

Table 6.39
Details of capital investment and employment in selected public sector enterprises in the fertilizers and chemicals industry in Kerala during 1998-99 and 1999-00

S.No.	Name of Industry	Investment in capital as on 31.3.99	(Rs lakhs) as on 31.3.00	Employment as on	
				31.3.99	31.3.00
1.	Fertilizers and Chemicals Travancore Ltd.	78584.74	79438.57	7696	7488
2.	Cochin Refineries Ltd.	50285.00	81459.00	1785	1964
3.	Hindustan Organic Chemicals Ltd.	3342.00	3342.00	–	504
4.	Hindustan Newsprint Ltd.	8253.99	8253.99	1533	1501
5.	Kerala Minerals and Metals Ltd.	3197.27	3093.27	1084	1985
6.	Kerala Clays and Ceramics Products Ltd.	131.82	131.82	423	407

Source: State Planning Board, 2001, pp.S.96 and S.102.

Table 6.39 shows significant levels of investment and employment in the Fertilizers and Chemicals Travancore Limited, Cochin. Cochin Refineries also show high levels of investment although the level of employment is not as high as in Kerala Minerals and Metals Ltd.

The performance of the above enterprises in terms of the value of production and sales turnover may also be looked at. Table 6.40 gives details of value of production and sales turnover of selected public sector enterprises in the fertilizers and chemicals industry of Kerala during 1998-99 and 1999-00.

Table 6. 40 shows significant values of production and sales turnover for Cochin Refineries and Fertilizers and Chemicals, Travancore Ltd.

A summary of performance of public sector enterprises of Kerala during 1999-00 presented by the State Planning Board shows remarkable performance by the chemical industries. Table 6.41 gives the summary of performance of public sector enterprises in the chemical and all industries group in Kerala during 1999-00.

Table 6.40

Details of value of production and sales turn over of selected public sector enterprises in the fertilizers and chemicals industry of Kerala during 1998-99 and 1999-00

(Rs in Lakhs)

S. No.	Name of industry	Value of production		Sales turnover	
		1998-99	1999-00	1998-99	1999-00
1.	Fertilizers and Chemicals Travancore Ltd.	NA	NA	113658.56	133511.39
2.	Cochin Refineries Ltd.	426429	597575	417091.00	576833.00
3.	Hindustan Organic Chemicals Ltd.	23403	22085	20889.00	22338.00
4.	Hindustan Newsprints Ltd.	23886	19577	22109.00	21249.00
5.	Kerala Minerals and Metals Lrd.	20250	34461	21831.00	25057.00
6.	Kerala Clays and Ceramics Ltd.	280	337	247.00	329.00

Source: State Planning Board, 2001, pp.S.97 and S.103.

Table 6.41

Summary of performance of public sector enterprises in the chemical and 'all sectors' of Kerala during 1999-00.

S.No.	Parameters	Chemical industry	All industries	Chemical industry as percent of all industries
1.	No. of units	11	111	9.90
2.	Total employment	7318	125814	5.81
3.	Paid up capital (Rs lakhs)	10296	458081	2.24
4.	Capital invested (Rs lakhs)	29312	1377040	0.02
5.	Units making profit (No.)	5	46	10.86
6.	Amount of profit (Rs lakhs)	14834	28544	51.96
7.	Units on loss (No.)	5	51	9.80
8.	Amount of loss (Rs lakh)	3035	33166	9.15
9.	Net profit/Loss (–) (Rs lakhs)	11799	-4622	-
10.	No. of enterprises declaring dividend	3	13	23.17
11.	Contribution to Central exchequer (Rs lakhs)	11267	17982	62.65
12.	Contribution to state exchequer (Rs lakhs)	2401	79448	3.02

Source: State Planning Board, 2001, p.S.110.

The most interesting point revealed in table 6.41 is the fact that out of a total profit of 28,544 lakh made by 46 public sector enterprises, Rs 14534 lakhs (52 per cent) was by five chemical enterprises. Interestingly, the sector has made a net profit of 11,799 lakhs when the 'all industry' group made a net loss of 4,622 lakhs during the year 1999-00. Twenty three per cent of the enterprises declaring dividend was in the chemicals sector. Most importantly 62 per cent of the remittance to central exchequer was made by the public sector enterprises in the chemical industry. Its contribution to the state exchequer was, however, only 3.02 per cent by 'all' public sector enterprises, indicating a 'weak' presence of state enterprises and a 'strong' presence of central public sector enterprises in the fertilizers and chemical manufacturing industry of the state.

In summing up this section, it may be noted here that the sustained operation of this sector is vital for the economy of the region and the state, notwithstanding the 'environmental costs' of their operation. It is significant to note here that the fear of pollution (a negative externality) caused by these units have disuaded the I.T. (Information Technology) giant 'Infosys' from entering into a major business venture in Cochin, either at Udyogamandal or Ambalamugal where it felt the presence of these enterprises will not be conducive to its operation (Shafi Rahman, City Express, Cochin, 11.8.2003).

The task before ICM in Kerala is to mitigate the negative externalities caused by this sector and to make their operation sustainable. These issues are discussed in the following chapters.

6.1.7. Tourism

Tourism, particularly coastal tourism, is a comparatively new entrant in the group of coastal activities. It has now become a leading claimant for coastal resource use and is expected to contribute significantly to coastal economic development. Currently, coastal tourism is a major component of the state's tourism sector, attracting foreign and domestic tourists to the state.

The major tourist attractions in the coastal zones are the backwaters and the beaches and the cultural and historical heritages of the coast. The backwaters of the state has been a major attraction for both domestic and international tourists. A graphic description of the picturesque backwaters as given in the Farmers of India, Vol.II of ICAR in 1961 is reported in the Kerala State Gazetteer. It notes that 'the journey through the backwaters is one of the most pleasant experience of those who travel in Kerala. During the rainy season the lakes are in flood and the passage through them difficult, if not dangerous.

But as the rain wears off, and the silver streaks of the moon illuminate the horizon on a cloudless night, the panorama presented to the eye of the traveller, viewing the scene from the deck of his boat, as it glides smoothly along the calm surface of the backwaters, is supremely beautiful. Myriads of fire flies, with their weird twinkle, light up coast line, fringed with luxuriant vegetation, while the starry heavens reflected in the blue, limpid water below make the fairy scene complete. The solemn stillness of the night is only ruffled by the splash of the oars or the darting of fish hither and thither, giving occasion for the phosphorescent water to make its glow appear and lend an additional charm to the already enchanting scene' (Kerala Gazetteer Department, 1989, p.646).

Equally attractive for the tourists is life in the backwaters. The Gazetteer notes that 'the life in the backwaters of Kerala reveals a strange pattern, the like of which cannot be seen in any other part of India. A boat journey from Kottayam to Alleppey will provide a fair sample of the area and its amphibious life ... The whole distance is about 30 km, of which about one-third is through canals and the rest through the Vembanad *Kayal.* Starting from Kottayam the canal passes through the middle of paddy fields which extend as far as the eye can reach on either side, interspersed with coconut palms which are generally planted on the main bunds of the paddy fields. During the rainy season the whole region from Kottayam to Alleppey is one large sheet of water. In the midst of these paddy fields are also small man made islands with houses surrounded by coconut palms and banana. The bunds on either side of the canal are often used by the people as dwelling places. Houses of well-to-do people have walls of timber or stone and roofs of red tiles. The poor people live in mud houses, thatched with palm leaves. All along the canal men, women and children can be seen bathing and washing clothes and utensils. The canal is, therefore, the most important source of domestic water supply for most people living in that area.

The canal is a very busy line of communication. Small boats pushed by men with poles and also motor boats are frequently seen hurrying through carrying men and material. Numerous branch canals take off from the main canal leading to places in the interior. Small bridges are provided at many places to facilitate crossing ... Coconut palms are planted in rows along the bunds adding charm to this nature's beauty spot. The *Kayal* or lake is full of activity. In the morning innumerable small canoes paddled by men can be seen going in all directions casting nets and catching fish. Big cargo boats with their sails spread can be seen speeding in all directions. Frequently motor tugs are also seen towing teams of boats loaded with produce. From all sides come the thud of engines pumping water from the paddy fields ...' (ibid, pp.647-648). The major backwater tourist centres of Kerala are Cochin, Pathiramanal, Kumarakom, Kottayam, Ararnmula, Kayamkulam, Varkala, Veli, etc.

On the shore side, the several sandy beaches with numerous promenades and the rocky palm fringed cliffs, ports, fortresses and other monuments like mosques, churches, etc. all have been a source perennial attraction for the tourists. Places of outstanding attraction on the coast now are, Kovalam, Sangumugham, Varkala, Thangassery, Alappuzha, Kochi, Kodungalloor, Kappad, Thalassery, Muzhappilangad, Kannur, Ezhimala, Bekal and Kasargode.

Tourism is now considered as 'the fastest growing and the second largest industry of the world' and 'having tremendous potentials for earning foreign exchange, yielding tax revenues' providing employment, promoting growth of ancillary industries and development of industrially backward regions' (Department of Tourism, 2001, p.4).

It would be interesting in this context to look at the Government's approach to tourism development in Kerala. The Economic Review of Kerala, 2000, notes that 'ever since tourism was declared an industry in 1986, several incentives, which were available to investors in other industrial sectors, were extended to the tourism sector. These include investment subsidies, electricity tariff concessions, technical guidance, marketing assistance, publicity through governmental publications, help in availing loans, etc. The plan allocation for promoting private sector investment increased from Rs 15 lakh in 1995-96 to Rs 300 lakh in 2000-01. Major projects in the tourism sector are now planned with private participation. Amusement park at Veli, tourism infrastructure at Bekal, development of Pathiramanal, Akkulam ... etc. are some of the initiatives undertaken through public-private partnership' (State Planning Board, 2001, p.130).

Translating this policy into practice, the Department of Tourism 'has been giving thrust to the development of basic infrastructure along the backwaters of the state. Construction of house boat terminals at major backwater nodes, tourist resorts, introduction of house boats, water side amenities at various centres, etc, were the activities carried out as part of the development (ibid, p.29).

Some of the major tourist sites developed/ proposed along the beaches and backwaters of Kerala are given in table 6.42.

Table 6.42
Major tourist sites developed/proposed along the beaches and backwaters of Kerala

S.No.	*Centre*	*Attractions*
1.	Poovar	Sandy beach
2.	Kovalam	Sandy rocky beach, bathing, boating
3.	Somatheeram	Rocky beach
4.	Sankumughom	Sandy beach
5.	Veli	Sandy-rocky beach, boating
6.	Varkala	Beach, bathing, cliff
7.	Thangassery	Beach, cliff, heritage site
8.	Thirumullavaram	Beach,bathing
9.	Pathiramanal	Boathing, anging, bird watching
10.	Kumarakom	Yatching, surf riding, skin diving, angling, swimming
11.	Punnamada	Boat race
12.	Poomalachal	Boat race
13.	Thamarkulam	Lake
14.	Thottappally feeder channel	Boat race
15.	Neerattupuram	Boat race
16.	Champakulam	Boat race
17.	Mararikulam	Beach
18.	Fort Kochi	Beach, Chinese nets, heritage sites
19.	Bolgatty	Boating, yatching, golfing
20.	Cherayi	Beach
21.	Ponnani	Beach
22.	Kappad	Beach, heritage site
23.	Thalassery	Fort, beach, cliff
24.	Dharmadom	Island, walk way
25.	Muzhappilangad	Beach, walk way
26.	Kannur	Fort, cliff
27.	Payyambalam	Beach
28.	Ezhimala	Beach, cliff
29.	Bekal	Fort, beach, resorts
30.	Kasargode	Beach, cliffs

Source: 1. State Planning Board (1973), pp.413-422.
2. State Planning Board (2001), pp.126-132.
3. Department of Fisheries (2001), Pan Fish Books, 1 and 4.

Many of the sites mentioned in table 6.42 are already developed, the most advanced being Kovalam. Kurmarakom has all the facilities for yatching, surf riding, angling, sun bathing, etc. Pathiramanal needs further development.

Fort Kachi is being developed as a heritage site. Bolgatty has facilities for yatching, outing, conference, etc. The whole stretch of the coast from Kappad to Kasargode is on the throe of a tourism development thrust. The most important project in this part of the coast is the Bekal project, and the Bekal Resorts Development Corporation Ltd (BRDC) was formed in the year 1995 as a joint sector company for the integrated tourism development in Bekal with the Government of Kerala as the chief promoter. Land acquisition and development of the project area for sale to potential buyers is the main activity envisaged in the project. Reviewing the progress of the project, the Ninth Five Year Plan (Mid-Term Appraisal) states that 'the original target was to acquire 687 acres of land, but the corporation could so far acquire only 151.87 acres of land. The short falls in land acquisition are reportedly due to the Coastal Zone Regulation Act, local sentiments, ecological factors, etc.' (State Planning Board, 1999, p.48). This observation by the Planning Board has real import for the sustainability of tourism venture in the region. This aspect will be looked in chapter seven.

The impact of tourism on the coastal economy of Kerala is felt through the employment and income multiplier effects of tourism development. It is well recognised that any expenditure by the Government or the industry in the sector will create new demand for inputs and services leading to new factor incomes, and the spending of these incomes by the recipients will work as the spring board for the first round of multiplier effects, and this process of working of the multiplier will continue as long as recipients of new income spend their incomes. In addition to this effect of initial investment in tourism by the Government and industry, the direct spending by tourists during their stay in the state will also create new demand for various goods and services, which will in turn lead to another wave of income/ employment generation and multiplier effects, as described earlier. Over and above this, tourism development can also lead to the expansion of producers' goods industry which will further accelerate the process of growth in the economy. It all, however, depends on the level and pattern of tourist spending in the course of their visit and how much of that spending flows or circulates in the local economy. Any leakage of that income from the local income stream is likely to retard the process of growth. In simple terms, the benefits the local community (economy) receives from tourism expansion will very much depend upon the extent of demand for local goods and services placed by the tourists. Assuming that the tourists spend considerable amounts during their stay in the state, an increase in tourist flow to the state is an indication of its contribution to the state's economy. Table 6.43 shows details of arrival of foreign tourists to Kerala from 1996 to 2000.

Table 6.43
Details of arrival of foreign tourists to Kerala from 1996 to 2000

Year	*No. of tourists*	*Per cent change over previous year*
1996	176885	23.70
1997	182427	3.15
1998	189941	4.12
1999	202173	6.44
2000	209933	3.84

Source: Department of Tourism, 2001, p.10.

Table 6.43 shows a continuous increase in the arrival of foreign tourists to Kerala, the last year recording 2,09,933 tourists.

Details of the arrival of domestic tourists is given in Table 6.44.

Table 6.44
Details of the arrival of domestic tourists to Kerala from 1996 to 2000.

Year	*No. of tourists*	*Per cent change over previous year*
1996	4403002	12.45
1997	4953401	11.11
1998	4481714	-9.52
1999	4888287	9.07
2000	5013221	2.56

Source: Department of Tourism, 2001, p.11.

Table 6.44 shows a general increase in the number of domestic tourists visiting Kerala, the terminal year showing the maximum number of 5013221. This is notwithstanding a fall in 1998.

Table 6.45 shows the trend in district-wise arrival of foreign tourists to Kerala during 1999 and 2000.

Table 6.45
District-wise arrival of foreign tourists to Kerala during 1999 and 2000.

S. No.	*District*	*No. of tourists*			
		1999	*per cent of total*	*2000*	*per cent of total*
1.	Thiruvananthapuram	96536	47.74	82803	39.44
2.	Kollam	7430	3.67	8997	4.28
3.	Pathanamthitta	141	0.06	208	0.09
4.	Alappuzha	10478	5.18	12013	5.72
5.	Kottayam	11832	5.85	12876	6.13
6.	Ernakulam	55546	27.47	55819	26.58
7.	Idukki	10719	5.30	24842	11.83
8.	Thrissur	1634	0.80	2057	0.97

(Contd.)

(Table 6.45 Contd.)

S. No.	District	No. of tourists 1999	per cent of total	2000	per cent of total
9.	Palakkad	1512	0.74	1517	0.72
10.	Malappuram	855	0.42	856	0.40
11.	Wayanad	449	0.22	561	0.26
12.	Kozhikode	2968	1.46	5159	2.45
13.	Kannur	1271	0.62	1415	0.67
14.	Kasargode	802	0.39	810	0.38
	Total	**202173**	**100.00**	**209933**	**100.00**

Source: Department of Tourism, 2001, p.29.

Table 6.45 shows that about 39.44 per cent of the foreign tourists visited Thiruvananthapuram during 2000, which was slightly less than the percentage for 1999. In 2000, the actual number of foreign tourists visiting Thiruvananthapuram has also come down. Ernakulam was the other district which attracted a large number of foreign tourists. About 27 per cent of the foreign tourists visited Ernakulam. Idukki showed an unusual increase in the flow of foreign tourists in 2000. Both Alappuzha and Kottayam attracted about six per cent of the foreign tourists during 2000. The northern districts did not attract any significant number or percentage of foreign tourists. This indicates the poor benefits realised by these districts from foreign tourists.

Table 5.46 shows the trend in district-wise arrival of domestic tourists to Kerala during 1999 and 2000.

Table 6.46
District-wise arrival of domestic tourists to Kerala during 1999 and 2000

S. No.	District	No. of tourists 1999	per cent of total	2000	per cent of total
1.	Thiruvananthapuram	755897	15.46	763345	15.22
2.	Kollam	110569	2.26	96103	1.91
3.	Pathanamthitta	76311	1.56	67041	1.33
4.	Alappuzha	111050	2.27	127719	2.54
5.	Kottayam	142143	2.90	140320	2.79
6.	Ernakulam	734837	15.03	810527	16.16
7.	Idukki	185579	3.79	209639	4.18
8.	Thrissur	1285029	26.28	1376692	27.46
9.	Palakkad	301861	6,17	300888	6.00
10.	Malappuram	250326	5.12	241740	4.82
11.	Wayanad	499062	10.20	496060	9.89
12.	Kozhikode	190559	3.89	171040	3.41
13.	Kannur	96918	1.98	76565	1.52
14.	Kasargode	148146	3.03	135542	2.70
	Total	**4888287**	**100.00**	**5013221**	**100.00**

Source: Department of Tourism, 2001, p. 31,

Table 6.46 shows that out of a total of 50.13 lakhs domestic tourists who visited the state in 2000, 13.76 lakhs (27.4 per cent) went to Thrissur district, the main attraction being Guruvayur temple. About 15-16 per cent of the domestic tourists visited Ernakulam and Thiruvananthapurara districts. Kozhikode attracted about 10 per cent of the domestic tourists. Palakkad drew about six per cent of the domestic tourists. Malappuram, Kollam and Idukki districts attracted between four to five per cent of the domestic tourists.

It appears from Table 6.46 that the number of domestic tourists visiting different districts is distributed with lesser amount of concentration in Thiruvananthapuram and Ernakulam districts and with a larger spread to other districts, notwithstanding its concentration in Thrissur district. A greater dispersal of the domestic tourist traffic can contribute to a wider sharing of tourism benefits. The ultimate benefits obtained from the tourist traffic might depend upon the amount of expenditure made by the tourists on a day and the duration of their stay in the state. Table 6.47 gives details of the per day expenditure by domestic and foreign tourists in Kerala during 2000.

Table 6.47

Details of per day expenditure by domestic and foreign tourist in Kerala during 2000

S. No.	*Item*	*Per day expenditure (Rs.)*	
		Domestic tourists	*Foreign tourists*
1.	Hotel	390	693
2.	Food on trip	38	80
3.	Beverages	28	85
4.	Local transport	70	116
5.	Health rejuvenation	19	59
6.	Entertainment	21	65
7.	Communication	16	60
8.	Personal care	12	13
9.	Shopping (handicraft)	13	182
10.	Shopping (textiles)	7	82
11.	Shopping (spices and cashew)	8	62
12.	Shopping (leather and rubber)	6	43
13.	Shopping (others)	24	165
14.	Miscellaneous	31	60
	Total	**682**	**1764**

Source: Department of Tourism, 2001, p. 43.

It appears from table 6.47 that the domestic tourists were spending Rs 682 per day, on an adverage, while the foreign tourists were spending Rs 1764 per day. The foreign tourist spends 159 per cent more than what a domestic tourist spends on a day. The duration of stay of the tourists may also be looked into. Table 6.48 shows the average duration of stay of domestic and foreign tourists at major tourist destinations in Kerala in 2000.

Table 6.48

Average duration of stay of domestic and foreign tourists at major tourist destinations in Kerala during 2000

S. No.	*Location*	*Average duration of stay (days)*	
		Domestic tourists	*Foreign tourists*
1.	Thiruvananthapuram	2.5	4.4
2.	Kovalam	-	4.6
3.	Kochi	2.5	3.5
4.	Thekkady/Munnar	2.7	2.7
5.	Kumarakom/Alappuzha	2.2	2.4
6.	Guruvayur	2.1	-
	Total	**6.5**	**14.1**

Source: Department of Tourism, 2001, pp.4-5.

It is evident from table 6.48 that the average duration of stay of foreign tourists in the state is much longer than that of domestic tourists.

The longer duration of stay and the greater expenditure per day by the foreign tourists make the global tourist a more attractive customer to the tourism industry. But the domestic tourists by their sheer number can compensate for the short fall in their daily expenditure and the shorter duration of stay. Yet, when earning the hard currency(foreign exchange) is the more important goal, foreign tourists will be encouraged with better amenities. In fact, the state has been following such a policy and it has succeeded in earning more foreign exchange from the global tourists. Table 6.49 depicts the trend in the earnings of foreign exchange by Kerala from foreign tourists.

Table 6.49

Trend in the earnings of foreign exchange by Kerala from foreign tourist arrivals from 1991 to 2000.

(Rs in crores)

Year	*Earnings*
1991	28.28
1992	59.75
1993	105.72
1994	116.11
1995	158.76
1996	196.38
1997	273.20
1998	302.08
1999	416.07
2000	525.30

Source: Department of Tourism, 2001, p. 26.

Table 6.49 shows a steady increase in the foreign exchange earnings by the tourism sector in the state. The foreign-exchange earned in 2000 marked an increase of nearly 18 times over the 1991 figure.

The total employment generated by the tourism sector in 2000 was estimated at 5.18 lakh persons of which 1.28 lakh was direct employment (Department of Tourism, 2001, p.43). What is emerging from all the above is that tourism, particularly coastal tourism consisting of beach tourism and backwater tourism, is an important component of the coastal economy and sustaining this activity is a major objective of ICM in Kerala.

6.1.8. Ports and harbours

Ports and harbours are the transit points on the coast and the 'international exchange' for the goods and services produced in the country. Historically ports have developed as the main window for foreign trade. Ports of ancient Kerala were the main centres for shipping timber and spices from the Kerala coast. In the early part of the last century, referring to the ports of Travancore, Velu Pillai wrote 'the long coast line is more or less regular. There are, however, some good ports, Alleppey, Quilon, Trivandrum and Colachal being the more important, (Velu Pillai, 1940, Reprint 1996, p.3). The last mentioned port now falls in Tamil Nadu. The 'major' ports in the Malabar region noted by William Logan in 1887 were Cannanore, Tellicherry, Calicut, Beypore, Cochin and Narakkal (Logan, 1887, Edition 2000, Vol.II, Appendix viii).

Kerala, at present, is having seventeen ports, of which one is the major port at Cochin, three intermediate ports at Beypore, Alappuzha and Neendakara and thirteen minor ports at Kovalam/ Vizhinjam, Valiyathura, Thankassery, Kayamkulam, Munambam/ Kodungalloor, Ponnani, Vadakara, Thalassery, Kannur, Azhikkal, Neeleswaram, Kasargode and Manjeswaram. The details of these ports have been given in the section on coastal infrastructure in chapter five.

To highlight the significance of ports in the economic milieu of the coast, an account of the working of the major port of Kochi during 1998-99 and 1999-00 as given in the Economic Review of Kerala is reproduced. 'Kochi port handled 128 lakh tonnes of traffic in 1999-2000 as against 127 lakh tonnes in 1998-99 registering an increase of 0.8 per cent. Contribution of Kochi port in traffic handled stood at 4.7 per cent of the total traffic handled by all ports in the country during the year under review.

While the total operating income of all ports in the country decreased to Rs 3357.30 crore in 1999-00 from Rs 3412.35 crore in 1998-99, the operating income of the Kochi port increased to Rs 180.41 crore as against Rs 162.9 crore in the previous year, registering an increase of 10.7 per cent. While the operating surplus of all ports decreased during the year under review to Rs 971.81 crore from Rs 1171.48 crore in the previous year, Kochi generated an operating surplus of Rs 33.15 crore in 1999-00 as against Rs 33.41 crore in 1998-99. Net surplus of the port decreased to Rs 2.71 crore in 1999-00 as against Rs 31.25 crore in 1998-99.

Regarding the operational efficiency of ships, the average turn around time recorded showed a decrease of 3.23 days during the year under review compared to 3.61 days in the previous year. The average pre-berthing waiting time during the year under review remained at the same level of 0.87 days as in the preceeding year. Total staff strength of the port decreased to 5277 in 1999-00 from 5447 in 1998-99' (State Planning Board, 2001, p.138). The above record of performance of the major port of Kerala indicates its increasing importance in the coastal economy of the state and the country.

Table 6.50 gives details of the number of ships called at Cochin port during 1998-99 and 1999-00 and their net registered tonnage.

Table 6.50 shows a remarkable increase in the net registered tonnage of ships that called at Cochin during 1999-00 indicating a sharp increase in the volume of goods handled by the port and the volume of employment and income generated thereby in the region. This is notwithstanding a slight fall in the number of ships that called at the port.

Table 6.51 shows the trend in the cargo handled by the Cochin port from 1994-95 to 1999-00.

Table 6.51 indicates a steady increase in the volume of import cargo handled by the port, which increased from 71.93 lakh tonnes in 1994-95 to 106.36 lakh tonnes in 1999-00, marking an increase of 48 per cent. The volume of export cargo handled was much less, never more than a quarter of this volume.

A general picture of the relative importance of intermediate and minor ports can be obtained from the number of harbour crafts

Table 6.50

Details of the number of ships called at Cochin Port during 1998-99 and 1999-00 and their net registered tonnage

S. No.	Type of vessel	No. of Ships		Per cent variation in 1999-00 over 1998-99	Net registered tonnage		Per cent variation in 1999-00 over 1998-99
		1998-99	1999-00		1998-99	1999-00	
1.	Container	377	359	-4.77	1427046	1247000	-12.61
2.	Break bulk	141	176	24.82	427198	588000	37.64
3.	Dry bulk	53	40	-24.53	582727	745000	27.84
4.	Liquid bulk	398	398	–	5992196	10217000	70.51
5.	Passenger carriers }						
6.	Others }	144	122	-15.28	333319	NA	–
	Total	**1113**	**1095**	**-1.61**	**8762486**	**12797000**	**40.04**

* % Variation as given in the source.

Source: State Planning Board, 2001, p.S.159.

Table 6.51

Trend in the cargo handled by the Cochin Port from 1994-95 to 1999-00

(in lakh tonnes)

Year	*Export*			*Import*		
	Coastal	*Foreign*	*Total*	*Coastal*	*Foreign*	*Total*
1994-95	5.24	9.14	14.38	42.46	29.47	71.93
1995-96	11.94	11.84	23.78	56.03	35.22	91.25
1996-97	10.65	11.90	22.55	49.90	44.97	94.87
1997-98	15.04	10.39	25.43	43.34	54.48	97.82
1998-99	14.78	9.52	24.30	40.82	61.69	102.51
1999-00	13.12	8.93	22.05	71.46	34.90	106.36

Source: State Planning Board, 2001, p.143.

registered with those ports. Table 6.52 gives details of harbour crafts registered at the intermediate and minor ports of Kerala during 1999-00.

Table 6.52

Details of harbour crafts registered at the intermediate and minor ports of Kerala during 1999-00

S.No.	*Name of port*	*Cargo boats including barge*	*Canoes including boats*	*Mechanised fishing boats*	*Others*	*Total*
1.	Kasargode	—	276	—	—	276
2.	Azhikkal	—	—	—	—	—
3.	Kannur	—	—	—	—	—
4.	Thalassery	—	—	—	—	—
5.	Vadakara	—	—	—	—	—
6.	Kozhikode/Beypore	—	—	18	—	18
7.	Ponnani	—	—	—	—	—
8.	Munambam	—	—	624	—	624
9.	Alappuzha	—	—	720	—	720
10.	Neendakara	—	1	333	—	334
11.	Valiathura	—	—	—	—	—
12.	Kovalam/Vizhinjam	—	—	—	—	—
	Total	**—**	**277**	**1695**	**—**	**1972**

Source: State Planning Board, 2001, p.S.161.

It appears from table 6.52 that most of the minor and intermediate ports have no crafts registered at these places, indicating the disuse of the facility. The Kerala State Gazetteer noted as early as 1989, that many of these ports have fallen into disuse mainly due to the inadequacy of infrastructure facilities to handle modern vessels efficiently and economically. The diversion of cargo traffic through rail and road has also contributed to the fall in traffic ...' (Kerala State Gazetteers, 1989, p.642).

Table 6.53 gives the number and tonnage of steamers and sailing vessels which called at the intermediate and minor ports of Kerala during 1999-2000.

Table 6.53
Number and tonnage of steamers and sailing vessels which called at the intermediate and minor ports of Kerala during 1999-00

S. No.	*Name of port*	*Coastal (C) Foreign (F)*	*Steamers*		*Sailing vessels*		*Total No. of vessels*	*Total tonnage*
			No.	*Ton-nage*	*No.*	*Tonnage*		
1.	Kasargode	C	—	—	—	—	—	—
		F	—	—	—	—	—	—
2.	Azheekal	C	—	—	35	4103.16	35	4103.16
		F	—	—	—	—	—	—
3.	Kannur	C	—	—	—	—	—	—
		F	—	—	—	—	—	—
4.	Thalassery	C	—	—	—	—	—	—
		F	—	—	—	—	—	—
5.	Vadakara	C	—	—	—	—	—	—
		F	—	—	—	—	—	—
6.	Kozhikode/	C	61	21699	243	36398.00	304	58097.00
	Beypore	F	—	—	—	—	—	—
7.	Ponnaini	C	—	—	—	—	—	—
		F	—	—	—	—	—	—
8.	Munambam	C	—	—	—	—	—	—
		F	—	—	—	—	—	—
9.	Alappuzha	C	—	—	—	—	—	—
		F	—	—	—	—	—	—
10.	Neen-	C	—	—	—	—	—	—
	dakara	F	2	38141	—	—	2	38141.00
11.	Vanliathura	C	—	—	—	—	—	—
		F	—	—	—	—	—	—
12.	Kovalam/	C	2	1396	31	4434.41	33	5830.41
	Vizhinjam	F	1	354	—	—	1	354.00
	Total		**66**	**61590**	**309**	**44935.57**	**375**	**106525.60**

Source: State Planning Board, 2001, p.S.161,

Table 6.53 indicates that only four ports at Azheekal, Kozhikode/ Beypore, Neendakara and Kovalam/ Vizhinjam attracted any sailing vessel or steamer in 1999-00.

Table 6.54 gives details of import and export cargo handled by the intermediate and minor ports of Kerala during 1999-00.

It appears from table 6.54 that the bulk of the import cargo was handled by Neendakara during 1999-00, whereas the bulk of export cargo was handled by Beypore and Neendakara.

Table 6.55 presents details of revenue collected at the intermediate and minor ports of Kerala during 1999-00.

Table 6.54

Details of import and export cargo handled by intermediate and minor ports of Kerala during 1999-00

(in tonnes)

S. No.	Name of port	Import			Export			Grand Total
		Coastal	Foreign	Total	Coastal	Foreign	Total	
1.	Beypore	27811	542	28353	30142	-	30142	58495
2.	Azheekal	2072	-	2072	207	-	207	2279
3.	Neendakara	-	-	-	-	52050	52050	52050
4.	Vizhinjam	5115	-	5115	845	1722	2567	7682
5.	Others	-	-	-	-	-	-	
	Total	**34998**	**542**	**35540**	**31194**	**53772**	**84966**	**120506**

Source: State Planning Board, 2001, p.S.160.

Table 6.55

Details of revenue collected at the intermediate and minor ports of kerala during 1999-00

(in Rupees)

S.No.	Name of port	Port dues	Export/import dues	Tug hire charges	Pilotage fees	Miscellaneous			Total
						Registration and other fees	Ground rent and shed rent, etc.	Private dredging charges	
1.	Kasargode	—	—	—	—	27350	352224	—	379574
2.	Azhikal	350	19647	—	—	418	37701	—	58116
3.	Kannur	—	—	—	—	—	48543	—	48543
4.	Thalassery	—	—	—	—	—	173042	—	173042
5.	Vadakara	—	—	—	—	—	—	—	—
6.	Kozhikode	86629	622455	—	—	23701	342094	—	1074879
7.	Beypore	200	—	768353	24328	1349963	144570	—	2287414
8.	Ponnani	—	—	—	—	—	28585	—	28585
9.	Munambam	—	—	—	—	167096	—	—	167096
10.	Alappuzha	—	—	—	—	245730	7762	—	253492
11.	Neendakara	129958	269995	4508622	—	159076	770882	111317	5949850
12.	Valiyathura	—	—	—	—	—	69655	—	69655
13.	Kovalam/Vizhinjam	22796	75490	—	—	1440	170950	—	270676
	Total	**239933**	**987587**	**5276975**	**24328**	**1974774**	**2146008**	**111317**	**10760922**

Source: State Planning Board, 2001, p.S.162.

Table 6.55 indicates that out of the Rs 107.60 lakhs revenue collected by intermediate and minor ports, Rs 52.76 lakhs constituted tug hire charges, Rs 21.46 lakhs ground rent, Rs 19.74 lakhs registration and other fees, Rs 9.87 lakhs export/import duty and the rest port fees, pilotage fees, etc. Among the various ports, Neendakara earned the maximum revenue, followed by Beypore, Kozhikode, Kasargode, Vizhinjam, Alappuzha, Thalassery, Munambam, etc. in that order. The export-import dues were collected only by Neendakara, Kozhikode, Azhekkal and Vizhinjam ports.

It appears that the working of the majority of minor and intermediate ports in Kerala have become unsustainable. Activating these ports must be considered as a major priority for integrated coastal zone management in Kerala. This issue is further discussed in the following chapter. A related industry, whose presence must be noted here is the ship/boat building industry. The ship building industry with the major public sector concern, the Cochin Shipyard, is an expanding economic activity in the region. The boat building industry in the state which had its moorings at Kozhikode has suffered many convulsions, with the focus now based in the three southern districts of Kollam, Alappuzha and Ernakulam. The state had 26 boat building yards in 1990, of which 10 were in Kollam, four in Alappuzha, 10 in Ernakulam and two in Kozhikode districts (Department of Fisheries, 1991, p.127).

6.1.9. Inland water transport

Among the many coastal activities of Kerala, inland water transport occupies a predominant position as the link between people and places, providing a valuable service. Describing this sector, the Kerala State Gazetteer gives an extensive note which is reproduced here to show its importance. It observes that 'Kerala is placed in a very favourable position in regard to inland water transport. The waterways of Kerala connect several minor ports with the major port of Cochin, and a number of industrial units, etc. situated close to them. The state enjoys a regular navigation system because of several west flowing rivers and a coastline interspersed with backwaters. Long before the development of road and railways, the coastal and inland waterways provided the main transport base in Kerala. The canal system, navigable all round the year, extends from Trivandrum in the south to Badagara in the north and is interlinked by backwaters and rivers through artificial canals. The total length of the navigable route in Kerala is 1895 kms, accounting for about

20 per cent of the total inland water route in India. This can be categorised under the following three main heads: (i) the interior coastal canal system; (ii) the river navigation system; and (iii) the inland cross canal system.

The 83 km long Vembanad lake constitute the centre of these inland waterways.

The inland waterways in the state are shallow in certain regions even for the vessels which are in use at present. These are unsuitable for carrying heavy vessels which will ultimately be more economical. Through traffic in waterways is therefore hindered. The state's waterways are at present maintained by the irrigation wing of the Public Works Department. Due to paucity of funds, this department has not been able to carry out adequate regular maintenance, which is a serious drawback. These waterways which were formerly navigable are now rendered unserviceable for want of proper maintenance. Side erosion and silting have reduced the draft and this has contributed to a reduction in traffic. Side protection works and deepening have not been done in most sections for decades.

The West Coast canal, which is the main waterway requires renovation. Land erosion during the rainy season prevents free movement of boats on this waterway. More landing places and jetties and better lighting arrangements are necessary. The existing landing places are not properly maintained. Besides, in the Travancore-Cochin area there is a need for constructing additional link canals in order to connect them with the main canals. For example, the Varkala tunnel which is of 9 metre width and 5 metre height with a draft of 1 metre only is the major bottleneck in the southern region.

In spite of all these limitations the inland water transport system in Kerala carried as much as 4 million tonnes of freight traffic in the year 1970 and 26.6 million passengers in the year 1976. Though there has been a high degree of competition from road and rail, the inland water transport has survived on account of its suitability for moving certain types of cargo over long distances, economy in the use of energy and its low cost. As the inland waterways connect en-route many villages and serve the rural region, they provide stimuli to develop small scale and cottage industries in rural areas. Moreover, Kerala being mostly rural, the inland waterways play an important role in the economic uplift of rural areas by providing transport connections, better irrigation and augmentation of pisciculture' (Kerala Gazetteers Department, 1987, pp. 650-651).

It also reports that 'a study conducted in Cochin Region by the National Traffic Planning and Automation Centre (NATPAC) revealed that the inland water transport provided direct and indirect employment to 19,058 people in the study region, and roughly this works out to 7 per cent of the working force in the region. The total employment, both direct and indirect, per Rs 1,00,000 of investment worked out to 33.59 man years' (ibid, p.652).

The Gazetteer also accredits it saying that, 'apart from their navigational importance and potentiality for fisheries, the inland waterways offer unique potential for the development of tourism. A coordinated development of inland water transport system and tourist infrastructure would increase phenomenally the tourist traffic, both foreign and domestic' (ibid, p. 652).

It appears that the Government of Kerala have incorporated these aspects in its programmes for the development of inland water transport in the state. The Economic Review of Kerala, 2000, notes that 'due importance has been given for development of inland waterways with a two-pronged strategy of reduction in the congestion in roadways due to the increasing volume of traffic and for tapping the tourism potential' (State Planning Board, 2001, p.139).

The major public sector organisations/agencies engaged in water transport operations in the State are: (1) State Water Transport Department (SWTD), (2) Coastal Shipping and Inland Navigation Department (CSIND) and (3) Kerala Shipping and Inland Navigation Corporation (KSINC) under the control of Coastal Shipping and Inland Navigation Department. The SWTD and CSIND mainly provide transport services to the public in the water logged areas of Alappuzha, Kollam, Kottayam, Kasargode and Kannur districts. The CSIND is orienting its activities towards the development of inland water canals and infrastructure facilities (ibid, p.139). The KSINC is engaged in transportation of passengers and cargo through the inland waterways of Kerala. Recently, it has also ventured into coastal shipping operation on a trial basis. It is reported that in 1999-00, it has also constructed two wooden passenger boats, one of which was put into service between Thekkumpadom and Valapattanam in Kannur district to cater to the needs of people residing in isolated places like Mattool, Azheekal, Thekkumpadom and Valapattanam in the district (ibid, pp.139-140).

Details of the working of public sector inland water transport agencies in Kerala during 1998-99 and 1999-00 are given in table 6.56.

Table 6.56

Details of the working of public sector inland water transport agencies in Kerala during 1998-99 and 1999-00

S. No.	Particulars	State Water Transport		Kerala Shipping and Inland Navigation Corportation	
		1998-99	1999-00	1998-99*	1999-00**
1.	No. of boats/Jhankars	81	86	12+2	12+2
2.	No. of boats/ Jhankars in operation	59	57	9+2	9+2
3.	No. of trips on schedule	399	865	43617	45840
4.	No. of passengers carried (in lakhs)	240.79	219.75	55.78	63.78
5.	Gross route distance (in kms.)	1549.86	8231.21	479800	470679
6.	Volume of cargo carried (tonnes)	-	-	6014	6140
7.	Total revenue receipts (Rs. in lakhs)	408.80	420.98	668.79	702.60
8.	Total revenue expenditure (Rs. in lakhs)	927.10	1105.43	618.16	658.21
9.	Profit/Loss (Rs. lakhs)	-518.30	-684.45	50.63	44.39
10.	Total No. of employees	1285	1285	317	328

* audited figures

** unaudited figures

Source: State Planning Board, 2001, p.S.162.

Table 6.56 shows that the Kerala Shipping and Inland Navigation Corporation was able to make profit in both 1998-99 and 1999-00, while the State Water Transport Department incurred loss in both the years. It appears that the profit earned by the KSINC was largely the result of the cargo carried by it and the comparatively low expenditure incurred by it. One probable reason for the loss incurred by the State Water Transport Department is its exclusive dependence on passenger traffic which apparently is not very lucrative. It, however, employed more persons.

The significant point emerging from this section is the continuing importance of inland navigation in the coastal economic and social milieu. Sustaining this activity, making it viable for the enterprises to continue this pursuit, should be considered as a goal of ICM in Kerala. Some of these issues are further discussed in chapter seven.

6.1.10. Urban development

Using the coast for urban development, predominantly for human settlement is a major activity that is fast expanding in the coasts of Kerala. This is certainly part of a global phenomenon. As Cicin-Sain and Knecht report 'two-thirds of the world's largest cities are located on coasts and populations of coastal areas are growing faster than inland populations. .... World Bank experts, estimated in 1994 that two-thirds of the population of developing nations would be living along coasts by the end of the twentieth century' (Cicin-Sain and Knecht, 1998, pp.15-16). Referring to such a development, Clark observes that 'shoreline real estate is in strong demand for human settlements, agriculture, trade, industry, amenity and marine support activities for shipping and fishing and recreation' (Clark, 1996, p.17). The consequence is that 'human settlements may crowd the seas with boats, over exploit resources, generate polluting industries, produce heaps of garbage, and create large amounts of chemical wastes ... while water front expansion may be necessary for coastal cities, it can jeopardise coastal resources. This demand which responds to essential needs for economic growth, leads to a linear approach to coastal development focussing on the land along the water's edge (e.g., the line of mean high water), wetlands that straddle the shoreline, or land with access to recreational beaches or that has an outstanding view of the sea ... Mangrove wetlands, tide flats, seagrass beds, and other critical habitats are often obliterated when settlements pre-empt these areas by land filling to create expensive real estate. Infrastructure impacts - from roads, air ports, sewage treatment, water supply, electricity, and other utilities and services may strain available resources and degrade natural systems' (ibid, pp.17-18).

The urban population of Kerala was 76.80 lakhs constituting 26.4 per cent of the total population of 290.98 lakhs in 1991. Table 6.57 gives the district-wise distribution of urban population in Kerala during 1991.

Table 6.57

District-wise distribution of urban population in Kerala during 1991

S. No.	*District*	*Total population*	*Urban population*	*Urban as per cent of total*
1.	Kasargode	10,71,508	1,76,226	16.46
2.	Kannur	22,51,727	11,45,476	50.87
3.	Wayanad	6,72,128	22,949	3.41
4.	Kozhikode	26,19,941	10,04,497	38.34

(Contd.)

(Table 6.57 Contd.)

S. No.	District	Total population	Urban population	Urban as per cent of total
5.	Malappuram	30,96,330	2,82,454	9.12
6.	Palakkad	23,82,235	3,74,577	15.72
7.	Thrissur	27,37,311	7,20,216	26.31
8.	Ernakulam	28,17,236	13,73,177	48.74
9.	Idukki	10,78,066	50,881	4.72
10.	Kottayam	18,28,271	3,20,918	17.55
11.	Alappuzha	20,01,217	6,09,610	30.46
12.	Pathanamthitta	11,88,332	1,55,034	13.04
13.	Kollam	24,07,566	4,46,036	18.52
14.	Thiruvananthapuram	29,46,650	9,98,243	33.87
	Total	**2,90,98,518**	**76,80,294**	**26.40**

Source: Directorate of Census Operations, 1999, pp.78-120.

It is evident from table 6.57 that six out of the fourteen districts of the state had an urban population component which is higher than or equal to the state average, and all these districts are coastal districts. The urban component was the highest in Kannur district, at 50.87 per cent. Districts like Ernakulam, Kozhikode, Thiruvananthapuram, Alappuzha and Thrissur come in the same order in their drive for urbanisation.

The propensity of the coastal zones for urbanisation (urban development) can be further understood from the distribution of urban agglomerations/cities in Kerala with a population of one lakh or more in 1991. Table 6.58 gives details of urban agglomeration/cities in Kerala with a population of one lakh or more in 1991.

Table 6.58
Details of urban agglomerations/cities in Kerala with a population of one lakh or more in 1991

S. No.	Name of urban agglomeration/cities	Urban population (No.)	Coastal / non-coastal
1.	Kanhangad	1,18,214	Coastal
2.	Kannur	4,63,962	Coastal
3.	Vadakara	1,02,430	Coastal
4.	Kozhikode	8,01,190	Coastal
5.	Malappuram	1,42,204	Non-coastal
6.	Palakkad	1,80,033	Non-coastal
7.	Guruvayur	1,18,632	Non-coastal

(Contd.)

(Table 6.58 contd.)

S. No.	Name of urban agglomeration/cities	Urban population (No.)	Coastal / non-coastal
8.	Thrissur	2,75,053	Non-coastal
9.	Kochi	11,40,605	Coastal
10.	Kottayam	1,66,552	Non-coastal
11.	Cherthala	1,32,883	Coastal
12.	Alappuzha	2,64,969	Coastal
13.	Kollam	3,62,572	Coastal
14.	Thiruvananthapuram	8,26,225	Coastal

Source: Directorate of Census Operations, 1999, pp.124-136.

Table 6.58 shows that nine out of a total of fourteen urban agglomerations/cities in Kerala with a population of one lakh or more in 1991 were coastal, and their urban population component was much higher in most cases.

The tendency for over-concentration of population and urban/slum development in the coastal areas can be partly understood from the area, population and density of population in the coastal panchayats, municipalities and corporations of Kerala as revealed in table 6.59.

Table 6.59

Area, population and density of population in the coastal panchayats, municipalities and corporations of Kerala in 1991

Name of the coastal panchayat/municipality /corporation	Area (km^2)	Households	Population	Density ($persons/km^2$)
Thiruvananthapuram District				
Elakamon	17.75	4460	21523	1213
Edava	9.14	4326	26537	2903
Vettoor	6.82	3403	18790	2755
Cherunniyur	10.87	3429	16325	1502
Ottur	9.47	2867	13142	1388
Manambur	15.08	4151	20575	1364
Anchuthengu	3.36	3128	16742	4983
Kadakkavur	10.39	4573	23037	2217
Kizhuvilam	14.74	5826	29314	1989
Chirayinkizhu	10.87	5635	29627	2726
Andoorkonam	13.96	4840	26201	1877
Azhoor	12.46	5363	26829	2153
Kadinamkulam	17.68	7630	40406	2285
Mangalapuram	21.66	6433	32919	1520
Kazhakkootam	19.47	6110	29469	1514
Ulloor	16.67	10013	47005	2820

(Contd.)

(Table 6.59 contd.)

Name of the coastal panchayat/municipality /corporation	*Area (km^2)*	*House-holds*	*Population*	*Density (persons/km^2)*
Attipra	16.03	7329	33880	2114
Kadakampally	8.14	5005	24541	3015
Thiruvallam	13.60	6756	33036	2429
Vizhinjam	12.62	1894	42402	3360
Kottukal	12.16	6293	28698	2360
Karumkulam	2.43	5721	25731	10589
Poovar	7.34	3752	18755	2555
Thirupuram	8.57	3682	16600	1937
Kulathur	11.24	6068	29417	2617
Karode	15.67	5661	27490	1754
Attingal Municipality	14.18	6733	32634	2301
Varkala Municipality	15.42	7115	38987	2528
Thiruvananthapuram Corporation	74.93	107892	524006	6993
Kollam District				
Poothakulam	16.56	7087	36391	1898
Chathannur	33.76	9632	46414	1375
Sakthikulangara	9.17	8831	44451	4847
Iravipuram	9.90	9930	54772	5533
Thrikkadavur	14.85	7403	35859	2415
Kilikkollur	11.21	10913	56773	5064
Kollam Municipality	18.48	26713	139852	7568
Paravur Municipality	16.19	6749	37185	2297
Mayyanad	17.57	7777	41011	2334
Neendakara	10.19	2984	15424	1514
Chavara	11.89	7549	38309	3222
Panmana	16.85	8585	45722	2713
Thekkumbaghom	20.26	3358	15813	781
Thevalakkara	15.71	7176	37717	2401
Munrothuruthu	13.37	2208	10380	776
Perinad	24.92	10547	50398	2022
Perayam	15.45	3889	19478	1261
East Kallada	12.20	4257	20811	1706
Thrikkaruva	18.39	4713	23122	1257
West Kallada	13.36	3651	17522	1312
Thodiyur	20.61	7882	40593	1970
Karunagapally	18.65	8397	43691	2343
Mynagapally	19.17	7087	36391	1898
Alappad	7.38	4456	24576	3330
Kulasekharapuram	16.75	8116	41464	2475
Clappana	17.49	4189	21114	1207
Kottayam District				
T.V. Puram	17.03	3610	18857	1107
Vechur	29.13	3271	16013	550
Chembu	18.42	3662	18828	1022
Thalayazham	22.40	3859	19488	870
Vaikom Municipality	8.73	4309	21788	2496
Udayanapuram	20.15	4748	24036	1193

(Contd.)

(Table 6.59 contd.)

Name of the coastal panchayat/municipality /corporation	Area (km^2)	House-holds	Population	Density (persons/km^2)
Alappuzha District				
Kayamkulam Municipality	21.79	12138	67151	3082
Devikulangara	7.07	4164	20145	2849
Kandallur	9.74	4063	19194	1971
Arattupuzha	22.80	5546	29621	1299
Thrikkunnappuzha	12.53	4820	25849	2063
Karthikappally	8.73	3648	18092	2072
Purakkad	23.19	5287	27912	1204
Ambalappuzha	24.17	8502	45103	1866
Punnapra	21.27	9036	46050	2165
Alappuzha Municipalify	46.77	33016	174666	3735
Aryad	6.87	5045	24043	3500
Mararikkulam South	19.07	9493	45335	2377
Mararikkulam North	16.97	5542	26883	1584
Cherthala South	18.34	6854	34884	1902
Kadakkarappaly	8.94	3502	17834	1995
Pattanakkad	15.36	5853	29235	1903
Vayalar	14.44	4654	22384	1550
Cherthala Municipality	16.18	8618	43326	2678
Arookutty	11.10	2828	15693	1414
Chennam-Pallipuram	25.53	5105	25391	995
Thanneermukkom	31.44	8071	38907	1238
Thuravur	19.18	6218	25583	1334
Aroor	15.14	6238	32662	2157
Panavalli	19.55	5078	26597	1360
Thaikattussery	13.82	3866	19287	1396
Perumbalam	16.38	1833	9352	571
Ezhupunna	14.08	4511	22633	1607
Kodamthuruth	10.81	3651	21590	1997
Kuthiathodu	9.80	4266	21590	2203
Ernakulam District				
Puthenvelikkara	16.83	5004	25615	1522
Udayamperur	24.86	5582	28545	1148
Chellanam	17.60	5955	32978	1874
Kumbalangi	15.77	4553	24601	1560
Kumbalam	20.79	4688	24143	1161
Maradu	12.35	6769	34995	2834
Mulavukad	19.27	4248	22322	1158
Kadamakkudy	12.92	2702	14668	1135
Cheranallur	10.59	4106	21407	2021
Ilamkunnapuzha	11.66	8971	47878	4106
Njarakkal	8.60	4350	22978	2672
Varappuzha	7.74	4372	22514	2909
Alangad	18.35	6071	31870	1737
Nayarambalam	12.19	4240	23166	1900
Pallippuram	16.66	7831	41100	2467
Edavanakkad	11.24	3645	19631	1747

(Contd.)

(Table 6.59 contd.)

Name of the coastal panchayat/municipality /corporation	*Area (km²)*	*House-holds*	*Population*	*Density (persons/km²)*
Kuzhuppilly	7.73	2325	11446	1481
Kottuvalli	20.82	6665	34352	1650
Ezhikkara	15.27	3335	17201	1126
Chennamangalam	10.83	5336	26825	2477
Cochin Corporation	94.88	108924	564589	5951
Tripunithura Municipality	18.69	10434	51078	2733
Parur Municipality	9.02	5450	27906	3094
Vadakkekkara	11.25	6196	31266	2779
Thrissur District				
Vengidangu	20.47	4442	25222	1232
Pavaratty	9.19	3280	19726	2146
Mullasseri	17.70	3683	19953	1127
Taikkad	8.08	2366	14079	1742
Vadakkekkad	13.72	4002	23575	1715
Orumanayur	5.19	1884	10990	2118
Engandiyur	5.68	4030	21464	1369
Vadanappally	13.18	4765	27003	2049
Thalikulam	10.89	4112	22491	2065
Edathiruthy	16.63	1593	27457	1651
Anthikkad	12.99	3855	19426	1495
Eriyad	16.75	7276	42011	2508
Methala	11.66	6494	33686	1889
Kodungallur Municipality	17.30	6027	31249	1806
Edavilangu	7.60	3478	18749	2467
Sree Narayanapuram	19.26	6580	34878	1811
Mathilakam	12.92	4706	25417	1967
Perinjanam	9.30	3736	19257	2071
Kaippamangalam	13.70	5511	30377	2217
Valappad	16.33	6249	33078	2026
Nattika	9.60	3642	19192	1999
Kadappuram	9.63	3576	22994	2388
Punnayur	16.60	4656	30715	1850
Punnayurkulam	18.71	4724	29795	1592
Tanniam	17.53	5349	27625	1576
Manalur	18.22	5954	31230	1714
Pookode	14.11	4766	26822	1901
Kattur	11.70	3231	16905	1445
Padiyur	18.57	3392	17204	926
Vellangallur	26.61	6321	32846	1234
Poyya	19.78	3950	20474	1035
Mala	28.35	6033	30787	1086
Puthenchira	22.29	3815	19804	889
Chavakkad Municipality	12.41	5860	37789	3045

(Contd.)

(Table 6.59 contd.)

Name of the coastal panchayat/municipality /corporation	Area (km^2)	House-holds	Population	Density (persons/km^2)
Malappuram District				
Perumpadappu	15.02	4039	27204	1811
Veliyancode	15.21	3982	26857	1766
Izhuvathirithi	1400	4779	30752	2197
Ponnani Municipality	9.32	6329	51770	5555
Marancheri	20.47	4412	28991	1416
Purathur	24.80	5240	36180	1459
Vettam	21.60	6297	48522	2246
Thriparangode	20.67	4705	32221	1563
Tanalur	24.68	7539	53628	2173
Tanur	19.49	6952	54243	2783
Parappanangadi	22.25	7489	53979	2426
Tirurangadi	17.73	6030	43645	2462
Vallikunnu	25.14	5625	35517	1413
Mooniyur	22.40	5552	38688	1727
Tenhippalam	36.23	7454	48612	1342
Vazhayur	21.19	3812	22948	1083
Chelambra	15.81	4035	24663	1560
Tirur Municipality	16.59	7031	49453	2981
Kozhikode District				
Thurayur	10.48	2180	12830	1224
Eramala	19.06	5145	30050	1577
Kadalundi	11.83	8879	35171	2973
Beypore	10.41	8580	56505	5428
Cheruvannur-Nallalam	10.31	7764	50556	4904
Peruvayal	39.83	9467	53190	1335
Kakkodi	18.59	5422	30024	1615
Ramanattukara	11.71	4252	25672	2192
Kozhikode Corporation	82.68	67468	419831	5078
Olavanna	21.43	7753	44398	2072
Thalakkulathur	21.54	4204	23708	1101
Atholi	21.06	5929	36787	2709
Elathur	13.58	5929	36787	2709
Chemancherry	16.76	5350	31326	1869
Chengottukavu	13.60	4202	23702	1743
Kizhariyur	13.69	2469	13482	985
Arikulam	23.12	4591	24587	1063
Naduvannur	22.20	4129	22258	1003
Chelannur	23.83	5664	30081	1262
Koyilandy Municipality	21.61	9142	57797	2675
Ulliyeri	25.89	5238	27805	1074
Thikkodi	14.15	3875	22998	1625
Payyoli	22.34	7206	42261	1892
Maniyur	31.03	6200	34600	1115
Vadakara Municipality	21.33	10981	72434	3396
Onchiyum	8.72	4002	24856	2850

(Contd.)

(Table 6.59 contd.)

Name of the coastal panchayat/municipality /corporation	*Area (km²)*	*House-holds*	*Population*	*Density (persons/km²)*
Cherode	13.41	5220	32947	2457
Azhiyur	9.77	3838	25700	2631
Edacheri	16.17	4053	23979	1483
Feroke	13.53	7096	44494	3289
Kannur District				
New Mahe	5.08	2308	17732	3491
Eranholi	10.08	3875	23584	2340
Kadirur	12.30	4207	26587	2162
Thalassery Municipality	23.96	15068	103579	4323
Dharmadam	10.66	4120	26705	2505
Kadambur	7.95	2516	16441	2068
Muzhappilangad	7.19	2665	18812	2616
Edakkad	18.26	5320	33261	1822
Pinarayi	20.04	4809	28759	1435
Mokeri	10.53	2772	17917	1702
Kannur Municipality	12.82	10396	70058	5465
Pallikunnu	6.90	3937	25057	3631
Azhikode	16.05	6357	42354	2639
Valapattanam	2.04	1114	8920	4373
Pappinissery	15.24	4820	30754	2018
Khirakkal	13.56	6070	39838	2938
Narath	17.24	3365	23584	1368
Cherukunnu	15.37	2669	16246	1057
Mattul	12.82	3108	24262	1893
Madayi	16.71	4792	33488	2004
Cannapuram	14.39	3177	18158	1262
Pattuvam	16.85	2289	14207	843
Kalliasseri	15.73	4143	25005	1590
Kolasseri	20.72	3358	23053	1113
Kariyad	9.81	2773	17995	1834
Mayyil	33.08	4044	25223	762
Ezhuvassey	49.09	3447	17752	361
Ezhome	18.95	3022	17715	935
Cheruthazham	32.18	4166	23099	718
Ramanthali	29.99	3224	21325	711
Karivellur-Peralam	22.23	3686	19062	857
Payyannur Municipality	54.63	10960	64032	1172
Taliparamba Municipality	43.08	9903	60226	1398
Kasargode District				
Thrikkarippur	23.31	4826	32626	1400
Valiyaparamba	16.14	1742	11917	738
Cheruvathur	18.37	4242	24504	1334
Padne	13.39	2607	17608	1315
Nileswaram	26.23	6458	36545	1393
Kanhangad Municipality	39.54	9639	57165	1446

(Contd.)

(Table 6.59 contd.)

Name of the coastal panchayat/municipality /corporation	Area (km^2)	House-holds	Population	Density (persons/km^2)
Ajanur	27.83	6644	42467	1526
Pallikkare	39.09	5584	34696	888
Uduma	23.54	5225	32441	1378
Chemmanad	40.11	6536	41651	1038
Kasargode Municipality	16.68	8047	50126	3005
Mogral-Puttur	14.24	3046	19256	1352
Kumbala	40.18	5566	35735	889
Mangalpathy	36.30	6150	37565	1035
Manjeswaram	24.40	4923	32097	1315

Source: Baba, *et al.* 1998, pp.103-107.

It appears from table 6.59 that the density of population in almost all the coastal zone panchayats, municipalities and corporations was far in excess of the state density of population of 749 in 1991 and 819 in 2001 (Directorate of Economics and Statistics, 2001, pp.4 and 11). The very few exceptions were in the case of panchayats like Thekkumbhagom and Munrothuruthu in Kollam district, Vechur in Kottayam district, Perumbalam in Alappuzha district, Mayyil and Ezhuvassery in Kannur district and Valiyaparamba in Kasargode district. In fact, these thinly populated panchayats were not coastal and were included in the CRZ because of their proximity to the backwaters or for being subject to tidal influence. On the other hand, the density of population in a large number of coastal panchayats, municipalities and corporations was exceptionally high. It was especially the case with panchayats like Anchuthengu, Kadakampally and Karumkulam in Thiruvananthapuram district, Iravipuram, Sakthikulangara, Kilikollur, Chavara and Allappad in Kollam district, Aryad in Alappuzha district, Elamkunnapuzha in Ernakulam district, Beypore, Cheruvannur-Nallalam and Feroke in Kozhikode district, and New Mahe, Valapattanam and Pallikunnu in Kannur district. Remarkably, the Karumkulam panchayat in Thiruvananthapuram district had the highest density of 10,589 persons per sq.km. Among the 24 coastal municipalities, only nine had a density higher than 3000 persons per sq.km. These were Kollam, Alappuzha, Parur, Chavakkad, Ponnani, Vadakara, Thalassery, Kannur and Kasargode municipalities. All the city corporations had densities higher than 3000 persons per sq.km. Details of rural, urban and total coastal area, population and density of population in Kerala in 1991 are given in appendix 6.5.

What is typical of the population concentration in some of the coastal panchayats is their endemic tendency to develop into urban/ slum sprawls. As early as the middle of the last century, the Census of India (in 1961) described the Vizhinjam settlement of fishermen thus: 'the houses are so crowded that there is not even moving space around them. The dense smell of fish attracts vast swarms of flies which cover the food, cooking utensils and the whole house as it were. During the rainy season the floors of the house will be damp and the roof leaky. Facilities for drainage being extremely poor, the colony presents such unhygienic surroundings during the monsoons that it is hardly worthy of human habitation' (Directorate of Census Operations, 1961,p.154). It is hardly possible for the situation to change with continuous increase in population and limited emigration from the coast.

The probable consequence of this population concentration in the coasts of Kerala, as hypothesised by Clark in the global context, and as noted earlier would be the obliteration of the mangrove wetlands, tide flats, seagrass beds, and other critical habitats. And with the demand for shoreline real estate for human settlements, agriculture, trade, industry, amenity, and marine support activities for shipping, fishing and recreation being on the increase, this certainly would be the outcome. The present position, as pointed out by the State Planning Board in 1997 is that "the development process followed by the state has led to the changing consumption pattern of the people even in interior rural areas of the state. Consequently, there is tremendous increase in demand for provision of services such as transport, communication, water supply, sanitation, solid waste disposal, area development, urban renewal, etc.' (State Planning Board, 1997, p. 212). It may be noted here that these are some of the predominant issues which coastal zone management in Kerala has to tackie in the prevailing scenario of development as noted in most of the previous sections of this chapter. Most of these issues are further focused in the next chapter.

6.1.11. Other uses

Included in this category are chiefly the non-economic uses of the coast by the community collectively for socio-cultural benefits. Some of the areas of outstanding beauty and historical heritage sites of the coasts of Kerala which offer non-economic value to the community have been noted in the last chapter. It may also be noted here that the non-economic value of the mangroves and wetlands of the state would be immense. Nevertheless it appears that many of these goods are either being destroyed or are becoming priced goods and their non-economic value either being lost or getting transformed into economic values, all in the wake of urbanisation and economic development. Maintaining the 'social' utility: of these goods is an issue for coastal zone management in Kerala, which is discussed in the next chapter. The socio-cultural value of the coast as noted by Throsby is a composite of its heritage value consisting of (a) aesthetic value, (b) spiritual value, (c) social value, (d) historical value, (e) symbolic value and (f) authenticity value (Throsby, 2001, p.84). Over and above the aforementioned non-economic values, the state's coast is extensively valued (used) for other purposes like national defence by the military and waste dumping by the local community. Waste disposal, is now considered as the most critical problem affecting the coast, which is being discussed in the next chapter. Some of the defence related institutions which use the coast are the Southern Naval Command at Cochin, the Naval Academy at Ezhimala and the Thumba Equitorial Rocket Launching Station (TERLS) and the Vikram Sarabhai Space Centre (VSSC) at Thiruvananthapuram.

6.1.12. Summary

This chapter gave an account of the major coastal activities of Kerala, which were broadly categorised as 'economic' and 'non-economic' uses. These activities were further considered as relating to the 'land-side' and 'water-side' uses of the coast. As a starting point, the land-use pattern of the demarcated coastal zone was examined to study the 'land-side' activities. The major activities discussed, however,0 included (1) fisheries, (2) aquaculture, (3) agriculture, (4) mining, (5) manufacturing (coir, cashew processing, fish processing, fertilizers and chemicals), (6) tourism, (7) ports and harbours, (8) inland water transport, (9) urban development and (10) other uses. The first nine activities were considered as representing the economic uses, while the last one, 'other uses' was meant to represent the non-economic or socio-cultural uses of the coast.

Throughout the discussion the economic and non-economic value of each activity to the coast, the need for sustaining them and the relevance of ICM in the context of sustainable development of the coast were highlighted.